The Stalin
Revolution

PROBLEMS IN EUROPEAN
CIVILIZATION SERIES

The Stalin Revolution

Foundations of the Totalitarian Era

Third Edition

*Edited, Revised, and
with Introduction and Notes by*
Robert V. Daniels
University of Vermont

D. C. HEATH AND COMPANY
Lexington, Massachusetts Toronto

Cover: Soviet poster by Vladimir Lyushin, 1931, entitled *The Young Communist League Is the Shock Battalion of the Five-Year Plan*. (The Granger Collection)

Published simultaneously in Canada.

Printed in the United States of America.

International Standard Book Number: 0-669-21165-6

Library of Congress Catalog Card Number: 89-84257

10 9 8 7 6 5 4 3

Preface

History never comes to a stop. A year is added to the human record every twelve months, and with the passage of time our view of the past changes, not only with the discovery of new information but more particularly with the new perspectives and the new concerns raised by the most recent events. So it has been, quite dramatically, with respect to Soviet Russia, in light of the remarkable changes, both in present policy and in access to historical truth, introduced under the leadership of Mikhail Gorbachev.

When the first edition of this collection of readings appeared in the mid-1960s, the Soviet Union had just experienced the failure of modest reform efforts under Nikita Khrushchev. It seemed that the totalitarian system of politics and economics known as Stalinism had sunk ineradicable roots in the old Russian soil or in the debris of the revolution, and that it would continue to dominate the USSR for the indefinite future. Given the current surprising and encouraging developments under Gorbachev, we can now reasonably begin to hope that totalitarianism was only a chapter in the history of Russia, ending finally in that nation's transition to a more open and law-based system of life and government.

Nevertheless, Gorbachev's changes—his new "revolution," as he likes to style it—do not make the study of the Stalinist past irrelevant. Quite the contrary; they make this study more relevant than ever, as a basis for understanding Soviet Russia today in terms of the system that it is reacting against and endeavoring to escape from. This means understanding how the Stalinist system came into being, and the forces and decisions that shaped it into the totalitarian structure of government and society that, in its essentials, prevailed in the USSR for half a century. Such understanding remains the goal of this revised edition of *The Stalin Revolution*. This objective holds for any and all readers who may wish to sample the most important international scholarship on Stalinism, and particularly for college students at any level in history or political science who are undertaking a study of Soviet Russia.

With the Gorbachev Revolution in mind, and with the resources of many more recent works of research and reflection on Stalinism now available—including that of contemporary Soviet scholars—this volume in the Heath series of anthologies on major problems in European history has been completely recast. Apart from the historic statements of Stalin, Trotsky, and Khrushchev, all but two of the selections are new (including a passage from the recently revised edition of Soviet historian Roy Medvedev's epochal study of Stalinism). The introduction, the list of suggested readings, and the annotations, also newly done for this edition, reflect the most recent events and the latest scholarship. The span of the selections is more international than ever; in addition to articles by Americans and by four leading Soviet historians and economists of the era of *perestroika*, there are contributions by British, French, Italian, Czech, and Yugoslav writers. The new selections also reflect the growing eminence of women in this field.

Earlier editions of this collection were worked out as classroom assignments, and thoroughly field-tested. The selections will serve not only as a basis for imparting an in-depth understanding of Stalinism as a crucial episode in European and world history but also as a resource for guided practice in the methods of research and in the skills of writing—two subjects that cannot be taught in a vacuum, without subject matter on which to practice. The twin pedagogical goals that this work, in both its earlier editions and this most recent one, has sought to serve are intake for enlightenment and output for growth in self-expression. I hope teachers will find that it meets these aims.

R. V. D.

Contents

Chronology of Events

1917	February Revolution (in March, by the Western calendar); fall of Tsar Nicholas II; Provisional Government
	October (November) Revolution; Bolsheviks (Communists) led by Lenin establish Soviet Republic.
1918–1921	Civil war and "war communism."
1921–1928	New Economic Policy (NEP).
1922	Stalin made General Secretary of the Communist Party.
1923–1924	Factional struggle against the Trotskyist opposition.
1924	Death of Lenin.
	Formation of the Union of Soviet Socialist Republics.
1925	Factional struggle against the Zinovievist opposition.
1926–1927	Factional struggle against the "United Opposition" of Trotsky and Zinoviev; defeat of opposition and expulsion from the CPSU at the Fifteenth Party Congress.
1928	Stalin defeats "Right Opposition" of Bukharin, Rykov, and Tomsky; becomes individual dictator.
1929	Beginning of the Stalin Revolution: First Five-Year Plan adopted (stepped-up industrialization); wholesale collectivization of peasants and dekulakization begun; end of NEP.
	Trotsky deported from USSR.
1929–1930	Bukharin group removed from leadership posts.

1931–1932	Second phase of Stalin Revolution begins (discipline and authority in place of utopianism and class war).
1932	First Five-Year Plan declared fulfilled in four years.
1932–1933	Collectivization largely completed; famine results from grain-collection campaign.
1933–1937	Second Five-Year Plan.
1934	Seventeenth Party Congress ("Congress of Victors"). Kirov assassinated (pretext for Stalin to begin purges).
1936	First Moscow Trial (Zinoviev, Kamenev, and their followers). Stalin Constitution; "socialism" and "classless society" proclaimed.
1937	Second Moscow Trial (Trotskyists); purge of military command (including chief of staff Tukhachevsky).
1937–1938	"Yezhovshchina" or mass purge of party and government officials.
1938	Third Moscow Trial (Bukharin and his followers).
1939	Hitler-Stalin Pact signed, World War II begins; Soviet Union and Nazi Germany partition Poland.
1940	USSR annexes Baltic republics. Trotsky assassinated in Mexico by a Soviet agent.
1941	Germany invades the Soviet Union.
1942	Battle of Stalingrad.
1945	Collapse of Germany, end of World War II; Soviet domination of Eastern Europe.
1953	Stalin dies; Khrushchev made First Secretary.
1956	Khrushchev's "Secret Speech" to Twentieth Party Congress, denouncing Stalin for crimes against the Communist Party.
1964	Fall of Khrushchev; Brezhnev made General Secretary; end of the first period of de-Stalinization.
1982	Death of Brezhnev.
1985	Gorbachev made General Secretary; *perestroika* and *glasnost* begin; de-Stalinization resumed.

The Stalin
Revolution

Introduction

In the mid-1980s, under the new leadership of General Secretary Mikhail Gorbachev, the Soviet Union entered a period of some of the most profound changes in its entire history. With the slogans of *perestroika* (restructuring) and *glasnost* (openness), Gorbachev launched an attack on the fundamentals of the Soviet system as it had stood for more than half a century — in other words, the entire era of Stalinism. Unlike his ill-fated predecessor Nikita Khrushchev, who confined himself to the repudiation of Joseph Stalin's terror and purges of the later 1930s, Gorbachev and his supporters turned against the basic institutions and policies that had constituted the Stalinist system of totalitarian government and society.

The institutions and policies that Gorbachev brought into his gunsights were not direct creations of the Revolution of 1917. He left unquestioned the legitimacy of the October Revolution, the Communist dictatorship, and the heroic role attributed to Vladimir Ilych Lenin. Instead, he directed his attack at a subsequent phase of the Russian revolutionary experience, when Stalinist despotism with all its political, economic, social, and cultural features came into being. This especially harsh regime was a product of the new era of revolutionary — or counterrevolutionary — change that the Soviet Union experienced in the late 1920s and early 1930s, when Stalin made himself a personal dictator and fashioned the programs of totalitarian power and national mobilization that bear his name. In short, these were the years of the Stalin Revolution.

Naturally, it is impossible to understand the Soviet Union of the 1980s and the issues addressed by the reformers under Gorbachev without an appreciation of the Stalin Revolution and the direction it laid down for Soviet Russia for the fifty years that followed. To review Gorbachev's reform initiatives is to catalog the features imposed on Soviet life at the time of the Stalin Revolution: Among the institutions and policies subjected to the severest criticism in the eighties were the centrally planned economy, the collective farms, the lack of economic incentives, the denial of real power to ordinary workers and peasants, the excessive power and privileges of the bureaucracy, and the straitjacket of Communist party control over intellectual and cultural life and the media of communication. Under Gorbachev, all of these evils in the Soviet system were held to be specific products of the Stalin Revolution.

Gorbachev did not venture beyond the legacy of the Stalin Revolution and begin to question Lenin and the political monopoly of the Communist party, except in the most oblique way. Examples are his initiatives to strengthen the local councils (the soviets) and the popular election of the Supreme Soviet (from among candidates largely screened by the party). The self-imposed limits to Gorbachev's reforms have led many outside observers to question whether they could really be fundamental or would remain only superficial. This issue in turn ties into the question, long debated by Western scholars, of whether Stalinism and the Stalin Revolution represented a fundamental break from Leninism and the early spirit of the revolution, or merely a logical extension and implementation of the Bolshevik principles of 1917. If the Stalin Revolution was truly something new and different, Gorbachev's rejection of it becomes highly significant. If Stalinism was only the extension of Leninism, and Gorbachev does not reject Leninism, then his reforms cannot be regarded as a fundamental change in the system.

Different authors represented in this collection of readings take very different positions on the Lenin-Stalin issue, and hence imply very different judgments about the reforms of the 1980s. But perhaps there is a way to combine the truth in both points of view and thereby put the Gorbachev reforms in a special long-term perspective. This resolution of the debate rests on recognizing that the Russian revolutionary experience was not an instantaneous event but a long process, as one phase and one set of circumstances led to the next. Like all the great revolutions of history, the Russian Revolution began (with the fall of the tsar in February 1917) as a moderate movement for liberal reform. However, radical emotions quickly escalated, carrying Lenin and the Bolshevik extremists into power in the October Revolution. Fanatical struggle and utopian endeavors marked the years of the Russian Civil War and "War Communism," from 1918 to 1921. Then, fearing a popular reaction that could overthrow him, Lenin proclaimed a "strategic retreat" and initiated the New Economic Policy, a partial restoration of capitalism accompanied by a spirit of pragmatism and remarkable cultural vitality. This was the "Thermidorean" era, which came to an end in the Stalin Revolution. Whether the NEP inevitably had to yield to the Stalinist system that followed it is still a vigorously disputed question among Western scholars and now among Soviet historians as well. But the place of this change in the revolutionary process is clear: it represents the advent of the postrevolutionary dictatorship, a characteristic aftermath to revolution. The postrevolutionary dictatorship that Stalin fashioned in Russia differed quite fundamentally from the kind of revolutionary dictatorship over which Lenin presided, though the latter prepared the ground. In the Russian case this basis was laid by Lenin's establishment of one-party government and by the habits of terror implanted during the Civil War years. We may thus view Stalinism as a natural sequel to Leninism, inherent in the condition of a country that had been torn by revolution, even if Lenin and his associates — perhaps even Stalin himself — did not intend or foresee the kind of totalitarian system that Stalin eventually set up.

Many American scholars in recent years have challenged the term *totalitarianism* and the "totalitarian model," seeing in these notions a propagandistic oversimplification of Soviet reality. I hold that the concept of totalitarianism is still meaningful and appropriate, if we understand it in the proper historical sense as a phenomenon that had, in each instance, a beginning and an end — a system that grew, flourished, and ultimately crumbled. The real onset of Soviet totalitarianism was the Stalin Revolution, and it has apparently come to an end in the era of reform more than a half-century later under Gorbachev.

Totalitarianism is really a matter of degree among types of dictatorships. It means that the political authority attempts intrusive, total control of all other aspects of life, in contrast to the milder *authoritarianism* at the other end of the scale. In an authoritarian dictatorship, those in power are content — or compelled by circumstances — to let nonpolitical life go on in a more natural way. Totalitarianism is always an outgrowth of revolution; it is the characteristic form of postrevolutionary dictatorship, in the name of the Left or of the Right, when twentieth-century resources of coercive organization and technology are available.

In this typology, we can describe the Soviet dictatorship as more "authoritarian" until the Stalin Revolution. From the thirties to the fifties it was severely totalitarian, and such relaxation as subsequently occurred up to the eighties did not end totalitarianism in principle. Only in the mid-1980s did the Soviet regime begin to back away from Stalinist totalitarianism and return to the less severe "authoritarian" category.

Where does Gorbachev stand in this scheme of things, in his attempt to escape from the system created by the Stalin Revolution? There are analogies in the history of other revolutions — the Glorious Revolution in England in 1688, for example — when a long era of postrevolutionary dictatorship or counterrevolutionary Restoration comes to an end in a new coup that allows the country to recover some of the spirit of the earliest, idealistic phase of the revolution. This appears to be the direction of the Gorbachevian reforms — toward a revival of the philosophy of liberal reform in a country that has become much more modern and stable than it was in the volatile years of the original revolution.[1]

For many years it was difficult for anyone to approach the history of the Soviet Union in a spirit of detachment. Soviet historians had to display militant partisanship, on pain of denunciation for counterrevolutionary falsification — yet another legacy of the Stalin Revolution. Even for outsiders, political preconceptions and emotional reactions, pro or con, often colored judgments of the Soviet record. With the passage of time and the perspective it affords, more objective appraisals have become possible, even for the Soviets themselves — which is one of the benefits of Gorbachev's new revolution. This new edition of *The Stalin Revolution*, incorporating selections from twenty Western and Communist sources (more than two-thirds of them new) endeavors to reflect a mature perspective on what remains one of the most stormy and painful episodes of twentieth-century history.[2]

All schools of thought about Soviet history acknowledge the years from 1929 to 1932 as a revolutionary turning point in the development of the Communist system, though they may differ widely in their estimates of the reasons, achievements, and implications of the changes

---

[1] The idea of a "moderate revolutionary revival" is spelled out in my recent book, *Is Russia Reformable?* (Boulder, CO: Westview Press, 1988), pp. 127–133.

[2] Footnote citations in the original selections have been eliminated or, where essential, retained selectively. Editor's notes have been added, as indicated, where clarification seemed necessary.

that came about during this period. Did Communism evolve according to plan, in line with the original revolutionary impetus of its founders, or did it turn onto a new path where practice contradicted theory and where a native dictatorship contradicted the international mission? Long after the event, the official Communist view of the Stalin Revolution presented it as the strict application of Marxist principles. Many Western writers agreed, though for some of them this meant only that Russia was driven from bad to worse. Dissident Marxists like Leon Trotsky, on the other hand, held that Stalin's revolution was a profound betrayal of Communist principles. Other observers have taken the position that Russian circumstances, for better or worse, induced or compelled Stalin to make fundamental changes in the Communist program. No one has denied that the Stalin Revolution brought about crucial changes, but why they occurred, and what they meant for the country's history, are questions that open the door to the most diverse interpretations. Was the Stalin Revolution a fulfillment (good or bad) of the Bolshevik promise of 1917? Or was it a betrayal (cynical or practical) of the aspirations of the October Revolution?

The actual steps of the Stalin Revolution were scarcely anticipated beforehand. By launching the NEP in 1921, Lenin had cut short the initial revolutionary period of terror, civil strife, and utopian experiment under War Communism. The NEP entailed restoration of a money economy, salary differentials, individual farming, private ownership of small business (by the so-called Nepmen), and considerable intellectual freedom, all on the premise that the Marxist movement would have to mark time in Russia while it awaited world revolution. The Communist party — ruling as a one-party dictatorship but still enjoying some freedom of controversy within its ranks — fell to disputing all manner of policy matters and especially the question of Russia's future industrial development.

The stakes were raised with Lenin's death in 1924 and the question of succession to the leadership of the party and the government. Trotsky, Grigory Zinoviev, and Nikolai Bukharin, the party theoretician, bid one after another for supremacy. All were defeated by the man who, as General Secretary since 1922, controlled the keys to power in the Communist party organization — Stalin.

Michal Reiman, in *The Birth of Stalinism,* describes how Stalin, with Bukharin's ideological support, mobilized the resources of the party apparatus to crush Trotsky and Zinoviev in 1926 and 1927, despite these two contenders' belated alliance. At the Fifteenth Party Congress in December 1927, the Trotskyists and Zinovievists were expelled from the Communist party. Trotsky was exiled to Central Asia in January 1928, and in February 1929, he was deported from the USSR altogether. Meanwhile, in a sharp new political struggle detailed by *Stephen F. Cohen* in his biography of Bukharin, Stalin turned against the Right Opposition led by Bukharin, Alexei Rykov (Lenin's successor as prime minister), and Mikhail Tomsky (the chief of the trade unions). He easily defeated this group in the fall of 1928, partly by borrowing arguments from the Trotskyists. By the spring of 1929 he was a virtually absolute personal dictator, even though he actually held no government post.

Stalin's radical steps of 1928 and 1929 were closely connected with the frustrating problems of economic backwardness and industrial development that Russia faced in the 1920s. Bitter controversies had divided the Communist leaders since 1921 over continuing the capitalistic concessions of the New Economic Policy or launching an ambitious governmental program of planned industrialization. These two alternatives — the Right policy of Bukharin and the Left program of Trotsky and Evgeny Preobrazhensky — are assessed in the second selection in this book, from *The Economic History of the U.S.S.R.* by *Alec Nove*. Nove shows the difficulties for either approach, against the backdrop of the Communists' commitment to hold power, which Stalin so effectively exploited. Does this mean that Stalin's answer of a violent break in agricultural and industrial policy was the inevitable sequel to Lenin's dictatorship, or was it really a unique program dictated by the problems of Russian backwardness?

Following his victory over the Right Opposition, Stalin intensified his dictatorial control over the country through the secret police and the Communist party organization. He made special efforts to impose controls on intellectual life — on writers, artists, scientists, and even Communist theorists. As *Giuseppe Boffa* explains, he took advantage of the trend toward popularizing Marxism-Leninism as a simplistic dogma, using it to brand his opponents as heretics. Were Stalin and his followers, then, making a genuine effort to clarify Marxism for the masses, or were they trying to get around the theory where it appeared to balk their determination to overhaul Russian society by political command? Was the Stalin Revolution based on a genuine revival of Marxism, or did it cynically manipulate the doctrine?

The two greatest policy innovations of the Stalin Revolution were the collectivization of the peasants and the Five-Year Plan of intensive industrialization. Actually, neither program was original with Stalin — he borrowed them to start with from the Trotskyists and used them, in exaggerated form, to discredit the Bukharinists. By the end of 1929 industrialization and collectivization were in full swing, and in his public speeches — typified by the two selections from his *Problems of Leninism* — Stalin was already congratulating himself on the victory of Marxism over Russian backwardness. According to Stalin, there was only one alternative to his program — surrender to the forces of capitalism. But as economists such as *Holland Hunter* suggest, there is reason to doubt that Stalin's high-speed program was really the most effective path to industrialism.

In the course of Stalin's industrial drive, many of the Marxist ideas and practices previously accepted by the Soviet authorities were sacrificed in the name of industrial efficiency. This was especially striking in the case of industrial labor, where revolutionary hopes for equality and industrial self-government gave way to a reality of bureaucratic power, inequality, and impoverishment of the workers. Part of Stalin's struggle with the Right Opposition involved a fight to remove Bukharin's ally Tomsky from the trade union leadership because Tomsky wanted the unions to represent the workers in any conflict with the state. The outcome, as depicted by *Donald Filtzer* in *Soviet Workers and Stalinist Industrialization*, was social atomization and depressed living standards, raising the question of what the "dictatorship of the proletariat" really meant.

The story of Stalin's forcible collectivization drive, paralleling the First Five-Year Plan, has prompted considerable questioning of the necessity and the cost of this radical transformation of the Soviet countryside, and the nature of the decision-making process involved. A major article by *Moshe Lewin*, reprinted here in abridged form, examines in detail the path by which Stalin arrived at his commitment to collectivize. Lewin sees Stalin's policy as a series of ad hoc and impetuous decisions taken at a moment of political and economic crisis. The actual impact of collectivization on the peasants is described in the remarkable *Pravda* interview of September 1988, with two Soviet experts — *Viktor Danilov* and *N. V. Teptsov* — who admit the damage done by Stalin's "dekulakization" program and the horrors of the famine of 1932–33.

What might be termed the secondary effects of Stalin's industrialization and collectivization drive were responses to the problems that the drive revealed or to the opposition that it engendered. We can speak of Soviet society becoming truly totalitarian in these years, in the sense of tight party control being imposed not only in political affairs but over all aspects of life. Autonomous economic activity came to an end with the nationalization of the small businesses of the "Nepmen," the subordination of the trade unions to the interests of production, and the elimination of individual farming. The basic social policies of the government — up to then a mixture of utopianism tempered by expediency — were deliberately revised in a conservative and disciplinarian direction. In the official view, these changes aimed at eliminating "petty-bourgeois" notions of equality and individual freedom. But the sociological analysis by *Hélène Carrère d'Encausse* contained in the selection from *Confiscated Power* suggests a contrary appraisal: to what extent did Stalin's acceptance of bureaucratic organization and inequality represent a permanent movement away from the revolution and toward an implicit conservatism?

Similar shifts of policy appear in other fields — in Soviet education, for example, as *Sheila Fitzpatrick* maintains in the selection from *Education and Social Mobility in the Soviet Union*. She describes the atmosphere of educational experimentation in Russia in the 1920s, and the abrupt rejection of such experiments when Stalin's industrialization program put a premium on mass training and technical competence. Again, the question is whether Stalin was finally getting Soviet Russia on the correct Marxist track or whether the requirements of political survival in industrial society compelled him to abandon the revolutionary ideal.

Most aspects of intellectual life felt the heavy hand of tightened Communist party control during the Stalin Revolution. In literature the impact of doctrinaire enthusiasm, as depicted by *Katerina Clark*, was particularly severe. However, constraints on the writers were not loosened when Stalin caused utopianism to be replaced by old-fashioned standards in Marxist guise.

Stalin's rule, in all its arbitrariness and harshness, was not quietly accepted by the Communist party, despite the defeat of the open opposition groups. As *J. Arch Getty* shows in his *Origins of the Great Purges*, dissension and disorganization were rife in the presumably totalitarian party until Stalin launched his campaign of terror against the whole of Soviet officialdom. The hopes of the anti-Stalinists rested with the

Leningrad party secretary, Sergei Kirov, who appeared to have some success in 1933 and 1934 in promoting a relaxation of Stalin's program. Stalin, however, was preparing to destroy all who stood in his way. He was probably responsible for the assassination of Kirov in December 1934. There soon followed the Great Purge of 1936–1938, the efficacy of which was underscored in the sensational secret speech by First Secretary *Nikita Khrushchev* at the Twentieth Party Congress in 1956. The document, blaming Stalin's pathological personality for the woes of the thirties, was widely read in closed party meetings and soon became known to the rest of the world, though it has only very recently been openly published in the USSR.

The final section of this book is directed at broader evaluations and explanations of the phenomenon of Stalinism. The selection by *James Billington* from *The Icon and the Axe* aims to show Stalin as a consistent product of Russian tradition (even though Stalin's native nationality was not Russian but Georgian). *Robert C. Tucker* analyzes Stalin's "revolution from above" as a natural stage in the revolutionary process in Russia, while the noted Soviet dissident, *Roy Medvedev*, using only internal sources that were available to him in pre-*glasnost* times, managed to work out a distinctive social explanation of the Stalin phenomenon.

To Stalin's Communist enemies in his lifetime, as well as to most present-day Soviet writers and non-Soviet Marxists, he represents the repudiation or undermining of everything the revolution stood for. *Leon Trotsky*, writing his *Revolution Betrayed* in exile, condemned Stalin in Marxist terms as the equivalent of the dictatorship of Napoleon Bonaparte and later on of his nephew Louis Napoleon Bonaparte in France. The present-day Soviet economists *Nikolai Shmelyov* and *Vasily Seliunin* reject the bureaucracy and "administrative methods" of Stalinism as a counterproductive obstacle to the modernization of the Soviet economy and Soviet society. Finally, the Yugoslav sociologist *Zagorka Golubović* finds that Stalinism represents a fundamental antithesis to the genuine ideal of socialism.

An overall review of the materials on the Stalin Revolution cannot fail to bring some profound problems into focus. The Stalin Revolution was an unprecedented event, calling for specific explanation in terms of the individual, the political institutions, the economic circumstances, and the national experience. As an aspect of the history of Communism, the Stalin Revolution requires an appraisal of the truth and relevance of Marxist theory and of the relation between Marxist theory and actual Communist behavior. Finally, outside the Communist frame of reference altogether, readers may wish to make their own informed judgments about the necessity or capriciousness of the Stalin Revolution. Was it driven by desperate need and old national habits of governance, was it the inevitable outcome of Lenin's revolution, or was it the unredeemed historic crime of a deranged despot?

Variety of Opinion

The open form of political crisis, seen in 1927, was coming to an end. It was replaced by a hidden crisis, related to the general economic and social situation in the USSR.

Michal Reiman

The protagonists shared many common assumptions . . . , the necessity of the retention of sole political power by their party . . . , the necessity of industrialization . . . , the limitations of individual peasant agriculture.

Alec Nove

The very concept of a new "revolution from above" which inspired Stalin's leadership contrasted radically with the developments that the Marxist debate had gone through. . . . Every dispute, however limited its cultural and theoretical scope, risked becoming intertwined with the political struggle.

Giuseppe Boffa

The question stands as follows: either one way or the other, either back — to capitalism — or forward — to socialism. There is no third way, nor can there be.

Joseph Stalin

Bolshevik objectives might have been achieved without the Draconian methods that Stalin used . . . , with far less turbulence, waste, destruction, and sacrifice.

Holland Hunter

No objective conditions could justify the violence against the peasantry that was committed in the Stalinist implementation of collectivization and dekulakization.

Viktor Danilov and N. V. Teptsov

After having exalted the army of the lowly for ten years, Soviet ideology hierarchized society according to utilitarian criteria.

Hélène Carrère d'Encausse

By the middle of 1931 there were signs that the Cultural Revolution had run its course. . . . The "bourgeois intelligentsia" was formally rehabilitated in a speech by Stalin.

Sheila Fitzpatrick

It would be naive to be taken in by Stalin's cult of personality and to accept Stalinist protestations of unity. . . . It may well be that where one finds the loudest affirmations of unity are the places where unity is most lacking.

J. Arch Getty

We must affirm that the party had fought a serious fight against the Trotskyites, rightists, and bourgeois nationalists. . . . Here Stalin played a positive role.

Nikita S. Khrushchev

When the Russian revolutionary process resumed in the Stalinist stage, it had a different character from the revolutionary process of destruction . . . , and this change of character is to be understood in terms of a reversion to a revolutionary process seen earlier in Russian history.

Robert C. Tucker

Stalin . . . in many respects . . . can properly be called a counterrevolutionary. But he also continued to rely on the masses, which was the chief peculiarity of Stalin's actions and the ultimate determinant of his success.

Roy Medvedev

It is perfectly obvious that the poorer the society which issues from a revolution . . . , the more crude would be the forms assumed by bureaucratism, and the more dangerous would it become for socialist development.

Leon Trotsky

The objectives set up by Stalinism as its practical program are diametrically opposed to socialist goals as they were defined by Marx.

Zagorka Golubović

Workers parading through Red Square, Moscow, on the thirteenth anniversary of the Bolshevik Revolution (November 1930). (Wide World Photos)

The Setting

Michal Reiman

The Forging of Stalin's Dictatorship

The most exhaustive study to date of the political beginnings of the Stalin Revolution is the work of the Czech historian Michal Reiman. A specialist in Soviet history, trained in Moscow, Reiman supported the 1968 reforms in Czechoslovakia and was compelled to emigrate to West Germany after the Soviet intervention; he is now a professor of political science at the East European Institute of the Free University of Berlin. In *The Birth of Stalinism*, first published in Germany in 1979 and excerpted here, he exploited every bit of evidence, including the German diplomatic archives, to tell the tale of Stalin's victory over his political opponents in the late 1920s.

From Michal Reiman, *The Birth of Stalinism: The USSR on the Eve of the "Second Revolution,"* pp. 19–20, 21–23, 27–33, 35–36, Indiana U Press. Copyright © 1987 Indiana University Press, reprinted by permission.

In 1927, the left opposition was not a new phenomenon in Soviet life. It had grown, in the preceding years, in proportion to the concentration of power in Stalin's hands after Lenin's death. During the spring and summer of 1926, an agreement was reached by the two most influential left opposition groups, the Trotskyists and the Zinovievists, both of which had been pushed to the political sidelines by Stalin. They were joined by the Democratic Centralists, a small but radical group led by Timofei Sapronov. It was assumed that an alliance of the three best-known leaders of the Lenin-era Bolshevik Party — Trotsky, Zinoviev, and Kamenev[1] — supported by a large number of important political, theoretical, and practical leaders of the party, would provide the opposition with enough weight to wage a successful fight against the new leadership.

The opposition's main point of attack was Stalin's manner of running the party — his regime within the party — but there were also important differences on questions of economic and social development, which have been mentioned earlier. Thus, the opposition's main blow was divided — it lacked a single focus — and since it aimed at the moderates as well as the Stalin group, it drove the moderates into Stalin's arms, giving him more room to maneuver.

The importance of the left opposition is often underestimated in the literature. It is considered an important current in Soviet ideological and political life, a kind of "revolt of the leaders" in the context of the power struggle with Stalin; and it is cited as evidence that alternate forms of Soviet development were possible. But many authors doubt that the opposition had any substantial influence on the mass of party members and even less on broader sections of the population. One can hardly agree with such views: they seem paradoxical indeed in light of the mountain of ammunition expended on the opposition by the party leadership in those years — the multitude of official declarations, reports, pamphlets, and books, not to mention the mass political campaigns that penetrated even the remotest parts of the USSR.

In the spring of 1926 the united opposition, based on a cadre of old and experienced party leaders, conquered some fairly significant positions. It consolidated its influence in Leningrad, the Ukraine, Transcaucasia, and the Urals region; in the universities; in some of the central government offices; in a number of factories of Moscow and the central

---

[1] Lev Kamenev, Zinoviev's collaborator and a deputy prime minister. — Ed.

industrial region; and among a section of the command staff of the army
and navy, which had passed through the difficult years of the civil war
under Trotsky's leadership. Repression by the party leadership prevented the opposition from growing, but its influence was still much
greater than indicated by the various votes taken in the party cells.
Although the top three opposition leaders, Trotsky, Zinoviev, and
Kamenev, lost their Politburo posts during 1926, they remained members of the Central Committee along with a number of other opposition
leaders. The unresolved economic and social problems did not develop
into a major crisis in 1926; in general, the country was still going
through a period of relative stabilization and growth. The leadership
was able to deal with the situation, which consequently did not prove
conducive to success for the opposition. In October, under very heavy
political and administrative pressure from the central party institutions,
the opposition was obliged to disarm, to renounce any further factional
activity. It fell silent, but it had not been broken.

In the spring of 1927, a new stage of the internal political fight
began. . . . Sensing that the leadership was in a shaky position, the
opposition increased its pressure. On May 26, Trotsky, Zinoviev,
Smilga, and Grigory Yevdokimov sent the Politburo a declaration
signed by eighty-four prominent oppositionist party members. Among
the points made in this document were the following: events in China[2]
had freed the imperialists' hands for war against the USSR; the party's
failures were the result of a wrong political line, which was contributing
to the growth of capitalist elements in the USSR at the same time that
conditions for the workers and poorer sections of the population were
getting worse; rightist forces were raising their heads, and inside the
Communist party itself there was a growing right wing, while the Politburo was trying to surgically remove the left opposition. The situation
could still be saved, but in order to do this, repressive measures would
have to be renounced, an open discussion permitted, and all decisions
arrived at collectively. In private conversations Trotsky was more concrete: the Stalinist parasites would have to be removed and a healthy
regime established in the party; everything else would follow naturally.

The Politburo, after suffering another heavy blow, the break in
relations with Great Britain, lost its usual self-assurance. To risk a split
in the party during a crisis in foreign policy seemed inadvisable. The

[2]Chiang Kai-shek's coup against the Chinese Communists. — Ed.

moderates in the leadership did not fully share Stalin's views and, sensing a future clash with him, showed no particular eagerness for fighting the opposition.

The Politburo — according to several sources — decided to negotiate. It proposed a truce to the opposition for the duration of the diplomatic break with Britain, promising a future agreement on certain questions (democratization of the soviets, a change in agrarian tax policies, and a revision of Comintern policy in China). The opposition — according to the same sources — responded with counterproposals insisting on immediate changes; they understood very well that the leadership was playing for time so that its wounds could heal. Meanwhile, opposition activity was spreading like a river in flood. The opposition organized mass meetings of industrial workers in Ivanovo-Voznesensk, Leningrad, and Moscow; at a chemical plant in Moscow shouts were heard: "Down with Stalin's dictatorship! Down with the Politburo!"

There were rumors of underground strike committees, in which oppositionists were said to be participating, in the Urals, the Donbass, the Moscow textile region and in Moscow proper — and of funds being raised for striking workers. The GPU[3] reported to the leadership that it could not guarantee "order" nor prevent the "demoralization of the workers" if it was not given the right to arrest oppositionist party members.

Stalin's supporters insisted on repression of the opposition. On June 9, 1927, on the crest of the wave of indignation following the assassinations in Warsaw and Leningrad, a notable event occurred. The opposition organized a meeting at the Yaroslavl Station in Moscow to say farewell to one of its leaders, Ivan Smilga, whom the Central Committee was sending away to the remote Siberian city of Khabarovsk, on the Manchurian border. As many as two thousand people turned out for this farewell demonstration. Trotsky and Zinoviev gave speeches. Smilga was borne aloft to his railcar by the crowd. The GPU did not intervene because members of the party, indeed of the Central Committee, were taking part in the demonstration. In party circles the incident was described as "an antiparty rally" at a time when there was a direct threat of war. The foreign press also commented on the incident. The demonstration had a big impact, but the negative interpretation

---

[3] "State Political Administration" was the name of the secret police, 1922–1934 — Ed.

placed on it by party leaders was clearly exaggerated. It was obvious that a convincing pretext was being sought for administrative measures against the opposition and intervention by the agencies of repression. The Central Control Commission[4] took up the case. Hardcore Stalinists raised a fuss behind the scenes, seeking to have Trotsky and Zinoviev expelled from the party. The situation inside the party became white hot. Aron Solts, a member of the CCC Presidium, one of many who was touted as "the conscience of the party," began talking about the history of the French revolution, about arrests and the guillotine. Among the oppositionists there was serious apprehension that this was more than rhetoric. Trotsky responded to Solts at the CCC session. It was then that he uttered the winged phrase about "Thermidorian degeneration"[5] of the leadership. Later on he added the point, in a letter to Ordzhonikidze, chairman of the CCC, that the danger of war did not eliminate the need for criticism and that replacement of the leadership might actually be a precondition for victory. . . .

Precise data on the scale of opposition activity in the fall of 1927 are not available. It is doubtful that such information has been preserved in Soviet archives to any significant degree. After the revolution, conditions for the free expression of opinion were lacking, and the evaluation of the strength of various tendencies was always more a matter of intuition and atmosphere than a comprehensive analysis of facts. Nevertheless, the small amount of existing material gives an impressive picture. Even after the plenum, the party organizations continued to be flooded — especially in the large urban centers and the two capitals — with opposition literature and leaflets. Reports of heightened opposition activity came one after the other from various cities and from entire provinces — Leningrad, the Ukraine, Transcaucasia, Siberia, the Urals, and of course, Moscow, where the greater number of opposition political leaders were working. There was a steadily growing number of illegal and semilegal meetings attended by industrial workers and young people. The influence of the opposition in a number of large party units became quite substantial. It hampered the former free functioning of the Stalinist party apparatus. The army was also strongly affected by opposition activity. Reports on a significant rise in the authority of the

[4]The party's disciplinary body. — Ed.
[5]Reference to the French Revolution after the fall of Robespierre in July 1794 (in the month of "Thermidor" by the revolutionary calendar. — Ed.

opposition came from the Leningrad military district and the garrison in Leningrad, from Kronstadt, and from troop units in the Ukraine and Byelorussia.

The main problem was not the increase in opposition activity, however, but the overall balance of power within the party. Quite a large number of famous political leaders were on the opposition side. The weakened authority of the party leadership, especially of Stalin and Bukharin, was insufficient to turn the setbacks and failures of party policy into gains. The leadership could not cope with the situation without bringing the GPU into the fight. But until then, GPU interference in internal party matters was strictly forbidden. (A precondition for GPU intervention in political cases was expulsion from the party.) In the upper circles of the party, more than among the rank and file, there was still a powerful fear of the consequences of bringing in the GPU. The experiences of the French revolution, which had been cited more than once since October 1917, were evident to all.

The problem of relations with the opposition was added to disagreements existing in the party leadership. Not all the political leaders, as one might assume, considered the opposition to be excessively dangerous. This fact made itself felt during the July plenum, as I have shown. After the clashes with Stalin in the spring and summer, plans apparently ripened within the moderate wing of the leadership to use the increasingly complicated internal party situation to make fundamental changes in top party posts. The details are hard to determine today. But it remains a fact that rumors were circulating — even reaching diplomatic channels — that in the interest of making peace within the party, Stalin would be replaced in his post by someone else. The name of Tomsky, head of the trade unions, was mentioned.

These plans — even if they were meant seriously — would have been hard to carry through. The opposition and the moderate wing of the leadership were separated not only by deep differences in political outlook but by the accretions built up in the course of a long drawn out internal fight, which affected the attitudes of the forces favoring a moderate policy. The moderates could not try to remove Stalin without placing their own positions in danger.

The political crisis threatened to become a governmental crisis. In early September, the opposition presented the leadership with a programmatic document, the Platform of the United Opposition, which had been written during the summer months. It was intended as the basis for a determined drive to win control of the central party institutions through the precongress discussion period. It was assumed that twenty to thirty thousand signatures could be obtained in support of the platform — this in itself testified to the extent of the opposition's connections.

Outwardly, the platform did not contain much that was new; it repeated arguments the opposition had made earlier. It restated the fundamental economic strategy worked out by the opposition in 1925–1926, and, in some respects, as early as 1923. Predicting inevitable economic difficulties and a crisis, the opposition proposed immediate steps to broaden the scope of Soviet foreign trade, using for this purpose an "administrative loan" of 150 million poods of grain from the well-to-do rural elements. At the same time, the opposition insisted on a radical improvement in the structure of the Soviet economy to increase its efficiency. It also called for a decisive reorganization and reduction of the swollen administrative and economic apparatuses, which caused huge losses of national resources because of their costly and incompetent character.

This was not the platform's only major point. The opposition shifted the weight of its criticism somewhat away from the failed foreign policy of the leadership. It attacked the system of internal policy, the way the NEP was carried out, the expansion of "money-commodity relations," and the related growth of the more well-to-do strata in the city and countryside. It called for a quick improvement in the social conditions of industrial workers and the rural poor (through such measures as wage increases, strict adherence to the law on fixed working hours, meaningful assistance for the unemployed, increased housing construction, government aid and exemption from taxes for the poorer peasant households, the expansion of poor peasant cooperative farming, and the organization of the rural poor). The platform also proposed that the vital core of workers and poor peasants in the party, the soviets, and public organizations be strengthened and that democracy within the party and state be expanded as a precondition for the active participation of working people in public life. At the same time, it urged that increased economic and administrative pressure be applied to the wealthy layers of the population and that their influence in the society and state be suppressed.

From this point of view, the platform sharply criticized the "Moscow centralism" of the party leadership, its crude interference in the national republics and national regions of the USSR, restrictions on national life, and instances of national oppression. It proposed the expansion of the rights and powers of autonomous action for soviet and party bodies in the union republics and national regions, the encouragement of their economic development, and a stronger role for the workers and poor peasants in those areas. At the same time, it demanded that workers of the Russian national minority in the union republics be protected from the consequences of the bureaucratic policy of "naturalization," which was used to conceal the real state of affairs.

The opposition extended its assessment of the situation in the society and state to the party as well. It especially stressed the danger of the rightward course, whose main proponents were said to include Rykov, Kalinin,[6] and Tomsky, in the central leadership, and, in the Ukraine, Grigory Petrovsky and Vlas Chubar. In this way an old error of the opposition was not only repeated but compounded: by striking at the moderates, the opposition made things easier for the Stalinists, whom they classified as "centrists."

The platform was far from being an ideal document. It misjudged the real social relations in the USSR, overestimating the wealth and economic power of the better off sections of the population. The implementation of its proposals would undoubtedly have endangered the NEP. In addition, and here Zinoviev's views played an important role, its assessments and recommendations on foreign policy were left-extremist. Nevertheless, it was an integrated political program that reflected fairly accurately the sentiments of a large section of party members and of politically active industrial workers.

There is no doubt that the platform made a fairly substantial impression on the party leadership, particularly — it can be assumed — on Stalin. He had to question the usefulness of Bukharin's political conceptions, which had resulted in serious setbacks. But the leadership, and Stalin in particular, must also have understood what serious consequences — under conditions of intensifying crisis — the circulation of the opposition's demands could have. On September 8, 1927, the Politburo categorically banned the platform. It was determined to do everything in its power to enforce this prohibition. . . .

Late in the night of September 12 and the early hours of September

[6] Mikhail Kalinin, Chairman of the Presidium of the All-Union Central Executive Committee (i.e., chief of state). — Ed.

13, events occurred that were fated to have momentous consequences for the Soviet future. The GPU raided the apartments of several opposition activists and discovered an illegal "printshop" (an ancient hectograph and some typewriters) where the platform of the opposition was being duplicated. By crude frame-up methods, this "printshop" was linked not only with "certain bourgeois specialists" but also with a "Wrangel officer"[7] (who turned out to be a GPU agent) and with alleged preparations for a "White Guard conspiracy" against Soviet power. Some of the individuals implicated in the case, including the civil war hero Mrachkovsky, were arrested; others were expelled from the party. Three leaders of the opposition, Preobrazhensky, Leonid Serebryakov, and Y. Sharov, attempted to save the situation by taking political responsibility for the "printshop," but they were also expelled.

It soon became evident that the whole operation had been carefully prepared and planned far in advance. News of organizational measures against the opposition and arrests of its supporters came from all major cities — Leningrad, Kiev, Tbilisi, Baku, Yerevan, Rostov on the Don, and elsewhere. Special "fighting units," organized by the Stalinist party apparatus as early as the summer of 1927, broke up opposition meetings with increasing frequency, turning off lights and creating other disturbances. In many instances, matters came to blows. Almost everywhere, oppositionists were fired and blacklisted, working-class members of the opposition being especially hard hit.

These organizational measures against the opposition moved higher and higher toward its top leaders. On September 27, the Presidium of the ECCI[8] returned to the question of Trotsky and Vujovic's[9] membership on that body. The two were charged with a policy of splitting the Comintern and the Soviet Communist Party, slandering the Soviet party leadership, and supporting underground oppositional activity in association with "alien elements." The Presidium corrected its earlier wavering and assumed the role of agent for the Soviet leadership, on which, in fact, it was totally dependent. Trotsky and Vujovic were expelled.

The decisions of the ECCI Presidium were merely a prelude. After a series of tactical maneuvers, confrontations, declarations, and angry

---

[7] The anti-Communist Civil War commander Baron Pyotr Wrangel. — Ed.
[8] Executive Committee of the Communist International. — Ed.
[9] V. Vujovic, a Yugoslav Communist representative. — Ed.

resolutions, on October 21–23, 1927, the question of Trotsky and Zinoviev was again brought before a joint plenum of the Central Committee and CCC. The moderate group in the Politburo, which by then was convinced of the dangerous consequences of the party crisis, abandoned its earlier intentions and retreated all along the line. It became obvious that the opposition, by itself, without the benefit of differences within the leadership, and despite the substantial sympathy and support it enjoyed among the ranks, could not stand up under the fire of organizational measures and repressive acts against its members.

The joint plenum proceeded in an atmosphere of white-hot tension. The leaders, Stalin among them, "apologized" to the Central Committee and CCC for their previously soft approach. When Trotsky and other opposition members of the Central Committee tried to explain their position they were unable to speak because of the constant interruptions of rude and hostile remarks. Ordzhonikidze and Bukharin were said to have shouted, "Trotsky's place is in the inner prison of the GPU," and Menzhinsky[10] seems to have accused the opposition of spying — apparently in connection with Herbette's dispatches.[11] Responding to protests by oppositional members of the Central Committee over the arrests of veteran revolutionaries, Stalin made an ominous remark that has echoed down through Soviet history: "Yes, we have arrested them and we will continue to arrest people like them."

Events quickly approached a climax. The opposition, mobilizing its considerable store of influence, tried to make a show of strength to turn the situation to its favor. During Leningrad's celebration of the tenth anniversary of the October revolution in mid-October 1927, the opposition suddenly received impressive support. Trotsky, Zinoviev, and other oppositionists, who found themselves by chance on one of the official reviewing platforms as the workers of Leningrad paraded past, found themselves the object of demonstrative greetings and cheers from the crowd of a hundred thousand. The authorities appeared to be powerless to control the crowd. The GPU reported with alarm, although this was not without a hidden motive, that units of the Leningrad garrison were politically unreliable.

Inspired by this success, the opposition decided on a number of further steps whose purpose was by no means realistic or rational. It

[10] Vyacheslav Menzhinsky, Director of the GPU. — Ed.
[11] J. Herbette, French Ambassador in Moscow. — Ed.

tried to organize mass resistance within the party and among politically-minded workers against the offensive of the leadership. In Leningrad, Zinoviev, who vacillated between fits of euphoria and panic, hastily arranged meetings with delegations of Leningrad workers. In early November, the opposition took over the auditorium of the Higher Technical School in Moscow and held a meeting with two thousand of its supporters; representatives of the Central Committee and CCC were not allowed in. Rakovksy, who had just been relieved of his post as ambassador to France and therefore enjoyed an aura of martyrdom, made a speaking tour through the Ukraine. He tried, mostly in vain, to get a hearing before audiences of workers. Beloborodov, people's commissar of internal affairs for the RSFSR, spoke for the opposition in the Urals region. The oppositionists' attention was focused, however, on the November 7 demonstrations celebrating the Bolshevik revolution. They wanted to repeat the experience of October's Leningrad demonstration in all the major industrial centers of the country.

The party leadership was seriously alarmed. If the opposition succeeded, it could destroy many well-laid plans. The leadership was apparently not certain what practical purpose the opposition thought to achieve, or what consequences its demonstrations might have.

The Politburo mobilized not only the party apparatus but also the GPU, with all its resources, against the upcoming opposition demonstrations. Emergency measures were taken in the garrisons of all big cities. Every attempt to hold an opposition demonstration on November 7 was suppressed before it could begin. The Stalinist goon squads ("fighting units") and groups organized by the GPU and party apparatus broke up the opposition columns as they formed and provoked scuffles that developed into full-scale brawls. Opposition leaders were greeted with derisive whistling and various objects were thrown at them; some had difficulty escaping from the violence of the hired mob.

Stalin, encouraged by the successful disruption of the opposition's plans, moved to take command of the situation. He was concerned not only by the opposition but also by the moderate leaders who still objected to direct intervention by the GPU in internal party affairs. . . .

Opposition influence remained strong, but it could no longer exert effective influence on the real relations of power. Party conferences held during November, as well as congresses of the Communist parties of the union republics held the same month, were totally controlled by the leadership. The opposition did not win any elected delegates to the upcoming party congress. The moderate leaders paid a heavy price for this new state of affairs. Against their own better judgment, they publicly stressed Stalin's role as leader of the party and expressed their willingness to defend him against the opposition, even with the help of the GPU.

The Fifteenth Party Congress, on which so many hopes had been pinned, convened in Moscow on December 2, 1927. It could no longer play any role in the fight for an alternative road of Soviet development. Its decisions were predetermined by the narrow circle at the party's top. The congress confirmed the expulsion of the opposition, which in fact had already taken place, and — such is the irony of fate — instead of witnessing a struggle against the leadership, it became the scene of an incipient split between the two original groupings in the opposition, the Trotskyists and the Zinovievists. The Zinovievists were hastily swimming back to the safe waters of party loyalty. Still, the leaders of both opposition tendencies were arrested in the first half of January and deported to remote areas of the USSR. The leadership felt that this method of rendering them harmless was tactically preferable to imprisonment.

The open form of political crisis, seen in 1927, was coming to an end. It was replaced by a hidden crisis, related to the general economic and social situation in the USSR. The resolution of the crisis, as is common in such conditions of society, independently of the wills and desires of individuals, brought about major shifts in political thinking and in the power structure.

Within two or three months of the events of September 12–13, 1927 (the raid on the opposition "printshop"), the basis for the existence of any kind of opposition whatsoever inside the Soviet Communist Party had been destroyed. From then on, opposition was an unequivocal political crime, bringing stern punishment in its train. Resistance to GPU interference in party matters was broken. To reinforce this state of affairs, Stalin presented a number of new proposals to the Politburo before the end of the year: that persons propagating opposition views be regarded as dangerous accomplices of the external and internal enemies of the Soviet Union and that such persons be sentenced as "spies" by administrative decree of the GPU; that a widely ramified network of agents be organized by the GPU with the task of seeking out hostile elements within the government apparatus, all the way to its top, and within the party, including the leading bodies of the party. "Everyone who arouses the slightest suspicion should be removed," Stalin concluded. "Humane considerations have no place here." In the fall of 1927, under the pretext that the army was unreliable, and at the price of conflict with the military command, an intensive reinforcement of GPU troop units began, which were contemptuously referred to in the army as the "Soviet gendarmerie." They were intended to combat the "enemy within." . . .

Alec Nove

The Challenge of Industrialization

Alec Nove, Professor Emeritus of Economics at the University of Glasgow, is one of the world's leading authorities on the history of the Soviet economy. In his *Economic History of the U.S.S.R.*, excerpted here, he recounts the genuine debates about future economic development that went on among Soviet economists and political leaders during the 1920s, while Stalin was consolidating political power.

What . . . was in Lenin's mind when NEP was fully established and fate removed from him the power of movement and coherent speech? Did he, as Bukharin believed, draw from the horrors and excesses of war communism a cautious, gradualist conclusion? NEP, he asserted, was intended "seriously and for a long time." How long is a long time? Lenin himself answered this question by hinting that twenty-five years would be a rather pessimistic view. Lenin and all his comrades must have believed that the advance would be resumed, otherwise they had no *raison d'être* as Bolsheviks at all. They were bound to regard the ultimate achievement of socialism as the one possible justification for their being in power. But when was the advance to be resumed? At

From Alec Nove, *Economic History of the U.S.S.R.*, pp. 122–127, 128–129, 132–133, 134–135, Copyright © 1982. Reprinted by permission of Penguin Books.

what speed? In what direction? Above all, what was to be done to convert or transform the peasant majority of the population, and how was the industrialization of Russia to be pursued after the period of reconstruction had come to an end? Questions such as these interacted with political issues, concerned with the power position of individuals and factions and the succession to Lenin.

In disentangling the various strands of the argument it is important to distinguish between a number of aspects of a highly complex situation. There was first and foremost the basic dilemma of a Bolshevik revolution, triumphant in the name of Marxism and the dictatorship of the proletariat in an overwhelmingly peasant country. The party had power, the prerevolutionary productive capacity had been, or was being, restored. By 1925–6 the party had to face a vast question of political economy: how to transform the entire social-economic situation by deliberate action from above. If this was to be done by planning, then by what kind, enforced by what mechanism? A large increase in savings, in accumulation of capital, would be necessary. Who was to bear the sacrifices, and how severe would these sacrifices be? . . .

If the emphasis in investment was to be on heavy industry, then the peasants could not be offered material incentives sufficient to persuade them to sell more produce. This in turn severely limited the power of manoeuvre of an industrializing Soviet government, within the context of the agricultural settlement bequeathed by the revolution. . . .

Agricultural production recovered fairly rapidly, but there was a persistent shortage in marketed produce, and the towns could only be fed at the cost of a drastic reduction in exports of grain. Yet urbanization called for a substantial increase in off-farm consumption of food and also for a large export surplus to pay for essential imports of capital goods. Could this problem be resolved within the traditional peasant methods of production, the three-field system, strips, tiny holdings? Was this not a bottleneck which would hold back the entire economic development of Russia? NEP was based on the so-called smychka with the peasants, the word implying a link, cooperation, harmony. Yet Lenin knew and said that a market-orientated private peasantry generated capitalism. It is true that Lenin, in his last year of political life, also said that the peasants had to be shown the advantages of socialism and cooperation, that they should not be coerced. This presented his successors with a very complex question. It was from the better-off peasants that marketable surpluses would come. Any peasant who specialized in providing marketable surpluses would increase his income. Would this be a dangerous growth of potentially or actually capitalistic elements? What alternative was there, without being in breach of both the assumptions of NEP and of the principles of the smychka? Bukharin, who had been a leader of the left wing during the war communism period, became the best known of the leaders of the moderates (the future "right-wing deviation") in the twenties. He reasoned as follows: NEP is to be persisted with for a long time, for a generation at least. It is out of the question to use force against the peasants. While support for the poor peasants may be politically preferable from the Bolshevik point of view, it is from the middle and better-off peasants that the needed farm surpluses will come, and in no circumstances must they be antagonised. On the contrary, they must be encouraged. The alternative policy would bring back the black days of confiscations, and gravely endanger the Bolshevik hold on political power, since it would lead to peasant rebellion. Bukharin was in favour of building socialism, but only at a pace which the individual peasant producers could be persuaded to accept. In his view, greater prosperity among the peasants, more commercial production, was not only essential but was also not dangerous. In the process of time these peasants too would "grow into socialism." Following his own logic, he launched in April 1925 the slogan "Get rich." The Russian word for this, *obogashchaites*, was the exact translation of a slogan coined in the 1840s by Guizot, the minister of Louis Phillipe of France: *enrichissez-vous*.

Parallels with French revolutionary history were never far from the minds of Bolshevik intellectuals. Guizot was a bourgeois statesman *par excellence*. The slogan was too much. While at this period Stalin was in political alliance with Bukharin, and favoured tax concessions to the more prosperous peasants, which were in fact accorded in 1925, he never committed himself as far as did Bukharin to the logic of his peasant policy. He declared to the fourteenth party conference in the same month: "The slogan 'get rich' is not our slogan." Bukharin was forced to withdraw the offending words and to admit that kulaks were an evil to be limited and squeezed.

However, this retreat from the logic of his policy made Bukharin's entire position untenable. A kulak is a prosperous peasant. A middle peasant is a less prosperous peasant. The official line in 1925–7 accepted the middle peasant as the indispensable provider of farm surpluses, while making political gestures towards the poor peasant (there were bitter complaints that the poor peasants' interests were in fact neglected). But this meant that any middle peasant who was successful in developing commercial sales, who sought to expand his holding by leasing or his production by employing a couple of labourers, would speedily convert himself into a kulak. Agriculture had to succeed, and yet it could not be allowed to succeed on the basis of a prosperous private peasant. This was not a sensible or logical policy. Yet what was the alternative?

This kind of dilemma has been faced in other developing countries. There is a tendency for the same people to demand both land reform and industrialization. Yet land reform often has the effect, at least in the short term, of reducing the volume of marketable production, and sometimes of total production, because an egalitarian land redistribution strengthens the traditional subsistence sector. The problem can in principle be resolved by the emergence of a commercially-minded peasant minority, though no one who knows anything about agricultural problems in developing countries would fall into the error of supposing that there is an easy solution. In the special case of the Soviet Union under Bolshevik rule, an advance in this direction came up against an ideological/political barrier.

The logic of the Bukharin approach necessarily involved an emphasis on the production (or importation) of goods the peasants wanted. The same logic called for relatively slow growth, since progress would be limited by the peasants' willingness to save and to supply the state with food surpluses. Bukharin himself spoke of "riding into socialism on a peasant nag." But could the peasant nag be persuaded to go in the right direction? Would the Party be able to control it? It must not be forgotten that Soviet power in the villages was weak, and that traditional peasant communal institutions were in effective command; within them the more prosperous peasants tended to become dominant as natural village leaders and because so many of their poorer neighbours depended on them.

The so-called left opposition challenged the validity of Bukharin's policies. As might be expected, their arguments were deeply influenced not only by their views on the particular issues but also by the logic of factional struggle. It is this same logic which in the middle twenties led to a temporary alliance between Stalin and the Bukharin faction. Zinoviev and Kamenev in 1923 found it politic to support both Stalin and Bukharin in a struggle against the left opposition. In 1925,

Zinoviev and Kamenev joined the Trotsky group, and thereupon saw virtues in the left opposition's case which had quite escaped their notice two years earlier. However, these and other policy zigzags should not cause us to suppose that the perplexing issues faced by all these men were unreal. Issues are often adopted by political men for their own purposes.

The most cogent theoretical statement of the opposition's case, and one which lights up most vividly the nature of the difficulties which faced the regime, came from the pen of Preobrazhensky. He had been a collaborator of Bukharin's in 1918, but unlike Bukharin he accepted NEP with many reservations and clearly wished to resume the offensive against the hated private sector at the earliest date. He therefore emphasized the dangers which the regime ran if it were to persist for long in the course set in 1921–4. Already in 1923 he was quoting with approval the concept of "primitive socialist accumulation," and his lectures on the subject in 1924 at the Communist Academy were later expanded and published as a book.

Primitive (or initial) capitalist accumulation was described by Marx using British models. Capital was accumulated through the expropriation of the peasantry, by the enclosures of agricultural land, colonial exploitation, the Highland clearances in Scotland. The resultant concentrations of capital came to be invested in industrial development. Applying this analysis to the situation of the U.S.S.R., Preobrazhensky pointed out that there were no colonies to exploit and the peasants could not be expropriated, and yet the necessary socialist accumulation had to come from somewhere. It would be necessary not only in order to finance industrialization, but also to expand the socialist sector of the economy at the expense of the private sector. Clearly the necessary resources could not arise wholly or even mainly within the socialist sector of the economy. Apart from the fact that it was too small to bear the burden by itself, it was wrong and politically dangerous that the sacrifices should be borne by the working class employed by nationalized industries. Resources would therefore have to be obtained from the private sector. The bulk of the private sector were the peasants. Preobrazhensky saw that the necessary capital would not be provided by voluntary savings. The better-off peasants were very unlikely to lend sufficient money to the government, and the Nepmen in the cities naturally used whatever capital they possessed to make hay while the sun shone, realistically fearing that it might not shine for long. Resources would doubtless have to be obtained by taxation, but most of all through unequal exchange, by "exploitation" of the private sector. The state should use its position as the supplier of the bulk of industrial goods, and as the foreign trade monopolist, to pump resources out of the private sector and so finance the state's investments into the expanding socialist industrial sector. Preobrazhensky never failed to emphasize the importance of this conflict between socialist and capitalist elements, and he wrote of the struggle between "the law of value" and the principle of primitive socialist accumulation, i.e., between the forces of the market and those of the socialist state expanding the socialist sectors.

Bukharin and other leaders of the party majority strongly counterattacked. This doctrine, in their view, was threatening the alliance between workers and peasants. The word "exploitation" and the principle of unequal exchange were severely criticized. After all, this was 1924, when the country was only just correcting the excessively unfavourable terms of trade for peasants which characterized the "scissors" crisis of 1923. . . . Every effort was still being made to compel a further relative reduction in the prices charged by state industry. Was this the time to speak of unequal exchange? It may well be that some reasoned privately thus: "Of course we will have to exploit the peasants in due time, but for goodness' sake let us keep quiet about it now."

Trotsky, Preobrazhensky and their followers developed two further criticisms. Firstly, they held that the official line had been too favourable to the better-off peasants. They spoke loudly of the kulak danger and envisaged the degeneration of the party into some sort of adjunct of the NEP bourgeoisie. (We shall see that this degeneration, such as it was, was of a very different kind, but this was not apparent to the opposition at the time.) The party majority was under continuous attack from the left for being soft on the kulaks. Secondly, the "left" opposition contended that the party's industrialization programme was too modest, that a major campaign to build up industry far beyond the levels of 1913 should be launched forthwith. Both Stalin and Bukharin argued at this time that higher growth rates and additional investments advocated by the left opposition represented an adventurist and unpractical policy, which would endanger hard-won financial stability and impose intolerable sacrifices. This would be inconsistent with the principles of NEP. It is true that the same Stalin was a few years later advocating tempos which were far more ambitious and ruthless than any which the opposition had proposed. . . .

The lines of controversy were by no means clear-cut. It must be emphasized also that the protagonists shared many common assumptions. All took for granted the necessity of the retention of sole political power by their party. All took for granted the necessity of industrialization and were under no illusions concerning the limitations of individual peasant agriculture. Peasant cooperation and collectivization were regarded by all as desirable aims. The difference lay in tempos, methods, the assessment of dangers, the strategy to be followed in pursuit of aims very largely held in common. Soviet historians are fond of contrasting the policies of the majority ("the party") with the negative, defeatist, anti-industrializing, pro-peasant policies of various oppositions. Such a picture is a most distorted one. The fourteenth congress of the party meeting in 1925, passed resolutions favouring industrialization, while the fifteenth congress (1927) declared in favour of collectivization and of the five-year plan. However, these resolutions were adopted with the support of the future right-wing opposition. Indeed the "industrial plan" resolution in 1927 was introduced by Rykov, who was Bukharin's most influential supporter.

Trotsky's views have also become distorted, not least by those who purport to be Trotskyists. Until 1925, when he was expelled from the Politbureau, he remained wholly within the assumption of NEP. In his speech to the 12th party congress in 1923, and on other occasions, he accepted the need to encourage the private peasant producer, and advocated more effective and comprehensive planning for the peasant market. He was better able than his ally Preobrazhensky to see the necessity for the coexistence of plan and market, and perhaps this helps to explain why Preobrazhensky broke with Trotsky when, in 1928, Stalin turned "left."

Does this mean that the argument was concerned only or mainly with who should wield political power? Such a conclusion would be totally misleading. The policy differences were deeply felt. It is true that Stalin later on stole many of the clothes of the left opposition, but Bukharin's entire vision of Soviet development differed radically from that which came to be adopted by Stalin, despite the fact that they shared some common aims. Bukharin wished to preserve NEP for a long time yet. Stalin destroyed it. The right opposition were horrified by Stalin's peasant policies and by his industrialization strategy, as well as by his political methods. There were deep and sincerely held policy differences. . . .

As with NEP so with theories of development, 1926 was a year in which the atmosphere changed. Perhaps this was due to the virtual completion in that year of the restoration of the pre-war economy, and a consciousness that a new investment policy was necessary. This too found its reflection in the politics of the time, with resolutions favouring industrialization high on the agenda. Needless to say, the arguments of the economists were also related to the political factions, either directly or indirectly. Thus the argument in favour of investment in agriculture and the consumers' goods industry would naturally fit into the Bukharin approach to NEP. Equally clearly, it would find little sympathy among the supporters of the left opposition, or, when he moved left, from Stalin. It is because of this (sometimes unwanted) association of theoretical arguments with factional struggles that so many of the able economists who expressed original ideas in the twenties died in prison in the thirties.

All planning, in the sense of deliberate decision-making affecting the use of resources, must represent some sort of compromise between two principles, which in Soviet discussions came to be known as "genetic" and "teleological." The first lays stress on the existing situation: market forces, relative scarcities of factors, rates of return, profitability. The second reflects a desire to change the proportions and size of the economy, to maximize growth, to emphasize strategy of development rather than adaptation to circumstances. The conflict between the two attitudes, on both the theoretical and the practical-political planes, increased in the second half of the decade. Naturally, neither side to the argument was unaware of the need for some sort of reconciliation of the opposing principles, though the original and intelligent ex-Menshevik economist V. Groman did assert that there was some "natural" relationship between agriculture and industry which remains (or should remain) constant over time. Most of the protagonists were concerned with relative emphasis. Surely, as Bazarov pointed out, any plan which ignored the existing situation was doomed to failure; any plan which saw no further than the demands of the immediate present was patently inadequate. The changing emphasis after 1926 led more and more to the stress on drastic change, and as party policy veered towards rapid industrialization one heard more and more voices advocate the priority of heavy industry, asserting the criterion of maximizing growth. The economist of this period whose name is now most familiar was Fel'd-man, whose growth model has been introduced to Western readers by E. Domar. Evidently, if the objective is the most rapid industrialization, the investment choices in any developing country are bound to be based on principles quite different to those which would minimize unemployment or economize scarce capital in the short term. As Collette[1] has pointed out, this type of thinking was found in the West only after 1955.

Much was made, by the supporters of a sharp rise in investments, of the phrase "extinguishing curve" (*zatukhayushchaya krivaya*). This was the forecast of a reduced rate of growth, made by a committee of VSNKн [Supreme Economic Council] . . . . Its conclusions followed logically from the inevitable slowdown which would be the consequence of the end of reconstruction. In part they assumed both a rise in the capital-output ratio and a fall in the volume of investment. But the idea of a slowdown was unacceptable to the political leadership; and indeed contradicted the dynamism and optimism without which the party rank-and-file would lose much of their drive and morale. It was sharply rejected. The fact that these and other bourgeois specialists were so very cautious in their prognostications later encouraged Stalin and his colleagues to ignore "moderate" advice. . . .

The issue of balanced *versus* unbalanced growth . . . was also discussed in Russia at this period. In part this was included in the "genetic-teleological" debate, and in part it came up as a problem of how to tackle existing or anticipated bottlenecks. Bukharin in particular advocated a careful attention to balance, and warned of the consequences of neglect of this factor which, after 1928, tended to discredit this approach, since it was associated with right-wing heresy. This was regrettable, since it affected the fate of another of the Soviet innovations: the "balance of the national economy." Using data from 1923–4, a group of gifted men led by Popov and Groman created the "grandfather" of the input-output tables of later years. They invented a new idea, without which planning could hardly begin. It was necessary to trace the interconnections of the sectors composing the economy; to discover how much fuel was (or would be) needed to produce a given quantity of metal, to take just one example. The attempt was in many

---

[1] J. M. Collette, author of *Politique des investissements et calcul economique* (Paris: Cujas, 1964). — Ed.

ways inadequate, many of the necessary data were missing. But it was the first such attempt, if one excepts Quesnay's *Tableau économique*,[2] to which Soviet economic literature makes frequent reference. The twenties were an intellectually exciting period. Not only were there debates among Bolshevik leaders and intellectuals, among whom were men of great eloquence and wit, but quite independent ideas were put forward by men who were not Bolsheviks at all. Gosplan [State Planning Commission] and VSNKн experts included many former Mensheviks, later to be accused of being plotters and saboteurs. Men like Groman, Bazarov and Ginzburg contributed significantly to policy debates. Ex-populists, ex-SRs, were active too, for example the famous economist Kondratiev, the agricultural experts Chayanov and Chelintsev. Even non-socialists, like Litoshenko and Kutler, could raise their voices. There was a one-party state, there were no legal means of organizing an opposition, but conditions were far from resembling the monolithic thirties. The communists were very weakly represented at this time among the planners. Thus in 1924, out of 527 employees of Gosplan, only forty-nine were party members, and twenty-three of these were drivers, watchmen, typists, etc.

The great debate, or more properly debates, must be seen as taking place at many different levels. There was the political struggle for power. There was the conflict at the political level between advocates of different policies towards the peasants, or on industrialization rates (tempos), or "socialism in one country." There were discussions and proposals put up by experts on investment criteria and growth strategies. Theory and practice, expert judgement and politics, interacted in various ways. Thus, not surprisingly, political men who were not allowed to express open dissent in a political way did so in their capacity as experts, just as others did so as novelists and poets. Politicians used experts, and selected statistics to suit their arguments, which eventually proved very dangerous for the experts. Thus the apparently abstract argument about peasant stratification became political dynamite, inevitably linked with the question of the kulak danger and the steps which could or should be taken to combat it. Even so statistical an issue as the volume of marketed grain became highly "political," as we have seen.

---

[2] Analysis of economic interrelationships by the eighteenth-century French "physiocrat" François Quesnay. — Ed.

Stephen F. Cohen

The Moderate Alternative

Stephen F. Cohen is a professor of politics at Princeton University and author of an outstanding biography of Nikolai Bukharin. In the excerpt reprinted here, Cohen gives special attention to the political crisis of 1928–29 when Stalin broke with the line of the New Economic Policy and crushed the resistance of Bukharin's "Right Opposition." Reflecting their rehabilitation of Bukharin, the Soviet authorities under Gorbachev agreed in 1988 to publish a Russian translation of Cohen's book.

How little the leadership's feigned unanimity reflected its internal discord was dramatized immediately after the plenum.[1] Speaking on the same day in Moscow and Leningrad respectively, the Politburo's two pre-eminent leaders, Stalin and Bukharin, gave radically different accounts of party policy and the situation in the country. Reviving his earlier bellicosity on the "grain front," announcing that Shakhty[2] was not "something accidental," and unveiling his "self-criticism" crusade, Stalin's theme was starkly uncompromising: "We have internal enemies. We have external enemies. This, comrades, must not be forgotten for a single moment." His target was unnamed but identifiable leaders who "think NEP means not intensifying the struggle," who wanted "a policy in the countryside that will please . . . rich and poor alike." Such a policy had "nothing in common with Leninism"; and such a leader was "not a Marxist, but a fool." Meantime, speaking in a very different tone on the same issues, Bukharin was expressing his first public apprehension over the "tendency" of "certain people" to regard the "extraordinary measures" as "almost normal" and "to negate the importance of the growth of individual economies and in general to exaggerate the use of administrative methods."

[1] The April 1928 plenary meeting of the Central Committee. — Ed.
[2] Trial of alleged saboteurs at the Shakhty coal mines in the Ukraine. — Ed.

From *Bukharin and the Bolshevik Revolution: A Political Biography, 1888–1938*, by Stephen F. Cohen, excerpts from pp. 282–335. Copyright © 1971, 1973 by Stephen F. Cohen. Reprinted by permission of Alfred A. Knopf, Inc.

At this point the grain crisis broke out anew. A severe winter, depletion of village reserves, and peasant withdrawal from the market suddenly brought another sharp drop in collections. In late April, the emergency measures were revived with greater intensity and scope than before. The role of Bukharin, Rykov, and Tomskii in this decision is not known; but if they supported it they must have done so with great misgivings. Kulak surpluses had been exhausted by the first campaign; now the measures would fall squarely on the middle — or majority — peasant, who held what stocks remained. During the next two months, the expanded collection measures and accompanying "excesses" provoked widespread discontent and sporadic rioting in the countryside. Reports of rural disturbances and food shortages stirred industrial unrest in the cities. The strain was too much for the fragile accord in the Politburo. In May and June, the split between Bukharinists and Stalinists became complete.

Until the spring of 1928, Bukharin, Rykov, and Tomskii seem to have regarded differences in the leadership as negotiable, and tried to resolve them in the Politburo. Now, however, they (and especially Bukharin) were alarmed by the Stalin group's increasingly radical, uncompromising posture. Differences of opinion were becoming large and systematic. At the center of the dispute were contrary analyses of the régime's current problems exemplified by the grain shortages and the Shakhty affair. The Bukharinists insisted that they were the result of secondary factors: the state's unpreparedness, poor planning, inflexible price policies, and negligent local officials. On the other hand, Stalin and the people around him were portraying the difficulties as having derived from structural or organic causes, and thus from the nature and deficiencies of NEP itself. In addition to kulak hoarding, Stalinists maintained, the grain crisis reflected the cul de sac of peasant agriculture; both it and the Shakhty episode were not transitory by-products of "faulty planning and chance mistakes," but evidence of an unavoidable intensification of the class war, a battle which had to be fought to the end.

Bukharin's analysis recommended moderate remedies, including assistance to private farmers, flexible price policies, and improved responsiveness by official institutions. Stalin's pointed to radical solutions. He had as yet no comprehensive alternative to prevailing Bukharinist policies, but he was moving in another direction: toward asserting and legitimizing the "will of the state," including coercive "extraordinary measures," on all fronts. In relation to this, he began to disparage private farming while heralding collective and state farms as "the way out." Though the dispute still focused on agriculture, its implications for industrial policy and the five-year plan then in preparation were equally great. Kuibyshev's reconstituted staff at the Supreme Economic Council was already challenging the cautious planners of Gosplan, whose views on proportional development and equilibrium market conditions were similar to Bukharin's. By May, echoes of the planning controversy could be heard in the Politburo. At stake, therefore, was the party's entire economic program and, once again, the future course of the Bolshevik revolution.

Taken together, Stalin's policy initiatives threatened the prevailing Bukharinist understanding of NEP as a system of civil peace and reciprocal market relations between town and country. They conflicted rudely with the Right's belief that problems could and should be solved "in the conditions and on the basis of NEP." More immediately, Bukharin complained, they distorted the party's general line ratified only four months earlier at the Fifteenth Congress. Embodying the Right's revised program, the congressional resolutions had promised a leftward turn toward an "offensive against the kulak," the creation of a partial, voluntary collectivized sector, and planned industrial development with greater emphasis on capital goods production. But each goal had been stated in a moderate, Bukharinist fashion, pointedly excluding extreme policies. Now, however, Stalin was seeking to legitimize his new militancy by reinterpreting those resolutions, portraying, for example, the "extraordinary measures" as a "normal" consequence of the congress's anti-kulak resolution. . . .

By late June, despite its public facade, there was neither pretense nor grounds for unity within the leadership. On the 15th, Moshe Frumkin, the rightist Deputy Commissar of Finance, sent the Politburo an anxious letter evaluating the situation in the countryside in terms even more pessimistic than Bukharin's. He reported that his views were supported "by many Communists." The Politburo voted to circulate his letter among Central Committee members with a collective reply. Stalin immediately violated the decision, sending a personal reply through the Secretariat. Outraged, Bukharin accused him of treating the Politburo as "a consultative organ under the general secretary." Stalin tried to placate Bukharin: "You and I are the Himalayas; the others are nobodies," a remark Bukharin quoted at a "savage" Politburo session to

Stalin's shouts of denial. No longer on speaking terms, the personal breach between the former duumvirs was total. Bukharin now refused to distribute written recommendations to the Politburo, reading them instead: "You can't trust him with a single piece of paper." He spoke of Stalin with the "absolute hatred" born of revelation — "He is an unprincipled intriguer who subordinates everything to the preservation of his power. He changes theories depending on whom he wants to get rid of at the moment." . . .

As events were to reveal, the Right's political position was far more vulnerable than its array of posts and allies suggested. Among other things, the advantages of Stalin's six-year manipulation of the party's Secretariat soon became evident in crucial ways: in the presence of strong Stalinist minorities in each of the Right's "principalities"; in the fact that virtually all initially uncommitted leaders went over to him; and in his overwhelming following among second-ranking leaders, especially party secretaries who currently sat as candidate members of high bodies, including the Politburo and Central Committee. If Bukharin and his friends formally prevailed in the high offices of the party-state, and monopolized its symbols of power, Stalin controlled a potent shadow government, "a party within the party." When the balance at the top, particularly in the Politburo, shifted to Stalin, his forces everywhere began to oust and replace entrenched leaders loyal or sympathetic to the Right, a process abetted by a decade of bureaucratic centralization and deference to orders from above.

But to participants and observers alike, the balance of power still appeared to be with the Right when the Central Committee assembled on July 4, a fact that helps explain Stalin's unwillingness to risk an open confrontation and his repeated concessions on major issues. It also explains Bukharin's shocked reaction to events at the plenum, whose public decisions bore little relation to what actually occurred during the week-long proceedings. On the surface, the Bukharinists emerged victorious. The principal resolution, while a compromise, spoke (for the last time) in the voice of the Right. It assured peasant farmers of their security and essential role under NEP, promised a final cessation of the emergency campaigns, and resolved, against Stalin's opposition, to raise grain prices. It was so conciliatory that exiled Left oppositionists lamented the Right's triumph. Trotsky predicted that Bukharin and Rykov would shortly "hunt down Stalin as a Trotskyist, just as Stalin had hunted down Zinoviev."

In fact, as Bukharin understood, the plenum represented a major setback for the Right. The rift was now partially exposed before the Central Committee. While the Politburo leaders continued their labored diplomacy, mostly criticizing each other only indirectly, their supporters exchanged sharp and explicit attacks. Molotov, Mikoyan, and Kaganovich[3] spoke for Stalin; Stetskii, Sokolnikov, and Osinskii for the Right (Osinskii, after years on the party Left, thereby rejoined Bukharin in a political friendship dating back to their Moscow youth). As the heated debate over peasant policy unfolded, the Right's hope for a majority faded. Bukharin had counted on the support of the important Ukrainian and Leningrad delegations; both failed to intervene, the Leningraders openly disassociating themselves from Stetskii, a member of their own delegation. Many delegates, genuinely worried about the rising tide of peasant unrest, spoke ambivalently; but they were unwilling to censure Stalin or endorse unlimited concessions to the peasantry at the expense of the industrialization drive. Their mood was not Stalinist, but it had shifted from the Right; at best, Bukharin reasoned, they "still don't understand the depth of the disagreements." Worse, it was also clear that the Right had lost its Politburo majority. Kalinin and Voroshilov, as their conduct revealed and Bukharin confided, "betrayed us at the last moment. . . . Stalin has some special hold on them."

Sensing the delegates' mood, the Stalin group became more daring. While Molotov openly criticized *Pravda*'s editorials on the procurement campaigns, and thus by implication Bukharin himself, Kaganovich defended the "extraordinary measures" so extravagantly as to justify them "at all times and in any circumstances." As the plenum drew to a close, Stalin and Bukharin rose to deliver the main addresses. The disheartened Bukharin tried to rouse the Central Committee. No sustained industrialization, he insisted, was possible without a prospering agriculture, which was now declining as a result of the requisi-

[3] Vyacheslav Molotov, party secretary under Stalin, successor to Rykov as prime minister, 1930–1941, foreign commissar, then foreign minister, 1939–1946 and 1953–1957; expelled from the leadership by Khrushchev in 1957. Anastas Mikoyan, Commissar of Trade and Politburo member, under Khrushchev Chief of State and supporter of de-Stalinization; Lazar Kaganovich, Politburo member, expelled from the leadership by Khrushchev in 1957. — Ed.

tioning. Moreover, faced with a "wave of mass discontent" and "a united village front against us," the régime was on the verge of a complete break with the peasantry: "two bells have sounded, the third is next." Stalinists retorted with hoots of "panic-monger." The general secretary was similarly unmoved. Dismissing the Right's admonitions as a "cheerless philosophy" and "capitulationism," he spoke instead of class war and collectivization, and suddenly introduced the theoretical rationale for a new, unspecified peasant policy: since Soviet Russia had no colonies, the peasantry would have to pay "something in the nature of a 'tribute'" to fund industrialization. Bukharin was stunned. His former ally had appropriated not only Preobrazhenskii's reasoning, but his draconian rhetoric as well.

Formally the plenum had decided nothing. Bukharin and his allies had not been directly defeated; the resolutions were largely theirs, and most delegates were perplexed rather than rigidly partisan. But Bukharin sensed the Right's perilous situation. A minority in the Politburo and unable to rally the Central Committee, they faced a ruthless, skilled adversary determined "to cut our throats" and whose policies were "leading to civil war. He will have to drown the uprisings in blood." Frightened by this turn of events, Bukharin took a desperate step, one that was to have adverse repercussions when it became known. Violating "party discipline," he made personal contact with the disgraced Zinoviev-Kamenev opposition. On July 11, the day before the plenum closed, he paid a secret visit to Kamenev.

What passed between them comes to us through Kamenev's elliptical notes acquired and published clandestinely by Trotskyists six months later. Bukharin, believing rumors inspired by Stalin of the general secretary's own impending reconciliation with the Left, had come to convert Zinoviev and Kamenev, or persuade them to remain aloof. He, Rykov, and Tomskii agreed: "it would be better to have Zinoviev and Kamenev in the Politburo now than Stalin. . . . The disagreements between us and Stalin are many times more serious than were our disagreements with you." As the "extremely shaken" Bukharin related the history of the rift, Kamenev had "the impression of a man who knows he is doomed." Bukharin was obsessed by Stalin's villainy — "a Genghis Khan" whose "line is ruinous for the whole revolution." Trapped in a Hamlet-like posture, Bukharin wanted, but was unable, to carry the struggle into the open because a fearful Central Committee would turn against any perpetrator of an open split. "We would say, here is the man who brought the country to famine and ruin. He would say, they are defending kulaks and nepmen." Bukharin could only hope that his discreet efforts or outside events would convince the Central Committee of Stalin's "fatal role." On this note, he left, swearing Kamenev to secrecy and warning that they were under surveillance. They were to meet twice again that year in equally melancholy and pointless sessions.

The July plenum was a pivotal episode in the struggle. Though it gave Stalin neither a decisive political victory nor a programmatic mandate, it emboldened him and reduced the Right to minority status in the leadership. With Stalin still groping toward alternative policies and uncertain of his political strength, and the Right's acquiescence in concealing the split, the pretense of Politburo unity continued. But the advantage was now Stalin's. . . .

One important policy issue still remained outside the controversy, the rate and pattern of industrialization. This came to the fore on September 19, when Kuibyshev, speaking for Stalin's faction, proclaimed a new industrializing manifesto. Bukharin's revised program, adopted at the Fifteenth Party Congress, was ambitious but restrained. In stressing balanced industrial and agricultural development, and consumer and capital production, it explicitly rejected "that formula which calls for maximum investment in heavy industry." Kuibyshev wholeheartedly embraced the formula, until now the clarion of the Left. Crisis and perils at home and abroad, he said, demanded a radical acceleration and concentration of investment in heavy industry at any price, including economic imbalances and "discontent and active resistance" among the population. Stalin, revealing his own thinking, cast the new industrializing philosophy in historical perspective a few weeks later. The imperative of "maximum capital investment in industry," he explained, was dictated by Russia's traditional backwardness. He referred his party audience to Peter the Great, another revolutionizer from above, who in an effort to break out of this backwardness "feverishly built mills and factories to supply the army and strengthen the country's defenses."

Bukharin responded in a famous article entitled "Notes of an Economist." Kuibyshev's Supreme Economic Council, with Stalin's encouragement and to the Right's dismay, was already escalating its proposed five-year plan targets. "Notes of an Economist" was a definitive policy rejoinder. Bukharin reiterated the Right's belief in proportional, "more or less crisis-free development" and a plan that specified and observed "the conditions of *dynamic economic equilibrium*" between industry and agriculture, and within the industrial sector itself. Defending the current level of investment but opposing any increase, he went on to a detailed indictment of Stalin's and Kuibyshev's "adventurism."

Two features particularly infuriated him. To increase capital expenditure without a requisite improvement in agriculture, indeed amidst an agricultural crisis, was to disregard industry's essential base and invite overall "ruin." Furthermore, in addition to the shortages of grain and technical crops, industry was already lagging behind its own expanded demand, creating acute shortages of materials and widespread bottlenecks. A further overstraining of capital expenditure could only disrupt construction already under way, reverberate adversely throughout the entire industrial sector, and "in the last analysis reduce the tempo of development." Instead, "upper limits" on industrial expansion had to be set, and that level of expenditure utilized efficiently for "real" construction, if only because "it is not possible to build 'present-day' factories with 'future bricks.' " Addressing the bravado of Stalinist industrializers, Bukharin added: "You can beat your breast, swear allegiance and take an oath to industrialization, and damn all enemies and apostates, but this will not improve matters one bit."

"Notes of an Economist" caused a major stir in the party when it appeared in *Pravda* on September 30, 1928. Though its target remained anonymous " 'super-industrialists' of the Trotskyist type," the long, strongly worded polemic was a transparent assault on Stalin's group and as close as Bukharin had come to making public the struggle. His supporters circulated and recommended the article as "showing the path that must be taken," while Stalinists, secretly trying to proscribe it, launched a press campaign defending their industrial line. On October 8, Stalin's Politburo majority, over the objections of Bukharin, Rykov, and Tomskii, reprimanded its "unauthorized" publication. The policy dispute was now total and seemingly beyond compromise. Its outcome awaited a political showdown.

With a Politburo majority to sanction his offensive, Stalin moved relentlessly against the Right's political bases in the late summer and autumn of 1928. Rykov's authority in high state councils was rudely challenged and a number of pro-Right officials in Moscow and the republican governments dismissed. Tomskii was savaged privately by Stalin as "a malicious and not always honorable person" — surely a classic piece of pharisaism — and his trade union leadership criticized in the Stalinist press for assorted sins, among them obstructing productivity. Much the same was afoot in the Moscow party organization in August and September, where Uglanov and his district secretaries were under the fire of a "self-criticism" campaign against "right opportunism." Meanwhile, the Bukharinist party bureau of the Institute of Red Professors was finally toppled by Stalinists. And in the Comintern, the dwindling band of Bukharin loyalists was locked in a losing battle for control of the Executive Committee apparatus, while Bukharin found himself powerless to stop the drive against Comintern "rightists," notably in the important German party.

Equally significant was Stalin's seizure of the party's leading press organs. Petrovskii, after criticizing the general secretary's "tribute" speech, was summarily transferred from the editorship of *Leningrad Pravda* to a tiny provincial newspaper. About the same time, probably in August or September, the young Bukharinist editors of *Pravda* and *Bolshevik*, Slepkov, Astrov, Maretskii, Zaitsev, and Tseitlin, were ousted and replaced by Stalinists. Bukharin remained editor-in-chief of *Pravda*, and with Astrov still sat on the seven-man board of *Bolshevik*; but he no longer decided their editorial policy or contents. This was an important development. Until the autumn, these authoritative publications of the Central Committee had interpreted disputed policy in a Bukharinist spirit, thus moderating the party leadership's official voice and its communication with lower officials. Now, though occasional dissonant articles and speeches by Bukharinists continued to appear, the party's official voice became Stalinist. The turnabout coincided in mid-September with the beginning of a strident press attack on a still unidentified "right danger" in the party. No such thin anonymity adorned the covert anti-Right campaign; by October, Stalinists were surreptitiously "working over" Bukharin as a "panic-monger" and "enemy of industrialization and collective farms."

Damaging as these developments were, they did not directly alter the uncertain balance of power in the Central Committee, where the struggle had ultimately to be completed. Here the key was the Moscow party organization, which continued to oppose Stalin with impurity, a fact no doubt carefully observed by party secretaries elsewhere. Since the July plenum, the Muscovites had persistently defended Bukharinist policies, including their own special interest in light industry. Indeed, Uglanov, a tough and determined adversary, was fighting back. Mounting their own press campaign, he and his associates had encouraged anti-Stalinists not to fear the word "deviation," denounced talk of a right danger as "slanderous rumors" by "intriguers," and suggested obliquely that Stalin was a negligent general secretary. Their daring worried even Bukharin, who cautioned Uglanov against giving Stalin a pretext to intervene in Moscow.

Considering the past efficiency of Uglanov's machine, Stalin's overthrow of the Moscow party leadership was remarkably swift. In the first weeks of October, Uglanov found himself besieged by rampant insubordination in lower ranks, unable to make personnel changes in his own organization, and forced to dismiss two of his most outspoken district secretaries, Riutin and Penkov. His hopeless situation was displayed at a full Moscow Committee meeting on October 18–19. Incited and sanctioned by directives from Stalin's central apparatus, insurgents censured Uglanov's conduct of the Moscow party and his toleration of "deviations from the correct Leninist line." On October 19, in the tone of a conqueror, Stalin personally addressed the gathering. His "message" was the urgency of conducting a relentless fight against the "Right, opportunist danger in our Party" as well as Communists who exhibited "a conciliatory attitude towards the Right deviation." Allowing that the apostasy was still only "a tendency, an inclination," and naming no offenders, he nonetheless magnified the peril: "the triumph of the Right deviation in our Party would unleash the forces of capitalism, undermine the revolutionary positions of the proletariat and increase the chances of the restoration of capitalism in our country."

Outgunned and humiliated, Uglanov and several aides issued semi-recantations, but to no avail. Further high-level dismissals ended their control of the Moscow organization on October 19. Uglanov and his deputy Kotov lingered on in their posts until November 27, when they were replaced formally by Molotov and Karl Bauman. A sweeping purge of Bukharin's Moscow supporters and sympathizers, high and low, followed. The overthrow of the old Moscow leadership was complete. . . .

Tomskii's downfall, preceded by subversion similar to that in the Moscow party, came at the Eighth Trade Union Congress on December 10–24. By early November, Stalin's campaign to discredit his leadership had led union officials to complain of "an atmosphere making it completely impossible to work." When the congress opened, Tomskii and his fellow leaders found themselves a minority in the party caucus which controlled the agenda, and were defeated on two crucial issues.

Nikolai Bukharin, Stalin's rival in 1928–29, photographed on a mission to London, 1931. (Sovfoto)

One involved endorsement of the Central Committee's November resolutions, and thus official trade union acquiescence in industrial policies bitterly opposed by its leadership. The fight was decided in the caucus, but it spilled over into a debate by innuendo at the public congress. While Stalinists led by Kuibyshev extolled all-out heavy industrialization, Tomskii and his associates objected to the prospect of an industrial drive that would victimize the working class and transform unions into "houses of detention." It was the Tomskii leadership's swan song, a defense of the traditional NEP role of unions: "Trade unions exist to serve the working masses," a conception now rejected as "narrow shop stewardism" and apolitical. The incoming order was heralded by a new Stalinist slogan: "Trade Unions — Face Toward Production!"

Tomskii's other defeat ended his decade-long control of the trade union organization. On Politburo instructions, the caucus voted to co-opt five Stalin appointees onto the Central Trade Union Council. Tomskii tried to block one nomination, that of the unpopular Kaganovich, charging that it created a "dual center" and imposed a "political commissar" on the unions. Defeated, Tomskii again submitted his resignation on December 23. It was rejected, but he remained trade union head in name only, refusing to return to his post. He and virtually the entire union leadership (most of them, like Tomskii, pioneers of the Bolshevik trade union movement) were removed officially in June 1929. This overthrow was so wholesale and arbitrary that it elicited an explanation by Kaganovich: "It could be said that this was a violation of proletarian democracy; but, comrades, it has long been known that for us Bolsheviks democracy is no fetish."

By November–December, Bukharin, Rykov, and Tomskii were no longer leading members of a divided leadership making decisions by compromise, but a minority opposition in Stalin's Politburo, powerless and with dwindling influence over policy. Apart from Rykov, their roles had become less than minimal. Formally still editor of *Pravda* and political secretary of the Comintern, Bukharin, like Tomskii, quit his posts in protest in December and never returned. . . .

Bukharin's most dramatic protest, however, came . . . in a long speech commemorating the fifth anniversary of Lenin's death. Its sensational title, "Lenin's Political Testament," alerted readers to its importance when it appeared in leading newspapers on January 24.[4] For,

---

[4]The speech was republished by the journal *Kommunist* in February 1988, preparatory to Bukharin's rehabilitation. — Ed.

while Bukharin was talking about Lenin's deathbed articles on party policy, his title recalled the dead leader's other "testament," unpublished but not unknown, with its damning postscript calling for Stalin's removal as general secretary. In the context of 1929, Bukharin's actual subject was no less provocative. He wanted to show that Stalin was violating Lenin's programmatic "testament" as well. The device was a straightforward exposition of the famous five articles that had inspired Bukharin's programs, and official policy, since 1923–4. Their legacy, he began, was "a large, long-range plan for all of our Communist work . . . the general paths and high road of our development. . . . To set out Ilich's entire plan as a whole — that is my task today."

Point by point, "adding absolutely nothing of my own," Bukharin reiterated Lenin's "last directives": The revolution's future depends on a firm collaborative alliance with the peasantry; party policy must center now on *"peaceful, organizational, 'cultural' work,"* on conciliating peasant interests, not on a "third revolution"; capital accumulation and industrialization must proceed on the "healthy base" of expanding market relations, with prospering peasant farmers joining into market-oriented cooperatives (which were not collective farms), and on a rational utilization of resources combined with a relentless cutback in unproductive and bureaucratic expenditure. The watchwords of Lenin's "testament" were caution, conciliation, civil peace, education, and efficiency. Its central directive was preventing a "split" with the peasantry, for this would mean *"the destruction of the Soviet Republic."*

Composed largely of Lenin's words and signed by Bukharin, "Lenin's Political Testament" was a ringing, anti-Stalinist manifesto, a defense of the NEP philosophy and policies being jettisoned by the general secretary. A year earlier it would have been an official homily. In January 1929, it was an opposition platform, attacked by the Stalinist majority as "a revision and distortion of the most important principles of Leninism," an attempt to portray Lenin as "a common peasant philosopher." It was also the last explicit statement of Bukharin's thinking and policies to be published in the Soviet Union. Sensing what was to come, he appealed to Bolshevism's tradition of critical thought, imploring party officials "to take not a single word on trust . . . to utter not a single word against their conscience." He added, plaintively, "conscience, contrary to what some think, has not been abolished in politics." . . .

On February 7 [1929] . . . Bukharin . . . drafted another detailed attack on Stalin which was signed by Tomskii and Rykov, who read it to the . . . Politburo session of February 9. This "platform of the three" seems to have been virtually identical to Bukharin's statement of January 30. Considered as a single document, it was his most important declaration of opposition, the strongest condemnation of Stalin and nascent Stalinism ever to originate in the Politburo. Never published and known solely from fragmentary accounts, it can only be partially reconstructed.

Its political theme was that behind a spate of participatory slogans, Stalin and his coterie were "implanting bureaucratism" and establishing a personal régime inside the party. The official line called for self-criticism, democracy, and elections. "But where in reality do we see an elected provincial secretary? In reality, elements of bureaucratization in our party have grown." Indeed, "the party doesn't participate in deciding questions. Everything is done from above." The same situation prevailed in party councils, where Stalin was usurping power: "We are against that practice where questions of party leadership are decided by one person. We are against that practice where collective control has been replaced by the control of one person, however authoritative."

Bukharin then specified Stalin's abuses of power. Among them were gross violations of party decorum, as in the surreptitious campaign against Bukharinists who were being "politically slaughtered" and subjected to "organizational encirclement" by Stalin's henchmen, "political commissars" like Kaganovich, "a wholly administrative type." These "abnormal conditions" made it impossible to discuss urgent problems. To point out that there was a grain shortage was to be "worked over" and accused of "every filth" by "a swarm of well-nourished, satiated functionaries." Meanwhile, Stalin was arbitrarily disregarding official party resolutions. Despite unanimous and repeated decisions to assist private farmers, for example, policy proceeded quite differently and these directives "remained merely literary artifacts." A similar process was under way in the Comintern, where policy was being revised "with scorn for the facts," and where Stalin's tactics of "splits, splinters, and groups" were leading to the "decomposition" of the international movement.

Turning to domestic policy, Bukharin charged Stalin with an irresponsible failure of real leadership in conditions of national crisis.

> *Serious, urgent questions are not discussed. The entire country is deeply troubled by the grain and supply problems. But conferences of the proletarian, ruling party are silent. The entire country feels that all is*

not well with the peasantry. But conferences of the proletarian party, our party, are silent. The entire country sees and feels changes in the international situation. But conferences of the proletarian party are silent. Instead there is a hail of resolutions about deviations (all in the very same words). Instead there are millions of rumors and gossip about the rightists Rykov, Tomskii, Bukharin, etc. This is petty politics, and not politics that in a time of difficulties tells the working class the truth about the situation, that trusts the masses, and hears and feels the needs of the masses.

Those economic measures actually advocated by the Stalin group, continued Bukharin, were only a disastrous "going over to Trotskyist positions." Industrialization based on the "impoverishment" of the country, the degradation of agriculture, and the squandering of reserves was impossible — "all our plans threaten to collapse." But Bukharin's harshest words dealt with peasant policy. Stalinists had written off private farming and talked only of collectivization; but "in the next few years . . . collective and state farms cannot be the basic source of grain. For a long time, the basic source will still be individual peasant economies." Then, in a never-to-be-forgotten "slander," Bukharin perceived a dark impulse behind the "overtaxation" and requisitioning in the countryside. Since the plenum of July 1928, he charged, Stalin had advocated industrialization based on "the military-feudal exploitation of the peasantry."

What in fact has determined subsequent policy? . . . Comrade Stalin's speech about tribute. At the Fourteenth Party Congress, Comrade Stalin was completely against Preobrazhenskii's idea of colonies and the exploitation of the peasantry. But at the July plenum, he proclaimed the tribute slogan, that is, the military-feudal exploitation of the peasantry. . . .

By 1929, Bukharin had come to share most of Trotsky's criticisms of the party's internal régime. Unlike Trotsky, however, having sanctioned its development, he was its prisoner. His dissent and accompanying pleas for the toleration of critical opinion in 1928–9 were regularly rebuffed with quotations from his own, earlier sermons against the Left's "factionalism," and his attacks on Stalin's "secretarial régime" with derisive jeers: "Where did you copy that from? . . . From Trotsky!" Still, despite his complicity in imposing the proscriptive norms, Bukharin was tempted to appeal to the whole party. He agonized over his dilemma: "Sometimes at night I think, have we the right to remain silent? Is this not a lack of courage? . . . Is our 'fuss' anything but masturbation?" Finally, believing that the party hierarchy he sought to win over would "slaughter" any leader who carried the struggle beyond its councils, he conformed to "party unity and party discipline," to the narrow, intolerant politics he had helped create. He shunned overt "factionalism," and so was reduced to ineffectual "backstairs intrigues" (like his Kamenev visit) easily exploited by his enemies. His position was politically incongruous: driven by outraged contempt for Stalin and his policies, he remained throughout a restrained, reluctant oppositionist.

Apart from public appeals too Aesopian to be effective, Bukharin, Rykov, and Tomskii therefore colluded with Stalin in confining their fateful conflict to a small private arena, there to be "strangled behind the back of the party." And it is in this context that Stalin's decisive victory must be explained. The customary explanation is uncomplicated: his bureaucratic power, accumulated during six years as general secretary and fed by successive victories over party dissidents, was omnipotent and unchallengeable; effortlessly and inexorably, it crushed the Bukharinists. The full truth is more complex. For while this interpretation emphasizes an important part of the story, it exaggerates Stalin's organizational power in 1928, underestimates the Right's, and discounts the substantive issues that hung in the balance and influenced the outcome.

Stalin's control of the central party bureaucracy was, of course, a major factor. Through its appointment powers, he had promoted loyalists throughout the party, especially provincial secretaries who sat also on the Central Committee. Like a fourteenth-century Muscovy prince, he had gathered party "principalities" and barons into his orbit. They were the backbone of his support in 1928–9. Equally important was the central bureaucracy's secretarial apparatus, which served the general secretary as a nationwide shadow government. On one level, its direct communication with all party organizations allowed him to interpret policy, manipulate party opinion, foster "pogroms," and generally offset the Bukharinist press. On another, its network of subordinate organs — whose secretarial cadres (133,000 to 194,000 strong) were sufficiently ubiquitous to obstruct Bukharin's return from Kislovodsk in November 1928 — functioned as virtual Stalinist caucuses in every institution headed by the opposition and its sympathizers. Minorities when the struggle began, these caucuses subverted and replaced rightist leaderships in places as diverse as the Moscow organization, the trade unions, the Institute of Red Professors, and even foreign Communist parties.

Their collective ascendency in 1928–9 imposed the hegemony of the party bureaucracy over "principalities," among them Rykov's governmental apparatus, previously outside its control. . . .

By November, the pillorying of Bukharin, "the right deviation," and "conciliationism" had become an ideological terror directed at policy moderation in general. Coupled with the purge (which was now victimizing all of Bukharin's known sympathizers, even Lenin's widow Krupskaya and his sister Mariia Ulianova), its immediate political consequence was to impose zealotry on a still predominantly recalcitrant party. Among other things, it repressed the widespread hostility to Stalin's agricultural policies and drove terrified party officials to the frenzied excesses that produced the rural catastrophe of the winter of 1929–30.

More generally, the campaign constituted an official repudiation of NEP's moderately tolerant, conciliatory practices, now assailed as "rotten liberalism" or, occasionally, "Bukharinist liberalism." It echoed a major transformation underway in Soviet cultural and intellectual life since mid-1929. Paralleling the persecution of private farmers, small merchants, artisan producers, and the nonparty intelligentsia, cultural diversity was falling prey to the "class struggle on all fronts." In the Manichean spirit of its warfare politics, the Stalin group began by elevating one of the several groups or schools as its instrument to silence the others: dialectical philosophers over mechanists (incriminated by their casual affinity with Bukharin's philosophical theories); "proletarian" writers and artists over fellow travelers; teleological planners over geneticists; "red" specialists over "bourgeois" specialists. The goal and eventual outcome, however, was simply the suppression of heterogeneity and the imposition of a monopolistic orthodoxy still in the making. Here, as in economic life, the principles and foundations of NEP society were under attack.

None of these radical developments during the second half of 1929 resulted from a formal party decision. Far exceeding the April resolutions of the Central Committee, which was scheduled to reconvene on November 10–17, they were initiated by Stalin and his chief lieutenants, notably Molotov and Kaganovich, who now dominated the party's executive bodies in Moscow. On November 7, in a *Pravda* article that for cowed party officials carried the force of a decree, Stalin went still further. He proclaimed "a great change" in agriculture and the central myth of his "revolution from above." Contrary to party legislation (as

well as to the actual situation), he asserted that the peasant masses,
including middle peasants, were voluntarily quitting their private plots
and "joining collective farms . . . by whole villages, groups of villages,
districts, and even regions." It was a call for immediate wholesale collectivization.

The Central Committee convened three days later. Exactly what
occurred during this crucial November plenum remains obscure. Despite serious misgivings even among Stalin's supporters, the assembly
was no longer able or willing effectively to deny the general secretary,
who demanded ratification of his related *faits accomplis*: the political
destruction of Bukharin and the turn toward mass collectivization. On
November 12, following a barrage of Stalinist threats that they recant or
face possible expulsion from the party, Bukharin, Rykov, and Tomskii
read a circumspect but unrepentant statement to the plenum. While
acknowledging certain "successes," it criticized Stalin's methods in the
countryside and their impact on urban living standards. It was immediately denounced by Stalin and Molotov; and on November 17,
Bukharin was expelled from the Politburo.

Even though public defamation had made Bukharin's continuation
in the leadership untenable, the Central Committee appears to have
acquiesced in his ouster without enthusiasm. (Rykov and Tomskii,
attacked less harshly in the press, temporarily retained their seats.) The
assembly then endorsed Stalin's call for mass collectivization, but anx-
iously and with some reservations. Unlike his spokesman, Molotov,
who urged the incredible goal of complete collectivization in key areas
by the summer of 1930, the plenum was vague on the tempo, stating
ambiguously that events "now confront separate regions with the task of
mass collectivization." Still hoping for some semblance of order and
moderation, it also recommended that a special commission be established to work out specific guidelines.

One political triumph eluded Stalin at the plenum, but only
briefly. Demoralized and broken, Bukharin's remaining Moscow supporters on the Central Committee had recanted during the proceedings.
Bukharin, Rykov, and Tomskii, however, continued to refuse with
"extraordinary obstinacy." But a week later, on November 25, they
finally relented and signed a brief statement of political error. Published
the next day, the conceding passage read:

> *We consider it our duty to state that in this dispute the party and its
> Central Committee have turned out to be correct. Our views . . . have*

turned out to be mistaken. Recognizing our mistakes, we will . . .
conduct a decisive struggle against all deviations from the party's gen-
eral line and above all against the right deviation.

Though considerably less than the abject self-renunciation demanded
by Stalin, it was political surrender and the end of the Bukharinist
opposition.

Giuseppe Boffa

The Role of Ideology

Giuseppe Boffa is a former Moscow correspondent for the Italian Communist daily *L'Unità*, a member of the Central Committee of the Communist party of Italy, and the leading Eurocommunist authority on the
history of the Soviet Union. In his many works he has challenged the
legitimacy of the use of Marxism under Stalin and the Soviet effort to make
their interpretation of the ideology binding dogma for Communists
throughout the world. The selection here is from Boffa's contribution to a
collection of essays honoring the 100th anniversary of Marx's death in
1883, entitled *Marx e i marxismi* (Marx and the Marxisms). The use of the
plural *Marxisms* in the title of the book reflects the "polycentrism" defended by the Italian Left.

The link between Marxism and the Russian Revolution of October was
not so simple. . . . On the contrary, it was a rather complicated relationship. First of all because not all its protagonists were Marxists. This is
not just speaking in a general way about the masses of workers, soldiers,
or peasants who were, even though with diverse motives, the motive
force of the revolution, but who had only rather rough notions about
Marxism or no notion at all. We are speaking about the political forces
who influenced these masses for quite a while: it is enough to think of
the role played at various times and places by anarchist groups or, at

From Giuseppe Boffa, "La rivoluzione d'ottobre e il marxismo sovietico" in *Marx e i
Marxismi*, 1983, Feltrinelli Foundation (Milan), pp. 196–201. Translated by Robert V.
Daniels.

least in the first months of the revolution, by the Socialist Revolutionaries of the Left, the heirs of Russian Populism. On the other hand, not all Russian Marxists supported the October overturn: though they were a minority in the country, a whole stream of them, the Mensheviks in their various shades, were opposed to it. Neither the one nor the other of these phenomena can be considered superficial or transitory. The first was a reflection of the various social elements who gave life to the revolutionary wave. The second was the result of an old division in Russian Marxism: a whole wing, specifically the Mensheviks, continued to regard Russia as unready for a socialist revolution. Now it is true that this wing was thrown into a profound crisis by the revolutionary process that was in the course of unfolding in Russia, but it is also true that it had important connections with a large section of European Marxist thought: therefore it was not negligible even amidst the events in Russia.

However, the fundamental fact remains: the political force that succeeded in providing a guide to the intricate revolutionary process, so much so as to emerge victorious from the dramatic engagements of the civil war and foreign intervention that followed October, was a force that was inspired directly by Marxism and gave it the most revolutionary interpretation. This force was identified specifically with the other wing of Russian Marxism, that of Lenin and the Bolshevik Party. In the subsequent phases of the struggle the party always viewed and defined its tasks in Marxist terms. But despite the immense respect that there was for theoretical thought, at least among the party's principal leaders, questions of theory were certainly not their dominant preoccupation during the violent struggles of that period. Further, the earliest dissemination of Marxist ideas that went on among the masses in this initial phase was governed above all by propagandistic and agitational criteria. Political slogans were more useful than books. The documents themselves and the few original works which succeeded in being published — such as the 1919 Program of the Bolshevik Party or the celebrated *ABC of Communism* by Bukharin and Preobrazhensky — were essentially popularizations, quite simple, with thick strands of utopianism: these too helped substitute in place of "communism" the simple socialization accompanying the grave privations of these difficult years ("War Communism," as it was later called).

The end of the civil war and the Bolshevik victory coincided with an internal and international crisis in the revolution, which remained isolated in a Russia that was exhausted and in ruins. But in this singular

combination of victory and crisis, Marxist thought found new suste-
nance rather than embarrassment. The circumstances of a country
emerging from civil war are not generally the most propitious for the
free development of theoretical reflection. The merciless struggle between different social and political forces had concluded not only with
the success but with the government monopoly of a single Marxist
party, the Bolsheviks. The force that had represented the other wing of
Russian Marxism, the Mensheviks, had been outlawed. Yet despite
these circumstances that were anything but favorable, Marxist debate
did not die out. On the contrary, to the extent of constituting one of the
most striking characteristics of post-revolutionary Russia, there was in
these same years a new flourishing of debate, perhaps the most conspicuous and certainly the most animated in Soviet history, even
though it would manifest even greater vitality outside the borders of the
USSR and decades later. This debate unfolded in the twenties on various levels.

The first was the philological reconstitution of Marxist thought in
all its complexity. In the very first days of 1921 the Marx-Engels Institute was set up in Moscow, with the task of finding, collecting, and
preserving manuscripts, letters, and documents of the two authors, and
of preparing a scholarly edition of their works. Direction of the institute
was entrusted to Riazanov, one of the most cultured of the Russian
Marxists, regarded equally among all the currents of the movement for
his competence and his scholarly passion for Marx. Under his guidance, the Institute conducted from its very first years a valuable effort to
recover texts in their integrity. In fact, as early as 1924, at the Thirteenth Congress of the Bolshevik Party, Riazanov could report that he
had succeeded in obtaining from Germany numerous original Marxian
manuscripts, often still ignored or unknown in their entirety, including
the complete correspondence between Marx and Engels and the unpublished writings preparatory to *Das Kapital*, which came to light only
some years later. Even then Riazanov could propose, on this base, to
proceed with a Russian edition of all the works of Marx and Engels,
with a subsequent academic edition of all their texts in the languages in
which they had originally been written, together with the vast informa-
tional and critical apparatus necessary to understand them fully. The
same year he began the publication of some of the volumes of the Marx-
Engels Archive, where new texts and documents, still unpublished,
were gathered. His suggestions outlined a vast program of work which
would engage the Institute for quite a few years.

A second direction of renewed Marxist study was that represented by genuine and accurate theoretical discussion. This too extended into quite diverse fields. But among all of them one had particular prominence, that of economics. An attempt was undertaken from the first years of the twenties to give the Soviet economy a conscious direction, beginning with the compelling need for accumulation and development. This involved economists of different tendencies and backgrounds in the va ,ous centers assigned to this task, however they might differ in their reading of Marxism in a country where all economic thought, including the less revolutionary (take the name of Tugan-Baranovsky above all) had already been strongly influenced by Marx by way of "Legal Marxism" at the turn of the century. The debate therefore proceeded from Marxian conceptions not only in its most celebrated expression — the confrontation between Bukharin and Preobrazhensky with their divergent visions of the choices to be made — but also in the controversies involving numerous other scholars, less known because they were less conspicuous politically, but certainly of no lesser value. The problem to be solved was entirely unprecedented: to industrialize and modernize a country in ways different from the capitalist path which had characterized the economic growth of the major countries of Europe and North America. Marxist thought and economic thought in general were enriched in this debate by a new theme, that of development, which would have great importance in the course of the events of the following decades.

Finally, there was a third level of discussion, less fertile, more heterogeneous, but still not to be underestimated. The force that had emerged victorious from the revolution was said to be the bearer of a new culture: a political culture above all, but also a culture in the wider and more universal sense. Now Marxism represented the basic nucleus of this new culture. From this came the trend that enriched its themes and defined its new progress in the most diverse directions and disciplines: not only in philosophy and history, as well as economics, where this development seemed more natural since Marxian thought had already dug widely there, but also in sectors of knowledge where it was more difficult to find really stimulating guidance from the masters, such as aesthetics, linguistics, ethnography, and so on. The results in the latter cases were rather more modest, especially considering the fate that lay in wait very soon for these debates. Still, it was not a useless effort, considering that some of these explorations made a comeback to draw attention in later years and in various countries.

Even at the time, there was already noted in these debates in each discipline a tendency to install the dominant schools, which tended to push aside certain lines of research even within the general stream of Marxism, which was by far the prevalent but still not yet the only one existing in culture, publishing, and the universities. One example, perhaps the most famous, of this propensity toward domination, if not toward monopoly, is represented by the dominance of the school of Pokrovsky in the whole field of studying and teaching history. At the time Pokrovsky was the most illustrious, the dean, of Marxist historians in Russia. (This, however, would not be the reason, as is sometimes asserted, that led to sidelining the same Pokrovsky off in silence; there would in actuality be another motive, of which we will speak more fully a little later.) As a whole it may be recalled that schools or tendencies within the same general current of Marxism continued to confront one another, giving rise to debates that were quite informal when they were not actually bitter polemics. Among these instances it is worth remembering just one thematic example chosen by the particular fortune which it had much later, in the sixties of our century, among scholars of various disciplines and in many countries, but interesting especially for the history of non-European societies: the discussion around the phenomenon that Marx had defined with the concept of the "Asiatic mode of production."[1]

Finally, in addition, the inflamed political struggles that upset the original Bolshevik nucleus and tore it apart went on with a continuous appeal, implied or explicit, to the foundations of Marxism. But here things quite soon became complicated, since another term of ideological and political confrontation had the upper hand from the beginning. Predominant in the heated discussions among the leading figures in the party was the theme of fidelity to Lenin, to his thought, and to his program of action. A new word that had never been employed during Lenin's lifetime appeared all of a sudden and quickly took hold: Leninism. As to the specific content of this term there was not, in truth, any agreement of opinions. If the public polemics were conducted almost always by hitting each other with quotations from Lenin that too often were taken out of context, one of the main reasons was precisely in the flourishing of diverse interpretations of Lenin's thought itself, at a time when everyone was coming to grips with novel problems that Lenin had

---

[1] Notion of a social system neither feudal nor capitalist, but dominated by the state bureaucracy; possibly applicable to both pre- and postrevolutionary Russia. — Ed.

not had time to resolve. However, it remained indisputable for all the contenders that discussion of Lenin always meant discussion in the framework of Marxism and its inevitable historical developments.

A more pervasive phenomenon accompanied these disputes. Originally there was an attempt, at least in part, to overcome the disparity that existed in the Civil War years between the Marxist preparation of what we can call the general staff of the revolution, and the meager political culture with which the masses who had made the revolution expressed their general emancipatory aspirations. There appeared rather quickly in the party, therefore, an educational or pedagogic concern, which often became intertwined with mere propaganda or "agitational" activity. . . . Soon enough, the problem involved not only the disparity between party and masses; within the party itself the divorce between the directing nucleus and the base grew more acute, in the sense that with the constant influx of new recruits and with the decimation of the old militants in political and military battles, "The number of comrades who have gone through a basic Marxist preparation (as Riazanov was still asserting at the Tenth Congress) is declining day by day." In fact the party could grow only by drawing its reserves from the broadest revolutionary masses, and was therefore compelled to dilute its original membership (accustomed to the theoretical disputes) with newcomers.

From this came the early tendency to set up schools or circles that would provide enrollees or sympathizers with rudimentary Marxist political instruction. This task took on vast proportions with the "Lenin Enrollment" of 1924, when the years of mass recruitment of new members began. What was taught in brief lessons to the new enrollees, who often had a very thin general culture besides, was in principle the simple rudiments of Marxism or "Leninism" — therefore, inevitably simplified and half-baked notions.

On the other hand, at least in the twenties, this simplification was less a problem at the higher levels of culture, if it was not entirely absent there. This can be understood in connection with the relation between Marx and Lenin. Lenin's thought, especially after his death, acquired in the eyes of the Bolsheviks a value of theoretical generalization, not merely a value of simple though valuable practical directions which it had mainly seemed to be previously. For everyone, Lenin was a great interpreter of Marx. His contribution to the theory, though not yet judged by everyone to be of the same importance, nevertheless came to be considered an important development of Marxism, its only true revolutionary development. But this still involved a dialectical chain, and thus an evolution of thought, and not just a pure and simple identification of the two masters and their ideas. Basically the real, true study of Lenin's thought was just beginning. Thus, when Lenin died, no one proposed to add such a task to the already existing Marx-Engels Institute. Instead, a special Lenin Institute was created in 1924 with the mission of collecting all the manuscripts of the deceased leader, even the simplest, and all the documents that dealt with his activities. Publication of the so-called third edition of Lenin's works was mainly the work of this institute, initially directed by Kamenev. This edition was the first one to be presented with a definite aim of completeness, and, even if it had more gaps than later editions, it is the one that even today has the most objective and in some respects most complete critical-informational apparatus.

The unification of the two institutes in a single Marx-Engels-Lenin Institute did not occur until 1931. But 1931 was a year that is noteworthy for our subject in many other ways. First of all, the fusion of the institutes coincided with the removal of Riazanov from his responsibilities under a cloud of slanderous though vague accusations that later research has shown to have been the very plausible fruit of sordid police frame-ups. His case was by no means an isolated one. In practice, all the debates that had been flourishing in various areas during the previous decade were rudely cut off and stifled. This applied above all to the discussions among the economists, which were reduced by Stalin to the category of simple "prejudices": many of the advocates of economic ideas found the theses and proposals that they had openly defended in official organs of the Soviet government now actually presented as counts of the indictment in prefabricated trials. Something analogous, though less obvious, happened with the historians. In practice every dispute was hushed up by authoritarian and threatening methods in 1930 and 1931.

These were the years of Stalin's "great turn," the time of accelerated industrialization and forced collectivization in the countryside. Both set off dramatic disturbances in society. The very concept of a new "revolution from above" which inspired Stalin's leadership contrasted radically with the developments that the Marxist debate had gone through in the post-revolutionary USSR up to this point. It was not just a matter of theory. There was no debate, not even the most seemingly specialized, that could remain unaffected by the grave social and political conflicts that were taking place in the country. The anti-Stalin oppositions had been defeated but had not disappeared: they were still nourished by Marxist and Leninist ideas. Their advocates were still alive, and their warnings were more and more being borne out by events. In these circumstances every dispute, however limited in its cultural and theoretical scope, risked becoming intertwined with the political struggle. The entire Marxist debate of the twenties was consequently suppressed. Still, it could break out again at any moment in spite of official prohibitions.

Today we know for a fact that the victory of Stalin and his concepts was by no means complete and absolute in the first half of the decade of the thirties. What was needed to make it definite was the "mass repressions" (Khrushchev's term) of the years 1936–1938, which, though they struck down an enormous number of people of diverse social origins and diverse cultural orientations, had as their primary objective precisely that Bolshevik Party that had emerged from the revolution, with its guiding origins, its political "cadres," its not yet exhausted tradition of Marxist debate. This tragic moment would nevertheless not have had the enormous importance that it had for the problem we are interested in, if it had not been accompanied by a clever political-cultural operation on Stalin's part that necessarily left what has remained up to now an indelible imprint on Soviet Marxism. The operation hinged on a facile book, easy to read, published in September 1938, after Stalin had spent some time personally supervising its preparation and drafting. The volume was presented as a manual — or rather, according to the official definition, a "short course" — in the history of the Soviet Communist party. But along with its conciseness it claimed something wider: to offer a synthesis of the principal ideas of Marxism and Leninism, or rather, as would always be said from that time on as a canonical formula, of "Marxism-Leninism."

It may seem exaggerated to attribute so much weight to a single book. The fact that it had little or nothing in common with an accurate reconstruction of Bolshevik history has since been amply documented. That it represented not a simplification but a real distortion of the thought of Marx and Lenin has been underscored even more often. But this was precisely the point of the operation, which was conducted from the very beginning on a vast scale. The publication of the book was accompanied by a resolution of the leading organs of the party, over which the steamroller of the Stalinist repressions had already passed. In this document it was asserted that the "Short Course" was "an encyclopedia of the fundamental ideas in the realm of Marxism-Leninism." Something else was added: it was also the only text that represented "the official and verified interpretation of the fundamental questions of the history of the party and of Marxism-Leninism, which does not allow any other arbitrary interpretation." Thus this volume of synthesis confirmed the transformation of the thought of Marx and Lenin into a corpus of doctrine, crude but ironclad, raised not just to the level of an official state ideology, but even to the level of dogmatic truth, with no other reading of it being allowed.

The consequences for Marxist thought in the USSR were drastic and long-lasting. The "Short Course" was disseminated in truly huge printings, quickly surpassing those of all the works of Marx or of Lenin previously published. It was made the basis of all education of every level and type, beginning with education inside the party. Study went on under the guidance of "politically selected leaders." All propaganda and dissemination of "Marxism-Leninism" was supposed to be conducted according to the theses of the "Short Course." It was capped by the reading of certain selected works by Stalin. The writings of Marx, Engels, and Lenin continued to be published according to selective criteria, but reading them was given mainly an auxiliary function: they could serve to illustrate but certainly not to dispute what was said in this basic work.

What was taught and propagandized in this manner had only certain points of contact with the original thought of Marx and Lenin: it reflected rather better Stalin's concepts (which we could indeed call Stalinism, if this term had not become a source of certain misunderstandings). But the observation is still true that the historian Rudolf Schlesinger[2] first made. Whatever one might think of how little had survived of Marxist theory in these formulations, the fact remains that "Marxism-Leninism" in this garb reached millions of people, above all the political cadres of that immense country that is the USSR. However, the operation was not confined to the borders of the Soviet Union. It was extended to the whole international Communist movement through translations of the "Short Course" into many languages. It was thus in this version that "Marxism-Leninism" and the history of the Bolsheviks became known in the widest circles of many different countries around the world (especially when so much sympathy gathered around the USSR during the antifascist war), and was often accepted by their critics abroad.

[2] German-born British Marxist scholar. — Ed.

Joseph Stalin as he appeared in the 1930s. (Culver Pictures)

The Revolution from Above

J. V. Stalin

The Socialist Drive

Joseph Vissarionovich Stalin (1879–1953) rose from humble beginnings in a worker's family (real name Dzhugashvili) in the Transcaucasian region of Georgia, to become General Secretary of the Russian Communist Party in 1922 and unchallenged dictator of the Soviet Union in 1929. During the middle part of his career — from the mid-1920s to the mid-1930s — he recorded his achievements and intentions extensively in his many speeches, the most important of which were collected and translated in the various editions of *Problems of Leninism*. In speeches of November and December 1929, Stalin set forth a résumé of the new industrial and agricultural policies he had initiated. In Stalin's mind there were only two possibilities — his own policy, "forward — to socialism," or the retreat to capitalism which he charged his Communist opponents with advocating.

From J. V. Stalin, "A Year of Great Change (On the Occasion of the Twelfth Anniversary of the October Revolution)" and "Problems of Agrarian Policy in the USSR (speech delivered at the Conference of Marxist Students of the Agrarian Question, December 27, 1929)," in *Problems of Leninism* (Moscow: Foreign Languages Publishing House, 1940), pp. 294–298, 302–305, 308–309, 325–326. Reprinted with permission of the publisher.

The past year witnessed a great change on all fronts of socialist construction. The change expressed itself, and is still expressing itself, in a determined *offensive* of socialism against the capitalist elements in town and country. The characteristic feature of this offensive is that it has already brought us a number of decisive *successes*, in the principal spheres of the socialist reconstruction of our national economy.

We may therefore conclude that our party has made good use of the retreat effected during the first stages of the New Economic Policy in order to organize the *change* in the subsequent stages and to launch a *successful offensive* against the capitalist elements.

When the New Economic Policy was introduced Lenin said:

> *We are now retreating, going back, as it were; but we are doing this, retreating first, in order to prepare for a longer leap forward. It was only on this condition that we retreated in pursuing our New Economic Policy . . . in order to start a persistent advance after our retreat.*

The results of the past year show beyond a doubt that the party is successfully carrying out this decisive advice of Lenin in the course of its work. . . .

The expansion of the creative initiative and labor enthusiasm of the masses has been stimulated by three main factors:

(a) the fight — by means of *self-criticism* — against bureaucracy, which shackles the labor initiative and labor activity of the masses;
(b) the fight — by means of *socialist emulation* — against the labor-shirkers and disrupters of proletarian labor discipline; and finally
(c) the fight — by the introduction of the *uninterrupted* week — against routine and inertia in industry.

As a result we have a tremendous achievement on the labor front in the form of labor enthusiasm and emulation among the millions of the working class in all parts of our vast country. The significance of this achievement is truly inestimable, for only the labor enthusiasm and zeal of the millions can guarantee the progressive increase of labor productivity without which the final victory of socialism over capitalism is inconceivable. . . .

During the past year we have in the main successfully solved the *problem of accumulation* for capital construction in heavy industry; we have *accelerated* the development of the production of means of production and have created the prerequisites for transforming our country into a *metal* country. This is our second fundamental *achievement* during the past year.

The problem of light industry presents no exceptional difficulties. We solved that problem several years ago. The problem of heavy industry is more difficult and more important. It is *more difficult* because it demands colossal investments of capital, and, as the history of industrially backward countries has shown, heavy industry cannot be developed without extensive long-term loans. It is *more important* because, unless we develop heavy industry, we can build no industry whatever, we cannot carry out any industrialization. And as we have never received, nor are we receiving, either long-term loans or credits for any lengthy period, the acuteness of the problem becomes more than obvious. It is precisely for this reason that the capitalists of all countries refuse us loans and credits; they believe that, left to our own resources, we cannot cope with the problem of accumulation, that we are bound to fail in the task of reconstructing our heavy industry, and will at last be compelled to come to them cap in hand and sell ourselves into bondage.

But the results of the past year tell us a different story. The significance of the results of the past year lies in the fact that the calculations of Messieurs the capitalists have been shattered. The past year has shown that in spite of the open and covert financial blockade of the USSR we did not sell ourselves into bondage to the capitalists; that, with our own resources, we successfully solved the problem of accumulation and laid the foundation for heavy industry. Even the most inveterate enemies of the working class cannot deny this now. Indeed, since capital investments in large-scale industry last year amounted to over 1.6 billion rubles[1] (of which about 1.3 billion rubles were invested in heavy industry), and capital investments in large-scale industry this year will amount to over 3.4 billion rubles (of which over 2.5 billion rubles will be invested in heavy industry); and since the gross output of large-scale industry last year showed an increase of 23 percent, including a 30 percent increase in the output of heavy industry, and the increase in the gross output of large-scale industry this year should be 32 percent, including a 46 percent increase in the output of heavy industry — is it not obvious that the problem of accumulation for the building up of heavy industry no longer presents insuperable difficulties? How can anyone doubt that in developing our heavy industry, we are advancing

[1] In 1929 the ruble was officially valued at about 50¢ U.S. — Ed.

at an accelerated pace, exceeding our former speed and leaving behind our "traditional" backwardness?

Is it surprising after this that the estimates of the Five-Year Plan were exceeded during the past year, and that the *optimum* variant of the Five-Year Plan, which the bourgeois scribes regarded as "wild fantasy," and which horrified our Right opportunists (Bukharin's group), has actually turned out to be a *minimum* variant?

"The salvation of Russia," says Lenin,

> lies not only in a good harvest on the peasant farms — that is not enough; and not only in the good condition of light industry, which provides the peasantry with consumers' goods — this, too, is not enough. We also need heavy industry. . . . Unless we save heavy industry, unless we restore it, we shall not be able to build up any industry; and without heavy industry we shall be doomed as an independent country. . . . Heavy industry needs state subsidies. If we cannot provide them, then we are doomed as a civilized state — let alone as a socialist state.

These are the blunt terms in which Lenin formulated the problem of accumulation and the task of our party in building up heavy industry.

The past year has shown that our party is successfully coping with this task, resolutely overcoming all obstacles in its path.

This does not mean, of course, that industry will not encounter any more serious difficulties. The task of building up heavy industry involves not only the problem of accumulation. It also involves the problem of cadres, the problem (a) of *enlisting* tens of thousands of Soviet-minded technicians and experts for the work of socialist construction, and (b) of *training* new Red technicians and Red experts from among the working class. While the problem of accumulation may in the main be regarded as solved, the problem of cadres still awaits solution. And the problem of cadres is now — when we are engaged in the technical reconstruction of industry — the decisive problem of socialist construction. . . .

The assertions of the Right opportunists (Bukharin's group) to the effect (a) that the peasants would not join the collective farms; (b) that the speedy development of collective farming would only arouse mass discontent and drive a wedge between the peasantry and the working class, (c) that the "high-road" of socialist development in the rural districts is *not* the collective farms, *but* the cooperative societies; and

(d) that the development of collective farming and the offensive against the capitalist elements in the rural districts may in the end deprive the country of grain altogether — all these assertions have also collapsed and crumbled to dust. They have all collapsed and crumbled to dust as old bourgeois-liberal rubbish.

Firstly, the peasants have joined the collective farms; they have joined in whole villages, whole volosts, whole districts.

Secondly, the mass collective-farm movement is not weakening the bond, but, on the contrary, is strengthening it by putting it on a new, production basis. Now even the blind can see that if there is any serious dissatisfaction among the great bulk of the peasantry it is not because of the collective-farm policy of the Soviet government, but because the Soviet government is unable to keep pace with the growth of the collective-farm movement in supplying the peasants with machines and tractors.

Thirdly, the controversy about the "high-road" of socialist development in the rural districts is a scholastic controversy, worthy of young petty-bourgeois liberals of the type of Eichenwald and Slepkov. It is obvious that, as long as there was no mass collective-farm movement, the "high-road" was the lower forms of the cooperative movement — supply and marketing cooperatives; but when the higher form of the cooperative movement — the collective farm — appeared, the latter became the "high-road" of development. The high-road (without quotation marks) of socialist development in the rural districts is Lenin's cooperative plan, which embraces all forms of agricultural cooperation, from the lowest (supply and marketing) to the highest (productive collective farms). To *draw a contrast* between collective farming and the cooperative societies is to make a mockery of Leninism and to acknowledge one's own ignorance.

Fourthly, now even the blind can see that without the offensive against the capitalist elements in the rural districts, and without the development of the collective-farm and state-farm movement, we would not have had the decisive successes, achieved this year in the matter of grain collections, nor the tens of millions of poods[2] of permanent grain reserves which have already accumulated in the hands of the state. Moreover, it can now be confidently asserted that, thanks to the growth of the collective-farm and state-farm movement, we are

---

[2] One pood equals approximately 36 pounds. — Ed.

definitely emerging, or have already emerged, from the grain crisis. And if the development of the collective farms and state farms is accelerated, there is not the slightest ground for doubt that in about three years' time our country will be one of the largest grain countries in the world, if not *the* largest grain country in the world.

What is the *new* feature of the present collective-farm movement? The new and decisive feature of the present collective-farm movement is that the peasants are joining the collective farms not in separate groups, as was formerly the case, but in whole villages, whole volosts, whole districts, and even whole areas. And what does that mean? It means that *the middle peasant has joined the collective-farm movement.* This is the basis of that radical change in the development of agriculture which represents the most important achievement of the Soviet government during the past year.

Trotskyism's Menshevik "conception" that the working class is incapable of leading the great bulk of the peasantry in the cause of socialist construction is collapsing and being smashed to atoms. Now even the blind can see that the middle peasant has turned towards the collective farm. Now it is obvious to all that the Five-Year Plan of industry and agriculture is a five-year plan of building a socialist society, that those who do not believe in the possibility of building socialism in our country have no right to greet our Five-Year Plan.

The last hope of the capitalists of all countries, who are dreaming of restoring capitalism in the USSR — "the sacred principle of private property" — is collapsing and vanishing. The peasants, whom they regarded as material for manuring the soil for capitalism, are abandoning *en masse* the lauded banner of "private property" and are taking the path of collectivism, the path of socialism. The last hope for the restoration of capitalism is crumbling. . . .

We are advancing full steam ahead along the path of industrialization — to socialism, leaving behind the age-long "Russian" backwardness. We are becoming a country of metal, a country of automobiles, a country of tractors. And when we have put the USSR on an automobile, and the muzhik [peasant] on a tractor, let the esteemed capitalists, who boast so loudly of their "civilization," try to overtake us! We shall see which countries may then be "classified" as backward and which as advanced.

Can we advance our socialized industry at an accelerated rate while having to rely on an agricultural base, such as is provided by small peasant farming, which is incapable of expanded reproduction, and which, in addition, is the predominant force in our national economy? No, we cannot. Can the Soviet government and the work of socialist construction be, for any length of time, based on two *different* foundations: on the foundation of the most large-scale and concentrated socialist industry and on the foundation of the most scattered and backward, small-commodity peasant farming? No, they cannot. Sooner or later this would be bound to end in the complete collapse of the whole national economy. What, then, is the solution? The solution lies in enlarging the agricultural units, in making agriculture capable of accumulation, of expanded reproduction, and in thus changing the agricultural base of our national economy. But how are the agricultural units to be enlarged? There are two ways of doing this. There is the *capitalist* way, which is to enlarge the agricultural units by introducing capitalism in agriculture — a way which leads to the impoverishment of the peasantry and to the development of capitalist enterprises in agriculture. We reject this way as incompatible with the Soviet economic system. There is a second way: the *socialist* way, which is to set up collective farms and state farms, the way which leads to the amalgamation of the small peasant farms into large collective farms, technically and scientifically equipped, and to the squeezing out of the capitalist elements from agriculture. We are in favor of this second way.

And so, the question stands as follows: either one way or the other, either *back* — to capitalism or *forward* — to socialism. There is no third way, nor can there be. The "equilibrium" theory makes an attempt to indicate a third way. And precisely because it is based on a third (nonexistent) way, it is Utopian and anti-Marxian. . . .

Now, as you see, we have the material base which enables us to *substitute* for kulak output the output of the collective farms and state farms. That is why our offensive against the kulaks is now meeting with undeniable success. That is how the offensive against the kulaks must be carried on, if we mean a real offensive and not futile declamations against the kulaks.

That is why we have recently passed from the policy of *restricting* the exploiting proclivities of the kulaks to the policy of *eliminating the kulaks as a class.*

Well, what about the policy of expropriating the kulaks? Can we permit the expropriation of kulaks in the regions of solid collectivization? This question is asked in various quarters. A ridiculous question! We could not permit the expropriation of the kulaks as long as we were pursuing the policy of restricting the exploiting proclivities of the kulaks, as long as we were unable to launch a determined offensive against the kulaks, as long as we were unable to substitute for kulak output the output of the collective farms and state farms. At that time the policy of not permitting the expropriation of the kulaks was necessary and correct. But now? Now the situation is different. Now we are able to carry on a determined offensive against the kulaks, to break their resistance, to eliminate them as a class and substitute for their output the output of the collective farms and state farms. Now, the kulaks are being expropriated by the masses of poor and middle peasants themselves, by the masses who are putting solid collectivization into practice. Now, the expropriation of the kulaks in the regions of solid collectivization is no longer just an administrative measure. Now, the expropriation of the kulaks is an integral part of the formation and development of the collective farms. That is why it is ridiculous and fatuous to expatiate today on the expropriation of the kulaks. You do not lament the loss of the hair of one who has been beheaded.

There is another question which seems no less ridiculous; whether the kulak should be permitted to join the collective farms. Of course not, for he is a sworn enemy of the collective-farm movement. Clear, one would think.

Holland Hunter

The Industrial Plan

Holland Hunter has for many years been a professor of economics at Haverford College and an authority on the history of Soviet industrialization. In an especially provocative 1973 article in *The Slavic Review*, excerpted here, he used "input-output" economic analysis to show the impossibility of realizing the targets of Stalin's First Five-Year Plan and the consequences of attempting it anyway.

From Holland Hunter, "The Overambitious First Soviet Five-Year Plan," *Slavic Review* v. 32, no. 2 (June 1973), excerpts from pp. 237–257 (including tables). Reprinted by permission.

Soviet economic growth since 1928, under nine five-year plans, attests to the power of Soviet economic planning. Yet the first plan, far from marking out the road then taken by the economy, proves on ex post analysis to have been unachievable. This essay describes a test of the plan's feasibility and sketches a few alternative feasible growth paths. Its analytic base rests on plan-testing methods that have developed out of work on problems that were initially confronted in the USSR almost half a century ago. It seems fitting, therefore, to apply these methods retroactively, forty-five years after the fact, to the First Soviet Five-Year Plan, formulated in the late 1920s to cover the period 1929–33. Though the testing methods are somewhat technical, their power deserves appreciation and evaluation by scholars in many disciplines. I am grateful for the opportunity to expose this approach to the critical scrutiny of informed students of Soviet history.

In thus using new tools to reopen some of the growth issues that were faced in the late 1920s, we are able to make quantitative comparisons between intentions and various hypothetical alternatives, and relate both to actual developments. This in turn provides a new basis for evaluating the factors that led to the plan's overambitiousness. But while an economist can offer evidence that the targets were too ambitious, he cannot answer the question, "Why were overambitious targets pressed for and accepted?" Political scientists and historians are needed to add breadth and depth to a narrow economic analysis. Ambitious targets, up to a point at least, may serve a useful function in galvanizing a dramatic campaign for rapid expansion of output. But up to what point? Statistical possibilities require evaluation in a setting that takes account of the political cross-currents of the time, the fears and tensions that shaped national policy. These issues of degree and extent require qualitative as well as quantitative judgment.

Examination of alternatives tempts one to reflect on the consequences for the USSR of imposing overambitious targets on a strained economy. Brief observations in this vein, while necessarily tentative, are cautiously offered at the end of the essay. Economists and others engaged in formulating national plans today may find this review of early Soviet experience instructive. It may also be generally useful to be reminded of the consequences of overambitiousness and related contributions of Stalinism to Soviet experience.

This analysis is focused on the First Five-Year Plan as approved (in its "optimal version") in May 1929. We find that its targets, taken together, simply could not be achieved, nor were they all achieved during the five years after 1928. But the actual shortfalls were due in part to serious economic difficulties not foreseen when the plan was formulated. The test reported on below does not examine the plan's feasibility under the unanticipated blows in agriculture and foreign trade that shook the Soviet economy in the early 1930s. Rather, it confines itself to the question whether the targets for 1933 could have been achieved under the optimistic parameters embodied in the plan. It is also confined to the official targets ratified in the spring of 1929, ignoring the wild target increases issued in 1930 and 1931. We place ourselves at the beginning of 1929 and search for the upper limits of the achievable.

The Main Features of the Plan in an Input-Output Framework

Tables 1 and 2 summarize the 1928 preplan situation of the Soviet economy and the dimensions that were to be achieved by 1933. In these flow tables, the rows show the amounts of domestic production that six major sectors of the economy actually delivered to major users of their output in 1928 and were expected to deliver in 1933. The receiving sectors are in part the same producing sectors and in part the major users of final output: households, government, inventories, fixed capital, and exports. A number serves twice in this compact format. A sector's column shows the source of its inputs, and a sector's row shows the destination of its output. Hence the name, input-output table. The columns on the left of the double line show the composition of each sector's input requirements, and the columns on the right show the internal composition of each category of final demand. It will be seen that the 1933 numbers are much larger than the 1928 numbers. The extent of intended growth differs widely, however, from one cell to another, as is brought out in table 3.

The two panels of table 3 show the plan's intentions with respect to the growth of each sector's total output, and also with respect to the growth of each category of final demand. All outputs were to grow, but one is tempted to paraphrase the pigs' slogan on equality in Orwell's *Animal Farm*: "All outputs will grow, but some will grow much more than others." The industry and construction sectors were to be expanded far more rapidly than the agriculture and housing sectors. The plan called for *disproportional* growth in sectoral outputs. Subsequent

TABLE 1 First Soviet Five-Year Plan, Base-Period Flow Table, 1927/28 (in millions of rubles at 1926/27 prices)

Inputs from:	Agriculture	Industry	Transport	Construction	Housing	Other sectors	Total inter-industry	Consumption	Government	Inventories	Fixed capital	Exports	Total final demand	Total domestic output
								Output to:						
Agriculture	1,818	1,382					3,200	10,024	134	50		199	10,407	13,607
Industry	528	5,685	750	711	110	217	8,001	3,794	981	344		303	5,422	13,423
Transport and communications	47	714	184	64	11	19	1,039	824	178	32		33	1,067	2,106
Construction											3,888		3,888	3,888
Housing								1,694					1,694	1,694
Other sectors	431	937	148	140		43	1,699	4,882	297	107		213	5,499	7,198
Total intermediate	2,824	8,718	1,082	915	121	279	13,939	21,218	1,590	533	3,888	748	27,977	
Value added	10,783	4,705	1,024	2,973	1,573	6,919	27,977							
Total inputs	13,607	13,423	2,106	3,888	1,694	7,198								41,916

73

TABLE 2 First Soviet Five-Year Plan, Terminal-Year Flow Table, 1932/33, "Optimal" Targets (in millions of rubles at 1926/27 prices)

	Output to:													
Inputs from:	Agri-cul-ture	Indus-try	Trans-port	Con-struc-tion	Hous-ing	Other sec-tors	Total inter-industry	Con-sump-tion	Gov-ern-ment	In-ven-to-ries	Fixed capi-tal	Ex-ports	Total final demand	Total do-mestic output
Agriculture	2,487	2,914					5,401	14,033	777	777		727	16,314	21,715
Industry	1,484	18,815	1,810	5,245	166	365	27,885	6,111	1,925	1,451		888	10,375	38,260
Transport and communications	137	1,248	388	480	17	34	2,304	1,263	329	154		101	1,847	4,151
Construction											13,726		13,726	13,726
Housing								2,561					2,561	2,561
Other sectors	916	1,368	300	863		60	3,507	6,282	603	524		413	7,822	11,329
Total inter-mediate	5,024	24,345	2,498	6,588	183	459	39,097	30,250	3,634	2,906	13,726	2,129	52,645	
Value added	16,691	13,915	1,653	7,138	2,378	10,870	52,645							
Total inputs	21,715	38,260	4,151	13,726	2,561	11,329	52,645							91,742

TABLE 3	Principal Dimensions of the First Soviet Five-Year Plan, "Optimal Variant"

	1927/28 (million rubles)	1932/33 (million rubles)	Absolute increment	1932/33 as percentage of 1927/28	1927/28 percent share	1932/33 percent share
Annual Deliveries to Final Demand						
Consumption	21,218	30,250	9,032	143	76	57
Government	1,590	3,634	2,044	229	6	7
Inventories	533	2,906	2,373	545	2	6
Fixed capital	3,888	13,726	9,838	353	14	26
Exports	748	2,129	1,381	285	2	4
Total	27,977	52,645	24,668	188	100	100
Annual Gross Output of Each Sector						
Agriculture	13,607	21,715	8,108	160	33	24
Industry	13,423	38,260	24,837	285	32	42
Transport	2,106	4,151	2,045	197	5	4
Construction	3,888	13,726	9,838	353	9	15
Housing	1,694	2,561	867	151	4	3
Other and margin	7,198	11,329	4,131	157	17	12
Whole economy	41,916	91,742	49,826	219	100	100

five-year plans have continued this stress on disproportional growth, though the usual Soviet phrase is "planned proportional growth." The first panel of table 3 also displays markedly disproportional growth in the various categories of delivery to final demand. Household consumption was slated to rise by 43 percent, comparing 1933 to 1928, but the rise in deliveries to fixed capital formation was to be 3.5-fold, and other deliveries to nonconsumption were expected to be three times as large in 1933 as they were in 1928.

The foundation for this output growth was to be primarily a very rapid expansion in the economy's stocks of fixed capital, along with an increase in the size of the labor force, especially outside of agriculture. Table 4 shows 1928 base-period data for the amount of fixed capital in each sector, together with the plan's 1933 terminal year targets for the stocks that each sector would have after all the investment carried out during the plan period. Again one sees sharply disproportional growth, and marked stress on industry and construction. Their capital stocks

| TABLE 4 | Fixed Capital Capacity in 1928 and Planned for 1933, at the Beginning of the Year (in millions of 1925/26 rubles) |

Sector	1927/28	1932/33	Abso-lute incre-ment	1932/33 as per-cent-age of 1927/28	1927/28 percent share	1932/33 percent share
Agriculture	15,162	19,503	4,341	129	25	22
Industry	6,489	15,640	9,151	241	11	18
Transport	10,724	15,308	4,584	143	18	17
Construction	595	2,100	1,505	353	1	2
Housing	21,729	25,863	4,134	119	36	29
Other sectors	5,808	10,054	4,246	173	9	12
Whole economy	60,507	88,468	27,961	146	100	100

were to rise 2.4 and 3.5 times, while housing capital was slated to rise by 19 percent and agricultural capital by 29 percent. . . .

What Actually Happened?

Soviet growth since 1928 has been rapid and very substantial, but for the first few years it was erratic and fell far short of these targets. Agricultural output not only failed to grow but declined in absolute terms, as indicated in the first panel of table 5 and chart 1. The corrected official Soviet agricultural output index that has been cited since 1958 shows a fall from 100 in 1928 to 81.5 in 1933, as compared with an intended rise from 100 to 155 set forth in the first plan. The livestock products part of the index fell from 100 to 44, "Liquidation of the kulaks as a class," not foreseen in the plan, was the cause of this agricultural setback.

Industrial output expanded markedly, though the extent of the rise cannot be measured unambiguously. The content of manufactured output changed quite sharply, with many new products entering the list, and alternative valuations used in weighting these components lead to alternative estimates of the rate of growth in industrial output. The official Soviet index claims a rise from 100 in 1928 to 213 in 1933. Nutter's careful assembly of individual output series for Soviet industry,

TABLE 5	Intended and Actual Output in the Agricultural, Industrial, Transport and Communications, and Construction Sectors, USSR, 1928–34 (1928 = 100)

Sector	1929	1930	1931	1932	1933	1934
Agriculture						
Intended	104	107	125	138	155	
Actual	98	94	92	86	82	86
Industry						
Intended	116	137	162	194	236	
Actual (1)	120	146	176	202	213	254
Actual (2)	114	130	140	140	149	178
Transport and Communications						
Intended	113	127	144	162	183	
Actual	122	164	191	227	222	244
Construction						
Intended	123	171	226	285	353	
Actual	125	166	180	180	155	189

multiplied by base-period price weights, yields an index that rises from 100 in 1928 to 140 in 1931, stays at the same level for 1932, and rises to 149 for 1933. Other sets of legitimate price weights would yield higher rates of growth, though no Western investigator has yet been able to assemble and weight component series in such a way as to equal the official Soviet series reproduced in the second panel of table 5. Even if one rejects the official Soviet series as reflecting improper price weights, it remains clear that industrial output expanded markedly, by at least 50 percent over five years and 80 percent over six years, though the aggregate target for 1933 was far from met. . . .

[C]omparisons of actual developments with plan intentions show clearly how badly achievements fell short of plan targets. We should recall that the years 1929–33 were difficult ones. After 1929 serious crises developed in the agricultural sector, in retail trade, and in Soviet foreign trade, but instead of slowing the plan, the party responded by demanding emergency efforts for still more drastic quick results. A sharp fall in available animal draft power led to an emergency increase in the target for tractor production. Turmoil in agriculture cut food, cotton, flax, and leather supplies. The shortage of raw materials for

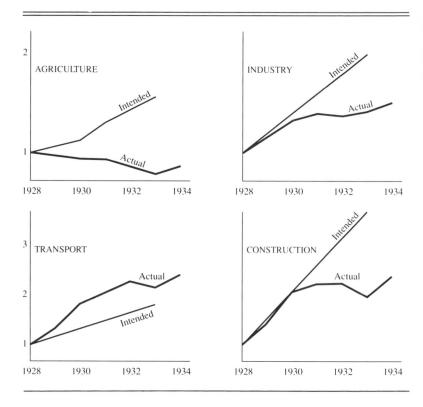

CHART 1 Intended and Actual Output Trends in Agriculture, Industry, Transport, and Construction in the USSR, 1928–34

textiles created a demand for emergency imports. Shortages of food and other consumer goods, combined with a drive on private retail trade, forced the introduction of rationing and stimulated a rise in money wage rates that played havoc with planned production costs. Delays in the completion of new capital capacity led for a while to emergency imports of steel, copper, and a wide range of machinery and equipment. Living standards plummeted, and parts of the country suffered famine in 1933. At the end of the first plan period, most large capital construction projects remained uncompleted. With the economy in the throes of a near breakdown, the plan was declared "completed" at the end of 1932 and a new five-year plan was not issued until early 1934.

It is obvious that the first plan did not "succeed," but perhaps this was not the planners' fault. Some of these difficulties reflected a series of unfavorable events not foreseen in the plan. The plan itself, for example, even in its third edition issued in the summer of 1930, did not recognize the drastic losses caused by the policy of "liquidating the kulaks as a class." Nor did the plan foresee the export and import crisis brought on by world depression. Emergency responses to these catastrophes could hardly prevent shortfalls in relation to the original targets of the plan's optimal variant. We can, however, ask whether the original targets would have been achievable in the absence of these heavy blows. . . .

The major question is a dynamic one: could the whole set of higher 1933 levels be reached in five years, starting from the 1928 foundation? Perhaps one or two of the targets could be reached, but could *all* of them? Stated differently, no doubt all could be reached over a longer period of time, but how much longer would it take? Clearly, we need to test intertemporal feasibility. Each sector's output in each year is limited by its capital capacity at the beginning of that year. Labor, raw materials, and imports are also potential limitations, but Soviet planners rightly took capital capacities to be the binding constraints they faced at this time. Our test therefore concentrates on limitations imposed by capital capacity.

Additions to capital capacity take time, up to seven years for very large projects. Current output goes into capital formation during a gestation period; in due course the sector gaining new capital capacity can produce more output. Meanwhile, however, current output is deflected into capital formation which will only lead to more output after a waiting period. Soviet planners were aware of these practical considerations, and a lengthy project list appended to volume 3 of the First Five-Year Plan recorded for over twelve hundred specific projects in the industrial sector the year they were to be launched, the year they were to be completed, their expected ruble construction cost, and some indication of the time pattern of outlays that was anticipated. Some were already under way as the plan period began, and some were not due for completion until after the First Five-Year Plan period was to end. Some quick projects could begin yielding output within a year. Two-year and three-year projects were more typical. Some very large and expensive projects would only begin yielding output after four years, and would not be fully completed for several years thereafter.

A composite weighted average of Gosplan expectations indicates a standard gestation-period pattern under which, if a sector's output was to increase in 1932 over 1931, for example, 8 percent of the value of the necessary capital increment for 1932 would have to be built in 1928, 16 percent in 1929, 41 percent in 1930, and 35 percent in 1931. This meant that three-quarters of the expense would be incurred over the two years preceding completion of the new capacity, but that the other quarter would have had to be launched earlier. Factories and other forms of productive capital cannot be built overnight; the growth and structural shifts called for in the First Five-Year Plan faced sharp physical limitations on this score.

Additions to capital stocks also are limited by the difficulty of diverting current output away from other uses, especially household consumption. The party was very conscious of this problem. It underlay the debate over terms of trade between the peasantry and the regime. The optimism and ambitiousness embedded in the First Five-Year Plan are epitomized by the fact that the plan assumed no belt-tightening at all! Household consumption was to grow throughout the plan period. Buried within detailed plan tables are indications that some categories of urban residents and some categories of the rural population were to be squeezed, but apart from these small minorities, all Soviet citizens were to improve their lot under the First Five-Year Plan. We shall shortly find that this optimism was unfounded. . . .

Alternative Expansion Paths . . .

The grim fact is — to repeat — that there was no easy way to pursue the first plan's objectives. The economy was already strained at the beginning of the plan period. Quick structural changes were impossible because of the gestation process required to build the desired new fixed capital, drawing directly and indirectly on every part of the economy. The intended sectoral growth rates were extraordinarily high by contemporary standards; and within the perspective of a quarter-century's development experience of dozens of countries, these rates appear even more obviously unrealistic today. . . .

The iron and steel works at Magnitogorsk in the Urals, constructed during the First Five-Year Plan. (Sovfoto)

The purposes embodied in the plan could have been sought through consistent and plausible programs, without any alteration in the structure of the terminal-year targets in the First Five-Year Plan or change in their level except to introduce a stern no-growth, no-fall policy toward per capita consumption standards. Lower growth rates and slower structural shifts might have brought the Soviet economy out of its strained situation by the middle 1930s, and might have done so fairly smoothly. A milder set of targets would still, of course, have required some difficult changes. The regime would have had to coax more off-farm output from the peasants, raising the level of 1928 procurements by perhaps 4 percent per year. It would also have been necessary to divert a larger share of the national income away from consumer goods and into capital formation. In the face of difficulties arising from the world depression, poor harvests, or construction delays, the plan period might have had to be stretched out. The likelihood of these developments cannot, however, be tested by the model used here, which merely accepts the parameters embedded in the 1928 flow table and its intended evolution.

Why Were Targets Set Too High?

These quantitative estimates demonstrate clearly that the targets in the "optimal" version of the plan accepted in the spring of 1929 were far too high to be achieved. Individual targets, especially those relating to industry and construction, had been sharply raised in successive versions of the plan over the preceding two or three years. Though linear programming tests in an intersectoral framework were not then available, it was generally appreciated that, taken together, the targets would require an enormous effort. What pushed them so high?

For one thing, recent experience seemed to justify optimism. In recovering from near chaos at the beginning of the 1920s, the industrial sector and the economy generally had shown extremely rapid rates of growth for several years. It was widely feared that when prewar levels were reached, growth would slow down. But after 1913 output levels were reached, there evidently still remained underutilized capacity, and rapid industrial growth continued during 1927 and 1928. Russian industry produced more in 1916 than in 1913, and despite territorial losses the capacity inherited by the new regime proved capable of being pushed above 1913 output levels. Party optimists could thus use recent experience to rebut the "extinguishing curve" school of thought.

A second important factor appears to have been fear of military intervention. In his November 19, 1928, speech to the plenum of the Central Committee, Stalin argued that rapid industrial development was necessary because the USSR was backward. In what was to become a familiar argument (vividly stated for the Soviet public over two years later, in February 1931), he argued before an intraparty audience that capitalist encirclement was a serious danger; he specifically mentioned Germany with its highly developed industry and technology.

An impending showdown with the peasantry was a third major factor appearing to require extremely rapid expansion of industry. In the same November 1928 speech Stalin argued that a crash program to produce more tractors and synthetic fertilizer would be required in order to modernize the agricultural sector promptly. A year later, with the plan targets approved and the first year apparently coming to a successful conclusion, Stalin launched his great assault on the peasantry, arguing that prompt and drastic change in both agriculture and industry would be mutually reinforcing.

A fourth major factor was social-psychological. S. G. Strumilin voiced the attitude of some party activists in the summer of 1927 when he paraphrased Marx to argue, "Our task is not to study the economy but to change it." He denounced Professor Kondratiev's cautious projections from the past and stressed the possibilities for imposing plan intentions on the existing situation. This view spread and by early 1931 was epitomized in Stalin's phrase, "There are no fortresses Bolsheviks cannot capture!"[1] A large group of cautious engineers and economists, skeptical of the increasingly ambitious targets emerging in successive drafts of a five-year plan, were pilloried as bourgeois wreckers and removed from office. Even Strumilin, an intelligent and competent economist, was swept aside. One can understand the rationale for a broad campaign to fire everyone with enthusiasm, enlist dedicated effort, "uncover hidden reserves," shake people out of stodgy habits, and provide encouragement to sustain people in a difficult period. In this context, ambitious targets would have some objective functional usefulness — at least up to a point. Clearly, the tragedy of 1928–29 was that this approach got completely out of hand. Perhaps if linear programing and input-output economics had been available to the planmakers, they would have been better able to stand up against the pressures for target increases.

A final factor that some have seen at work here, however, suggests that quantitative feasibility tests might have made no difference. Stalin's struggle for personal power introduced noneconomic considerations of decisive importance. He was prepared to push policy positions to an extreme degree in whatever direction would advance his drive against his opponents. Availability of the results reported in the present essay might not have added much to the arguments of those calling for reasonable targets. As Eugène Zaleski[2] suggests, "Stalin was a man of action, and industrialization meant for him the intensified construction of factories, the development of new branches of industry and new regions, the improvement of labor skills, and the reduction of economic dependence on the outside world. His vision of industrial development was of a vast program of large works, but works carried out under the impetus of a drive imbued with ideological fanaticism. Under these

[1] Actually Strumilin's phrase, lifted by Stalin. — Ed.
[2] A French economic historian; the quoted work is *Planning for Economic Growth in the Soviet Union* (Chapel Hill, N.C.: University of North Carolina Press, 1971). — Ed.

conditions, what would it matter whether these immense works were completed in three, four, or ten years?"

Conclusions and Implications

Some years ago, Alec Nove raised the crucially important question "Was Stalin really necessary?" and argued that, in order to accomplish Bolshevik objectives, he was. The present exercise in ex post planning provides some crude quantitative estimates indicating a modified reply. Stalin certainly was "necessary" for the drive to achieve the impossible targets of the First Five-Year Plan. But if Bolshevik targets are reinterpreted as calling for a very substantial increase in the economy's capacity (especially in industry and construction), put in place as quickly as conditions permitted, then the estimates presented above suggest that these Bolshevik objectives might have been achieved without the Draconian methods that Stalin used. A number of alternative paths were available, evolving out of the situation existing at the end of the 1920s, and leading to levels of capacity and output that could have been as good as those achieved by, say, 1936, yet with far less turbulence, waste, destruction, and sacrifice.

The "necessary" steps that Stalin took left behind them a permanently weakened agricultural sector, an embittered population, and a terrorized party. The policy of "liquidating the kulaks as a class" gave the regime control over the grain supply, but the agricultural sector after 1929 clearly supplied less output to the economy than it could have under fully plausible assumptions about its terms of trade with the regime. If economic expansion during the first plan period had proceeded along the kind of gradual path computed in illustrative solutions above, both the fixed capital base of the economy and the morale of its people would have permitted sustained expansion during the second plan period and thereafter. The serious external difficulties imposed on the Soviet economy by world depression would have been easier to handle.

Despite the disarray in the economy by the end of 1933, the practice of hortatory overtautness was continued in the Second Five-Year Plan and became standard operating procedure for the Soviet economy. The expansion rates embodied in Second Five-Year Plan targets were not as high as those bandied about during the "Bacchanalian planning" of 1930–31, but preliminary inspection suggests that, subjected to a feasibility test such as the one employed here, the 1937 targets would also prove overambitious. It is also clear that the practice of enforcing overfulfillment for targets related to construction and heavy industry, while permitting substantial shortfalls in targets related to living standards, carried over from the first plan period into subsequent standard Soviet operating practice. The regime mastered the art of "overfulfilling infeasible plans," in the felicitous phrase of Herbert S. Levine.

The overambitious First Five-Year Plan has thus had very long-run historical consequences. It started the USSR on the road to massive economic power, but the analytic model employed here to examine the plan's workability raises serious questions about the plan's impact on Soviet society. Soviet history cannot be revised after the fact, but perhaps other countries can draw useful conclusions from this way of reviewing Soviet experience.

Donald Filtzer

The Mobilization of Labor

Donald Filtzer is an American-born, British-trained historian of the Soviet economy presently working at the Centre for Russian and East European Studies at the University of Birmingham in England. In his first major publication he described the impact of Stalin's industrialization campaign on the Soviet working class. In the selection from that book reprinted here, he finds the nature of this social group profoundly transformed by the new command economy under the First Five-Year Plan.

The Soviet working class under NEP had no independent organizations through which to defend its position or to reconstitute itself as a political

From Donald Filtzer, *Soviet Workers and Stalinist Industrialization: The Formation of Modern Soviet Production Relations, 1928–1941*, Copyright © 1986, excerpts from pp. 22–70, 255–257. Reprinted by permission of Pluto Press, Oxford, England.

force. The trade unions found themselves in an excruciatingly ambiguous position. On the one hand, they were to defend the workers against abuses inside the enterprise; on the other, they had to obey and implement party policy, which was clearly for higher productivity, even if it meant speed-up, higher work quotas, and the more extensive application of piece rates. The unions' contradictory position was embodied in the institution of the so-called collective agreements, which were contracts reached between the unions and industrial management stipulating conditions, wage rates, and output quotas. Introduced in 1922, they initially embraced fewer than half the country's industrial workers, but they eventually came to govern shop-floor conditions for virtually everyone. By the late 1920s the agreements were reached directly between unions and the central economic authorities responsible for given branches of industry. The unions were clearly in a compromised position, for as an arm of the state and of the latter's industrial policy they were hamstrung in any attempts they might make to defend the interests of their members which might run in a contrary direction. The unions were not unaware of this political schizophrenia. At the start of NEP they openly complained of a return to capitalist-style management—replete with the emergence of mass unemployment. But the opposition was short-lived. Tomskii, head of the trade unions, resolved the problem by identifying the "interests" of the working class with the restoration of productivity, and thereby with the interests of the state. Henceforward the direction of the trade unions' allegiance was unambiguous. By 1924 they were offering little more than token opposition to the drive to extend the application of piece rates or to the massive rises in output quotas being imposed by many managers. . . .

This evolution of the trade unions' role made perfect sense from their position as agents of state economic policy. It was equally logical from the standpoint of the different oppositions to Stalin, including those organized around Trotsky, so long as they all accepted that the revolution's long-term survival depended on the political monopoly of the Bolsheviks. But the servile role of the unions was catastrophic in terms of the part it played in preparing the way for Stalin's eventual triumph. Instead of militant organizations preserving the combative traditions of the working class under market conditions — even the controlled market of Soviet NEP — the unions began increasingly to restrict their role to the provision of social, cultural, and educational amenities. Finally, in December 1928, at the Eighth Congress of the

All-Union Central Council of Trade Unions (VTsSPS), the old leadership of the trade unions under Tomskii was purged and the unions made completely subordinate to the state. Whatever their role in weakening the working class's ability to defend its position during NEP, the Tomskii leadership, which was politically allied to Bukharin, opposed the breakneck pace of the industrialization drive launched in 1928 and 1929 and the heightened pressure it placed on the industrial workers. It thus became necessary for Stalin to replace potential enemies in the unions with loyal adherents who would be faithful to official policy. After stripping Tomskii and his supporters of their positions of authority within VTsSPS, they were purged *in toto* in May 1929 and removed from the Central Council's Presidium. . . .

The rapid expansion of industry naturally created a huge demand for labour power, far exceeding the numbers foreseen by the original five-year plan. Total unemployment in April 1928 was over 1.5 million; among wage earners it was 1,274,000. In April 1929, at the start of the plan, it actually rose, to a total of 1.74 million including 1,335,000 wage labourers. By contrast the five-year plan had projected the number of workers and white-collar employees in the whole national economy to rise from 11.3 million in 1928 to 15.8 million in 1933, the end of the plan period (the first five-year plan was eventually declared "fulfilled" in 1932, nine months ahead of schedule). This was an increase of some 40 per cent, and allowing for natural population growth and migration from the countryside into the towns would barely have soaked up the pool of unemployed. This was even more evident from the planned increases in industry and construction. The number of industrial workers and employees was to go up from 3.5 million in 1928 to 4.6 million in 1933, an increase far below the number of urban unemployed. In construction the anticipated growth was more rapid, from 623,000 in 1928 to 1,883,000 in 1933. Even taking the combined number of workers and employees for the two sectors, the plan anticipated that some 511,000 unemployed would remain, much of it urban.

Reality was to prove otherwise. As production targets in industry and construction were pushed up, so too were the annual plans for employment, so that the plan for 1931 already foresaw 5.2 million workers and employees in industry and another 2.1 million in construction, both far in excess of the original plan for 1933. Yet even these figures were surpassed, as they were in every year until 1933, when a temporary moratorium on industrial recruitment was imposed. By 1932 the total number of workers and employees for the whole economy had more than doubled, to 24.2 million. Taking workers alone, that is, excluding white-collar employees, the rise was as shown:

	1928	1932	% Increase
Industry	3,124,000	6,007,000	92
Building	630,000	2,479,000	293
Transport	894,000	1,474,000	65

The question was where these new recruits were to come from. Initially it had been assumed that the pool of urban unemployed, in large part made up of dependents of heads of households already in employment, would provide the main source. This idea was soon dispelled, as unemployed began steadily and rapidly to decline from late 1929 onwards. This was accompanied by a marked change in the structural pattern of unemployment. Traditionally unemployment reached a nadir in the summer months when such seasonal industries as construction and peat were in full swing, and a peak in the spring, when the activities of seasonal industries were curtailed by the winter weather. In April 1930 this pattern was broken and never reappeared. Unemployment in that month was far below the autumn trough of September 1929. The social composition of unemployment also changed. The fall was most pronounced among those in industrial occupations, for example, metal-working and textiles. There was therefore a corresponding drop in the share of industrial workers among the unemployed, and a corresponding rise in the proportion of unskilled workers. Of these, most were now women and youth. Although absolute levels of unemployment fell amongst women as well, by January 1930 they were over half the unemployed. Most were young women under the age of 23; and some 90 per cent of the unemployed youth of both sexes were unskilled.

The urban "reserve army of the unemployed" was therefore practically exhausted by early 1930, a fact reflected in the increasing inability of the labour exchanges, organized by the People's Commissariat of Labour, to meet the demand for workers. The labour exchanges had started to experience a shortage of registered workers as early as 1926/7, when for every 100 people on their books they had 125 job offers. In 1928/9 the shortage had worsened, as there were 142 job offers for every 100 workers. By 1929/30 the ratio of offers to the number of available workers had nearly doubled, to 255 offers per 100 workers. The other side of this picture was a marked drop in the proportion of workers hired through the auspices of the labour exchanges, as opposed to being directly recruited by enterprises "at the gates." In April 1929 between 85 and 90 per cent of hirings were filled by the exchanges, depending on the industry. In April 1930, the range was 55 to 60 per cent; mining showed the sharpest drop, from 85 to 28.5 per cent.

If industry and construction were to find the workers they needed they would have to look to the countryside. Here the policy of forced collectivization fulfilled an historical function similar to the primitive accumulation of capitalism: using methods no less brutal than its capitalist predecessor, it forced millions of peasants off the land to seek work in the towns. . . .

As a result of collectivization and the peasantry's reaction to it the social composition of the Soviet working class underwent a profound transformation. From being an old, experienced working class with long traditions of struggle and organization it became a predominantly young, peasant-based, and unskilled workforce with little proletarian cultural tradition. In both industry and transport over half the workers newly recruited to the trade unions during the last half of 1931 (a good measure of the overall number of new workers in general) were peasants, and only a third workers; in construction some 77 per cent of new union members were from peasant background and only 18 per cent from the working class. By 1933 fewer than 20 per cent of workers in most industries had worked previously as wage labourers before taking up industrial employment, while those coming from agriculture ranged from around a quarter in most branches of engineering, to about a third in the iron and steel, motor vehicle, and paper industries, to 60 per cent in the cement industry and construction, and 88 per cent in the peat industry (a traditionally seasonal industry which always relied heavily on peasant labour). This trend was graphically illustrated in the Ukraine, especially the Donets Basin (Donbass), the heart of Soviet coal mining and the home of major industrial centres such as Dnepropetrovsk (iron and steel), Stalino (iron and steel), and Kharkov (engineering and iron and steel). In the Donbass between 1930 and 1932 the peasantry provided 80 per cent of new coal miners (as opposed to 66 per cent in 1926/7), and between 63 and 75 per cent of new iron and steel workers. In January 1931 nearly half of all Donbass coal miners were under the age of 24; as expected, the young workers were concentrated primarily in unskilled jobs. In the Ukrainian engineering industry the proportion of workers from peasant backgrounds rose from 34 per cent in 1928 to 43 per cent in 1931.

Alongside this process, the rapid industrial expansion created an enormous social mobility. The country found itself short of skilled technicians, industrial mangers, and low-level supervisory personnel, a need which it could meet only by rapidly promoting workers from the bench into responsible positions. New, streamlined education and training courses prepared these people to assume their new positions, which served as their entrée into the new intelligentsia and for many into the emerging elite. The number of these "promotees" [*vydvizhentsy*] was substantial: between 1930 and 1933 some 660,000 "worker communists" rose into the administrative and educational apparatus. This amounted to between 10 and 15 per cent of the industrial workers in 1930. Thus for a large number of workers the way out of the material hardships of industrialization was not to protest but to try and get out of the working class and move up into the bureaucracy, and for many into the ruling elite itself. The "promotees" in this way became a major base of support for the Stalinist elite, if not actually joining it. Their movement into positions of authority was accelerated after the Great Purges of 1937 removed much of the older industrial managerial stratum and allowed a new wave of upwardly mobile ex-workers to take their place. It has become fashionable among some historians to see this process as inherently progressive, as evidence that through Stalinism the Soviet Union achieved modernization not simply in a technological sense but in terms of acquiring a stable social structure appropriate to a modern industrial society. But this can only be done by turning a blind eye to the concrete content of Soviet industrialization, its class struggles, and its inherent deformities and inefficiencies. The rapid accession of working-class and peasant youth to responsible places in the elite did not in any way change the class character of the society which promoted them. The working class as a whole, together with the peasantry, remained ruthlessly exploited and deprived of any control over the political apparatus or over the social groups who made the decisions affecting their lives. However fluid access to social advancement became, it never altered the basic fact that *the Stalinist elite was at war with its own society.* It could win that war only by suppressing the last remnants of collective opposition and virtually destroying the working class *as a class.* . . .

The 1930s, in particular the period up to 1933, saw a veritable revolution in the position of women in the workforce. Although their share in industry as a whole rose by only about a quarter, they entered industries and trades that before industrialization had been virtually closed to them. The process was not all that it seemed, however, as women were channelled into the lowest-skilled and worst-paid jobs, where they had little prospects for promotion. To this day women in the USSR, although they make up half the workforce, are vastly under-represented in the higher skill grades relative to men, even in those industries, such as textiles, baking, and sewing, where they are the vast percentage of the total workforce.

From the start of industrialization it was understood that women were a major source of potential labour power. Most female "labour reserves" lived in cities and were members of workers' families. Their recruitment was therefore cheaper than that of men from the country-side, since they could be brought into production without major outlays on new housing or social amenities other than child-care facilities. The potential pool of untapped female labour was large, although never sufficient to cover the growing labour shortage. Surveys of women living in various centres claimed to show that between 80 and 90 per cent of women members of workers' families were not employed, including in some cases half the women who had no children. Estimates on just how many of these women were free to leave the home and enter production varied, but in at least some large engineering works it was close to 40 per cent. . . .

If the regime was going to realize its fantastic production programme it had necessarily to extract more work from the workforce, or put another way, to raise the rate of exploitation. Nominally this was to come from improvements in efficiency and extensive re-equipment, which would increase productivity without lowering workers' living standards. In reality this policy — even if conscientiously undertaken and not a cynical exercise in propaganda — collapsed almost from the start. Production costs did not fall as predicted, and productivity was far below planned levels. At the same time the failure of collectivization and the deepening capitalist depression meant that agricultural exports could not provide a compensating source of accumulation. On the contrary, collectivization became an unanticipated drain on the economy. The collapse of private agriculture, the slaughter of livestock, and the ensuing shrinkage in the hoped-for levels of private investment forced the regime to divert resources into the countryside that it had not planned for. The peasantry were in the unique position of suffering merciless exploitation without creating a surplus product sufficient to finance industrialization.

This left the industrial working class as the primary agent from whom an adequate surplus product could be extracted. To some extent the regime tried to motivate significant sections of workers voluntarily to increase their work rate in the interests of "socialist construction." The idea that with industrialization the USSR had embarked on a radical new path and was at last setting about the task of creating socialism after the years of drift during NEP no doubt appealed to many both in and outside the Communist Party, especially the young. The regime fuelled this enthusiasm through its rhetoric of heightened class struggle, its attacks on the "kulaks," private traders, and speculators, and the "unmasking" of alleged bourgeois industrial saboteurs. In 1928 the first of the fake show trials was staged, the so-called "Shakhty" affair, which claimed to unmask a group of bourgeois specialists engaged in sabotage in the coal industry of the Donbass. This was followed by the manufacture of other, equally spurious "conspiracies": the "Toiling Peasant Party" (1930), the "Industrial Party" (1930), and the so-called "Union Bureau of the Central Committee of the Menshevik Party" (1931), the latter two of which became victims of show trials. Each of these mythical organizations was charged with plotting to undermine the Soviet regime from within as a means of preparing the road for a capitalist restoration. Among the victims of these witch-hunts were many prominent ex-Social Revolutionaries and ex-Mensheviks who for years had worked loyally in Soviet government or academic institutions and whose commitment to Marxism was unquestioned. N. D. Kondrat'ev and V. G. Groman, for example, were professional economists who had actively engaged in the discussions around the drafting of the five-year plan. Another was Isaac Rubin, an academic economist whose interpretive works on Marx's *Capital* and the history of the labour theory of value rank among the outstanding Soviet theoretical writings of the 1920s. Despite the blatant transparency of the evidence and "confessions" (extracted through torture) on which these trials were based, it is probable that the vast majority of politically inclined Soviet citizens accepted the allegations at face value and perceived a genuine threat against the Soviet socialist experiment. The effect was to heighten the tensions and confrontational atmosphere of the period, and at least in the short run to strengthen the resolve and commitment of those who supported industrialization.

The appeal of moral incentives, although it mobilized thousands of young workers to make considerable sacrifices during the first five-year plan, was unsuccessful, as proven by the fact that these never played a dominant role in the regime's policy towards the working class. On the contrary, . . . the tactic of promoting "class struggle" came into open conflict with the main thrust of the regime's strategy, which was to impel workers to raise their work effort through speed-up and the increased centralization of managerial authority (*edinonachalie*, or one-man management). Output quotas, known in Russian as "norms," were repeatedly "revised" each year. The "revisions" were only one way — upwards, usually accompanied by cuts in piece rates. At first the norm revisions formally specified that although output norms were to go up the cut in job prices was to be limited, so that if workers could meet the new, higher targets, they would at least keep their earnings unchanged. This provision, clearly intended to make the rises more palatable, still required the workers to exert more effort just to maintain their old position. It did not accompany the revisions in following years. More to the point, even in 1929 managers took the rises as a signal that they were free to impose their own, unilateral wage cuts. In the Moscow sewing industry, for example, the trade unions officially complained that managers had slashed wages by half.

These statutory rises in output quotas and reductions in wage rates were not, in fact, the main vehicle for imposing the new policy. The centrepiece of the speed-up drive were the twin campaigns of "socialist competition" and "shock work" (*udarnichestvo*). Superficially socialist competition consisted of agreements — often arrived at after "challenges" from the workers of one factory or shop to the workers of another — between enterprises, ships, brigades, or individual workers to improve on various production "indicators," be it gross output, cost reductions, or quality. The agreements were made in the form of pledges or contracts, and could involve whole enterprises or groups of workers, either within the same factory or engaged in comparable work in different plants.

Shock workers (*udarniki*) were those who exceeded their production quotas and/or "volunteered" for extra work (overtime was technically illegal), to work so-called "Communist Saturdays" (*subbotniki*) helping to gather crops on nearby collective farms, or to raise their work norms. At first the incentives offered to shock workers were quite modest, but as the policy of intensified piece work and wage differentiation took hold shock workers became a privileged elite entitled to quite substantial bonuses and access to scarce foodstuffs and consumer goods. The regime, of course, insisted that workers participated in shock work campaigns out of socialist enthusiasm, but the reality was that for the vast majority the overriding incentive was the need to boost earnings at a time of extreme hardship and high inflation. . . .

[T]he main thrust of regime policy was to break down the working class, to undermine its cohesion and solidarity, divorce it once and for all from its militant traditions, and destroy its ability to act collectively as a self-conscious historical force. The old working class was ultimately eliminated and the new workforce that took its place encountered political, working, and living conditions that made it virtually impossible for it to reconstitute itself as a militant class able collectively to define, and fight for, its own radical needs.

The regime accomplished this by several means, all of which operated simultaneously and reinforced one another: physical repression; flooding the ranks of the working class with peasants having no traditions of industrial life and therefore of industrial militancy and collective action; driving many older workers out of production; undermining the cohesion of the proletariat by offering a sizeable minority opportunity to advance into the bureaucracy and the elite; the imposition of extreme economic hardship; socialist competition and shock work, and a concomitant radical individualization of work and labour incentives. Hardship and the more stringent working conditions made the fight for individual survival take precedence over collective protests, even those of a purely defensive character. For a minority upward mobility was therefore an even more attractive alternative and they opted to use it as a means of escape from the deprivations of the period. A sharp differentiation *within* the working class further undermined its internal cohesion by dividing the privileged shock workers from the rank and file.

The regime in this way finally succeeded in breaking down the working class as a collective force. The other side of this process was the actual recruitment of many of its members from the working class, who once having entered the apparatus behaved not as workers but as people exercising power over the workers. Hence the Soviet Union presented the seeming paradox of a society undergoing increasingly sharp class divisions at the same time as the exploiting class was becoming more "proletarian" in its social origins. Even so, the extent and effect of this upward mobility should not be overestimated. Despite the upward mobility of some 10–15 per cent of the workforce, for the mass of workers this avenue of escape was precluded. For them the only alternative was to defend their position as best they could. At times this expressed itself in collective action: strikes, demonstrations, industrial slow-downs. But at no time did these involve the large mass of workers or pose a serious political threat to the regime, which reacted sharply to any challenge from below. Thus for the mass of workers individual responses were the only avenues open, namely high labour turnover, absenteeism, insubordination, alcoholism, damage to machinery, physical attacks on lower-level management and shock workers, defective output, and an indifferent attitude towards work. The "rational kernel" of these responses was obscured by the peasant origins of most of the new workforce, whose lack of experience and knowledge of the industrial regime, with its demands for order and skills, were responsible for many of the early difficulties in production. But the fact was that the peasantry, like the older workers whom they joined, were in the main hostile to the regime and had little incentive to adapt to the rigours and strains of forced industrialization. Leaving aside their lack of knowledge of how to operate complex equipment, in all other respects the peasant workers behaved little differently from the older generation with longer industrial experience.

Deprived of any means to defend their interests collectively, the labour shortage and the subsequent breakdown of the traditional labour market, in particular the disappearance of the threat of unemployment, placed the workers in a position to appropriate considerable control over the individual labour process, most notably their work speed, how they organized their work, and the quality of the products they produced or the operations they performed. Managers, under their own pressures to meet production targets under near chaotic conditions, had little choice but to accommodate. Managerial concessions to workers were of two types. First were those to do with violations of labour discipline. This was a simple function of supply and demand: workers were scarce and managers could not afford to fire workers who committed grave violations of discipline regulations. As the regime imposed more stringent penalties for absenteeism, lateness, alcoholism, and insubordination, managers found themselves having to take a more active role in insulating workers from these sanctions. The second type of concessions was more complex and had a more direct bearing on the relations of production within the Soviet enterprise, as managers increasingly had to accept the workers' partial control over the work process. Managers needed not only to hold on to their workforces, but to achieve some basic degree of co-operation in order to minimize the disruptions to production endemic in the Stalinist system. They therefore came to tolerate workers' substantial control over how they used their work time, did little to combat the persistence of irrational and inefficient forms of work organization, accepted relatively high levels of defective or poor quality output, and took steps to protect workers' earnings by keeping output norms low and inflating their wages.

The result was the creation of an historically unique system of relations of production which conformed neither to the production relations of capitalism, geared to the creation of surplus value, nor to those of socialism, where the associated producers collectively determine the purposes to which they will put their labour and the methods by which they will carry it out. In the USSR the associated producers did not — and do not — have any positive control over the organization of their society. Goals are set by the elite, including what is produced and how. The fact that these goals are rarely met arises from the elite's loss of control over the actions of managers and workers alike, each of whom distorts central instructions to their own purposes.

Moshe Lewin

Collectivization: The Reasons

Western scholarship long ago began to challenge the view that Russia's economic difficulties made forcible collectivization of the peasants a necessary accompaniment of the industrialization drive. The Polish-born, Israeli- and French-educated historian Moshe Lewin, who presently teaches at the University of Pennsylvania, has re-examined the background of collectivization in great detail, particularly in his book *Russian Peasants and Soviet Power*. In an earlier article based on this work, excerpted here, he demonstrates the existence of real alternatives facing the Soviet leadership.

The Role of the Grain Crisis

It would be wrong to look upon the great leap at the end of 1929 as having been conceived all of a piece at the very last moment. For, in a sense, the decision to undertake overall collectivization had its roots in the grain crisis at the beginning of 1928. Stalin's ideas on policy germinated during the testing time of this crisis, though only in essentials, for *at that stage he was concerned only with a short-term policy of moderate aims*, but by reason of the growing crisis he was constantly obliged to extend the objectives with which he had set out at the beginning of the year.

Indeed, the grain crisis was of crucial importance in the shaping of future events, among other reasons because Stalin derived from it a whole series of new conclusions and the elements of a new plan of campaign. During his visit to Siberia, where he had gone to urge and compel the party officials to take the grain ruthlessly, he had felt that, in addition to the weapons of compulsion, he ought to have something to

From Moshe Lewin, "The Immediate Background of Soviet Collectivization," *Soviet Studies*, v. 17 (Oct. 1965), pp. 170–172, 179–197. Reprinted by permission of Longman Group Ltd., England.

offer these officials in the way of a long-term policy and a more optimistic perspective. None of his statements in Siberia was published at the time, but we now know in what terms he spoke.

It was at this juncture that he became aware of the urgent necessity for establishing strongpoints in the countryside, similar to those the regime had built up in the towns. So it appeared that the hitherto accepted thesis to the effect that cooperation could serve as this strategic position was in practice dropped. This was replaced by the discovery, which was new coming from Stalin, of kolkhozy [collective farms] and sovkhozy [state farms] — those feeble organisms hitherto the Cinderellas of the regime. It is at this point also that he expressed the thought that the Soviet regime was "walking on two unequal legs" — the socialist sector in the towns and the private sector in the villages — and that this could not go on indefinitely. It can be deduced from this (and Stalin in fact admitted it explicitly the same year) that he no longer believed in NEP as a viable policy. The more his methods intensified the crisis, the more his scepticism increased.

Towards May [1928], his faith in the kolkhozy and sovkhozy as the sovereign remedy was further strengthened. He discovered that these organisms had a considerable marketing potential; it was suggested that this was four times greater than that of the private peasants. At this time Stalin was also greatly preoccupied with another important problem; how was the regime to ensure that kolkhozy and sovkhozy would hand their grain over to the state? Here he went straight to the heart of the matter. He believed, and rightly so, that what would be impossible with the existing 25 million farms would become more practicable if they were merged into a smaller number of large farms.

Stalin's strategy, as it emerged at this stage, took the following form: there was an imperative need for a new policy, comprising a renewed effort on the industrial front and the establishment of a powerful kolkhoz-sovkhoz sector. The private sector in the countryside would remain, and would in fact continue to function as an essential element in grain production, but this was no longer enough. In Stalin's view, the scale of the socialist operation in the countryside would be determined by the quantitive target which he had set himself. As he saw it, matters must be so arranged that the state would be absolutely sure of having at its disposal some 250 million poods of grain (in other words, about a third of the quantity required by the end of the Five-Year Plan). Sovkhozy, kolkhozy and contracts signed with peasants' associations would

produce this quantity, and the state would thus be able to supply ʌ
sectors of the economy and the army, and to operate on the naʌ
(and international) markets, thereby forcing the peasants to sell t ʌ
surpluses to the state because of competition due to the reserves it had in
hand. Stalin would have liked to achieve this objective within three to
four years. His colleagues were of the opinion that it would take four to
five years.

The regime was, therefore, still a long way from any kind of total
collectivization but, as we know, it was already on the road, although it
was hardly aware of it at the time.

Stalin's thoughts about the situation had crystallized by the July
plenum and still followed the same main lines, irrespective of his maneuvers in the internal struggle against the right wing, which, brought
into the open by the procurement crisis, was now at its height. Stalin
knew, and told the Central Committee in a speech which was secret at
the time, that the peasants would have to pay a tribute (*dan*) for the
requirements of industrialization. This was Preobrazhensky's theory,
but with none of the latter's scruples or reservations. Stalin realized that
the workers, too, would have to be made to pay, and that this would
give rise to increasing social contradictions. How, then, were things to
be kept going for another four years or so, until such times as the state
and collective sector would bring an improvement in the situation?
Stalin had made up his mind: in the meanwhile, the regime would use
emergency measures to collect the grain. He had already done this in
the course of the year. He suggested it again in July, and had made
official policy of it by April 1929. Bukharin scarcely exaggerated when
he said to Kamenev: "He will have to drown the risings in blood," —
but this Stalin was prepared to do. . . .

The Five-Year Plan and Stalin's Attitude . . .

The Five-Year Plan had no convincing answer to the question of easing
current supply difficulties while waiting for the plan to bear fruit. At all
events, it was decided that, until the end of the Five-Year Plan, there
would be no export of grain.

No one had yet dreamed of mass collectivization as a rapid and
effective means of solving both current and long-term problems at one
and the same time. The plan was ratified by the Congress of Soviets in
May 1929. The great majority of the *Party leadership* did not, either at

this stage or in the autumn, foresee what decisions were to be taken some six months later. At that time, everyone was uttering warnings about over-hasty action in relation to changes of organization in the countryside. The party were convinced, as Kalinin and Rykov put it at the time, that the scale of collectivization must be related and adapted to the state's actual ability to provide machines and specialists. They all sincerely believed that the entire operation would be carried out exclusively on the basis of voluntary membership.

But it was precisely at this moment, when the plan, with its relatively moderate and feasible aims for the agricultural sector, had just been launched, that Stalin arrived at quite different conclusions. At the plenum in April 1929, his lack of faith in the private agricultural sector and in NEP finally came to the surface. Just about this time another procurement campaign had been carried through in the face of enormous difficulties, and had yielded *less grain than in the previous year*, despite the use of a whole body of coercive measures, which had been applied more or less throughout the country but especially in the Urals and in Siberia.

It was clear that Stalin was already planning to launch a really large-scale operation. He informed the Central Committee that the kulaks and other hostile forces were preparing to undermine the Soviet regime — a type of assertion which, as we now know, was a sign that he was either preparing to attack or to drive home his attack. Indeed, he told the Central Committee (it should be borne in mind that his speech was secret at the time) that "the days of the capitalists and the kulaks are numbered." . . .

The violent and impetuous character of the decisions which were taken is more readily explicable by certain internal factors. Stalin expressly stated in April that he was relying on emergency measures to solve the grain crisis. He was well aware that such a policy could not last long without leading to a disastrous clash with the peasantry. This was the reason behind the attack on the Nepmen and industrial specialists in the towns, and on the better-off peasants in the countryside, for care must be taken to weaken any elements which might eventually rally an outraged peasantry. The same motive underlay subsequent decisions (towards the end of 1929). Again, the antikulak measures, apart from their role in the campaigns for wresting grain from the peasants, were a maneuver aimed at the social encirclement of the middle peasants, designed to divide them and to block all their escape routes, leaving them only one way out.

Here one recognizes the hand of Stalin, the master tactician. In fact, his social and political tactics were much better than his strategy, for the latter calls for a greater capacity for theoretical analysis, which he did not possess. At all events, could it be said in April–May 1929, when he had already made his intentions quite clear, that the practical program embodying ideas on the scale of the reforms which were to take place and the methods by which they were to be achieved had received consideration, preparation or ratification from any organization whatsoever?

In the writer's view, Stalin at this point still did not know where his actions would lead six months later. It would seem that his aims, and those of his immediate lieutenants, were still in line with the provisions of the Five-Year Plan, although in certain respects going beyond these. Several months were still to elapse, until about the end of September, before the economic results of the year would be known, when Stalin and his Politburo would *once more revise* the existing plans, involving decisions on an unprecedentedly large scale.

The Results of the Year 1928/29 and the Part Played by Them

The economic results of the year 1928/29 were much worse than had been expected. This was admitted by Mikoyan. The better-off peasants had cut down their sowings and the authorities struggled to make good the loss by increasing the areas sown by the rest of the peasants. The results thus obtained were not encouraging. Worse still, the numbers of livestock began to decline for the peasants were short of fodder and food. The towns too were short of food. Ration cards were introduced in February 1929, while in the factories the management were putting increasing pressure on the workers to step up production. The workers retaliated by mass defections from one factory to another, and by an enormous wave of *brak* (faulty production) for which they could not of course be held entirely responsible. The rise in the price of bread grains and other agricultural products caused a rise in prices throughout the economy. Speculation was rife; bread tended to disappear from the towns into regions which had none, especially those which did not produce bread grains, or into provincial towns which the government was not supplying. Living standards dropped and all the time administrative pressure and state tyranny were growing. Grain procurements, as we know, had been very inadequate, whereas the private middlemen had succeeded in buying more that year from the peasants than in previous years.

Thus, the upheavals taking place in agriculture were clearly having repercussions on the national economy. In the view of the majority of the Politburo, the bad state of agriculture was entirely to blame for the crisis.

However, in addition to the part played by faulty economic policy, the great effort which was going into industrialization contributed enormously to the strain and was very largely responsible for the crisis because, as Bukharin had said, it was excessive. And yet the leadership were convinced that their only hope lay precisely in an ever higher rate of industrial growth. Moreover, they were borne out in this by the fact that, to all appearances, the annual industrial plan for 1928/29, which had been officially declared to be the first year of the Five-Year Plan, was going well. However, this was in appearance only, a point of capital importance in understanding the change in policy which took place at the end of the year. . . .

On the agricultural front the plan failed utterly. Agricultural production, including industrial crops, was on the downgrade. The food-processing industry also declined and the chemical industry and agricultural machinery plans were not fulfilled. It should be recalled that the trade networks had been gravely disorganized as a result of the offensive against the private traders.

It can readily be understood that in a situation of this kind the leaders would feel that they had their backs to the wall and that the regime would be impelled to bring to bear the full coercive power of its dictatorship.

In the view of the party leaders, it was exclusively the rural sector which was to blame for the disequilibrium. This sector had recently opened a second front against the regime, being now engaged on a livestock offensive, in addition to the grain offensive which had already assumed serious proportions by the beginning of 1928.

The pace of industrialization was not thought to be excessive; on the contrary, the Politburo thought it both desirable and possible to step up rates of growth, a decision which was to be taken at the Central Committee meeting in November 1929. In this way, the authorities hoped to rescue the country from its troubles and steer it into calmer waters with the minimum of delay. In the minds of the leadership, the state of agriculture was the biggest obstacle to their aims.

In September 1929, when the leadership were already aware of the year's economic results, it seems that the small Stalinist leadership, having evaluated the situation, made up their minds: if in the course of the coming months, which were the only ones in which a state campaign could be launched in the countryside (before sowing was begun) some radical change did not take place on the rural front, the drive for industrialization would unquestionably have lost its impetus by 1931, if not sooner.

It was this reasoning, at this precise moment, which dictated Stalin's change of policy at the end of 1929, particularly in view of the fact that the results of the forced collectivization which had been started in the summer seemed to give grounds for much optimism.

On to the Attack

It was not until June 1929 that any significant and far-reaching attempt at implementing the new policy in the countryside became apparent, and even then the exact nature and extent of the course which was to be followed had still not assumed any definite form. The development of the new program, or rather the new course of action (for there was as yet no definite program, in the accepted sense of the term) seems to have been characterized by a continual process of sliding, as it were, towards the objectives in question, while the latter were continually being enlarged. This curious process lasted from the beginning of 1928 to the end of 1929, with a period of extreme acceleration which set in in the summer of 1929. The incessant changes which the plans for agriculture underwent will serve to illustrate this sliding process.[1]

The Politburo were constantly changing their directives because they had no definite system of objectives. Events, some of a negative

---

[1] The Five-Year Plan spoke of 5 million households collectivized towards the end of the quinquennium, covering an area of 21–22 million hectares. In June 1929 *kolkhoztsentr* [the Kolkhoz Center] announced an aim of 8 million hectares with 7–8 million souls for the single year 1930, and half the rural population (and three times the area envisaged in the initial plan) by 1933. In August Mikoyan spoke (for 1930) of 10 million hectares. In September Gosplan fixed, still for 1929/30, a target of 13 million hectares with 10 percent of the total population in kolkhozy. In October and November the "control figures" for 1929/30 were altered to 15.2 million hectares with 12 percent of the population. In December Sovnarkom wanted to collectivize 30 million hectares — and this was not the end.

character, and others which appeared positive and encouraging, spurred the leadership to action. Thus, from summer onwards, a whole series of measures showed that the center had begun to act in earnest, and in great haste. . . .

In summer 1929 the Soviet press was already mentioning a new phase, that of mass collectivization. The countryside was mobilized by thousands of agitators and activists of all sorts. The rural Communists, under threat of disciplinary measures for the first time, were instructed to join the kolkhozy in order to set an example.

The *Kolkhoztsentr* was granted wider powers and began to set up its network at oblast, okrug and raion[2] level, while another organization, *Traktortsentr*, was set up to administer the MTS [machine-tractor stations] and to create a fairly large number of these stations as quickly as possible.

For the first time, the trade unions found themselves faced with an imperative demand to assist in the collectivization of the villages, an unfamiliar task for which they were in no way equipped. In fact, at this period almost all the state and party organizations were called upon to collectivize and to direct the process of collectivization. In its feverish haste, the Politburo delegated responsibility to so many organizations that there was soon a veritable administrative tangle, the results of which were harmful in the extreme.

In addition, the party and the specialized services spent that year preparing, with a degree of energy and efficiency rarely to be encountered in other fields, for the procurement campaign, which in fact was to be more successful than ever before because of the unprecedented extent of the resources mobilized for the purpose. Once the procurement task had been accomplished, the enormous forces which had been concentrated in the countryside were redeployed and instructed to apply themselves to the task of collectivization. After the procurements, the bulk of these forces were available mainly as from January 1930. The actual process of organizing the kolkhozy now began to develop in a number of interesting ways. There was marked progress. *Kolkhoztsentr* decided to double (between June and October) the area occupied by the giant kolkhozy, and during this period the kolkhoz movement as a whole was doubled, increasing from 3.9 to 7.6 percent of holdings

---

[2] Region, sub-province, and district. — Ed.

collectivized. At this stage the movement consisted mainly of poor peasants who had been influenced by propaganda and attracted by the quite unrealistic promises showered on them and by the state aid which was being channelled to the kolkhoz sector. This success ought to have been consolidated before any further advance was attempted, but the effect of it was rather to encourage the leadership to step up the campaign and to exert even greater pressure.

In its initial stages this movement, although not strictly speaking a spontaneous one, was nonetheless not the result of coercion, although some elements of administrative pressure had been in evidence as far back as the beginning of 1928. According to recent statements from Soviet sources, coercion began to play an increasing part from the early autumn of 1929, and one might add that, with the onset of winter, it had become the regime's main weapon. . . .

The more specific decisions about the great turn in collectivization appear to have been taken by the Politburo in the month of October, though the evidence for this assumption is still incomplete. At all events, a short time previously no such decisions had existed.

Towards the end of October, *Pravda* finally stated the problem in unequivocal terms: all the forces which had been massed for the procurements campaign, it said, must be thrown into collectivization. In view of what is known about the methods employed during the procurements campaign, the order is not without significance. In fact, from this time onward the press was to be full of denunciations of the kulaks and appeals for mass collectivization. The incitement to violent methods was barely concealed, though no definite indication was given about the nature or extent of these methods, or how they were to be applied. This was no accident. The leadership had now opted not for reforms but for revolution.

On 7 November Stalin published his famous article on the "Great Turn," in which almost every element of his appraisal of the situation was incorrect. In particular, he stated that "the middle peasant has opted for the kolkhozy," which according to present-day Soviet sources, was not at all the case. According to these same sources, Stalin was anxious to induce the forthcoming meeting of the Central Committee (the November meeting) to adopt the decisions he wanted by presenting the members of the Central Committee with a view of reality colored to suit his own aims.

The November meeting accordingly complied, though with certain reservations attested by present-day sources. The plenum adopted an unrealistic plan for industrial growth, called for a more rapid rate of collectivization, with a move towards "kolkhoz-sovkhoz composites" — mythical organizations which never in fact existed. At this meeting, it was decided to set up a new all-Union commissariat for agriculture, to build two new tractor factories and two more for combine-harvesters.

Molotov, who presented the principal report on the problem of collectivization, suggested "dekulakization" without explicitly saying so (and indeed, there were instances of confused antikulak measures in a number of places very shortly after); he spoke disparagingly of the five-year plans for agriculture, since in his view it was "the coming months, weeks and days which counted." He said that before long not only okrugs but whole republics would be completely collectivized, and the time which he thought such an undertaking should take was exactly five months.

The leadership were plainly reluctant to impose any terms of limitations on the activities of the officials. Some members of the Central Committee insisted that a commission be set up within the Politburo to direct collectivization and to see that the whole operation, particularly the process of dekulakization, was carried through in an orderly manner. We can but guess at the reasons why the Politburo took three weeks to set up this commission, which was made up of the most experienced representatives of the oblast authorities and specialists from the central departments.

Two weeks later the commission produced a draft resolution and a detailed plan of action, but Stalin altered their proposals to give them greater urgency and wider scope, his main preoccupation apparently being to give the least possible excuse for delay, and the freest possible rein to uninhibited action.

The subcommittee responsible for the draft proposal on dekulakization was even dismissed and replaced by another in January 1930. Without waiting for its conclusions, Stalin on 27 December publicly gave the green light to the "liquidation of the kulaks as a class," without putting forward at the time any suggestions or directions about the manner in which this terrible operation was to be carried out.

Some weeks previously, on his fiftieth birthday, Stalin had been hailed, for the first time, as the greatest Marxist-Leninist and the greatest strategist of all time, and so forth. From now on, he was the infallible leader, the object of a cult.

Was There Any Choice?

The historian is often perplexed when faced with the question: was there any other way out? And yet this is not a question which one can easily evade unless one is convinced that in fact no alternative existed.

As for the problem at present under discussion, the following argument suggests a number of replies:

Compulsory collectivization was launched under pressure from a crisis which threatened not only the country's drive for industrialization but also the stability of the regime itself. There may be reservations about the truth of this allegation, but the fact remains that this is how the situation appeared to the effective leaders of the party at the time.

It is true that the weaknesses inherent in the structure of agriculture had a disruptive effect on the national economy, that they threatened to reduce the country to famine and served as a breeding-ground for a number of adverse social elements, and so forth. But it is undoubtedly true that agriculture was not exclusively to blame for the crisis.

1. The measure of industrialization which was already going on at the time represented an enormous burden, the size of which was largely the result of the excessive rate of industrialization. But a particular rate or speed of growth is not exclusively dictated by the pressure of objective needs (in the case of Russia rapid industrialization as such may be accepted as an objective necessity); *they are also the result of a choice, an appraisal, a certain level of political and economic planning and administrative capacity.* Here there exists an enormous margin of error in decision-making and the conduct of affairs. In this particular context, it is our view that the leaders did in fact make mistakes over a whole number of questions, and that the quality of their administration was poor, and at times disastrous. In particular, the rate of industrial growth was excessive, and the decisions taken by the leaders were often quite arbitrary, since the leaders themselves had little inclination to listen to the suggestions put forward by experts or those of moderate opinions. Bukharin was right (and Trotsky agreed with him) when he said that it was absurd to embark on a building program knowing in advance that the requisite materials would not be available.

In fact, the excessive rate of growth and the lack of administrative skill in the handling of affairs were such that:

a. In practice the progress of industrialization during the First Five-Year Plan was not the result of the Five-Year Plan or of any other coherent plan. Such was the extent of the confusion in the administration of the Five-Year Plan that it led, among other things, to the famous method of priority (shock) projects (*udarniye stroiki*) in which everything was sacrificed for the achievement of a handful of objectives which were judged to be of key importance. The method was a salutary one, no doubt, in the given situation, but it originated in confusion and gave rise to excessive waste. This was not planning in any sense of the term.

b. The excessive growth rates which ruined the Five-Year Plan as a planned and properly organized operation also contributed to the resultant wastage of resources. It is impossible to say just what the *excess* cost of the Five-Year Plan was, but it is a fact that, in a country which was short of resources, what human and material resources they had were all too often recklessly squandered and consequently yielded no advantage. . . .

2. An analysis of the second major contributory factor in the crisis, that is the state of agriculture, discloses a number of ills which might have been avoided or mitigated if steps had been taken in time:

a. During the years of NEP, especially from 1925 onward, the leaders placed overmuch reliance on the ability of NEP to function automatically and either did not perceive, or neglected, a number of factors which were to cause them untold difficulties at a later stage; in this connection, the future right wing undeniably bears a great deal of the responsibility. At this stage, there was already some substance in the allegation made by the Left Opposition that a more serious attempt at industrialization could have been begun at a much earlier date. We previously cited as a significant example the case of the tractor factory at Stalingrad. Whatever might have been the practical considerations which led to a failure to implement this project in 1924, they reflect a poverty of statesmanship.

b. We have referred to agricultural price policy during the NEP period, which Molotov described . . . as a series of colossal stupidities. If these colossal stupidities had been avoided, could it possibly be said that subsequent events, particularly the grain crisis in the winter of 1928, need have been as severe as they in fact were?

c. The total neglect of the collective movement in the countryside was a blatant and unpardonable error. The same was true of the sov-khozy, which were in a notoriously backward state. We have already mentioned the views of Rykov, when he asked in 1928: Why was a major campaign on the sovkhozy not launched earlier? He had in mind a number of other measures which might have encouraged agricultural progress, but which were never introduced.

The idea of a powerful state and collective sector, which would be limited in scope but well-organized, might have played a part of the very greatest importance. Nor can it be said that the Bolsheviks were incapable of conceiving such an idea prior to 1928. And yet the fact remains that it was not until 1929 that this discovery was made, and energetic action was taken to build up this sector. How it was done, in what conditions and with what results, is well know. Having failed to pursue a reasonable policy, the regime found itself thrown back on the disastrous alternative of mass collectivization.

d. Prior to 1928, and for some time after this date, there were a number of elements in the social structure of village life which could have been of the greatest importance as a starting-point for promising developments in the collective and cooperative field. The institution of the *mir* [village community] itself could have been used to form one of the many variants of the producers' association (*tovarishchestvo*), as had been suggested by Gosplan in 1929. But this avenue was first neglected and then finally left unexplored.

There were abundant examples in the countryside of spontaneous cooperative movements, particularly the simple producers' associations (*prostiye proizvodstvenniye tovarishchestva*). We cannot discuss these at length in the present context, but they were in fact spontaneous, owing nothing to the initiative or support of the authorities. In most cases they did not even form part of the official cooperative movement (the same was true of a great many of the kolkhozy) and they were, therefore, described as wild or beyond the pale. But this need not have been so.

e. The way in which the authorities handled the cooperative movement, both before and after the grain crisis, left much to be desired. Behind the figures which recorded quantitative results, one could discern a movement stifled in the grip of a bureaucracy which left the mass of the peasantry no scope for genuine initiative and hence for constructive education. Lenin's dream of cooperation was in no way utopian. Furthermore, "kulak domination" of the cooperative movement was neither as real or as unavoidable as it was made out to be in the subsequent official interpretation. The party never deployed any appreciable forces in this sector, either in terms of quantity or quality, nor did it devote much thought to the problem. This is why the future process of collectivization, curious and paradoxical though it may seem, was in fact carried out on the ruins of the cooperative movement.

f. Up until the end of 1929, the kolkhoz movement consisted for the most part of *tozi*, a not very highly collectivized form of organization which was plainly favored by the peasants, and also by the majority of the party activists concerned with this problem. The directive calling for the abolition of these organizations and the imposition of the *artel;* the fact of *having made one single form of organization obligatory* in a country which had a whole range of such structures; the fact that no opportunity was afforded for experimentation with other possible types of organization — all these facts add up to a policy which it is impossible to endorse with the seal of inevitability. We have no hesitation in suggesting that these were fatal errors.

3. Whatever the circumstances may have been which led the Stalinist group to interpret the grain crisis as a sign that NEP was doomed, and which set them on the road to mass collectivization, all of their decisions and appraisals are open to criticism and to question.

a. It may be admitted that the grain crisis in the winter of 1928 called for a series of administrative measures, although this point of view was in fact disputed at the time by certain party experts, as well as by the Right Opposition. What is open to question is the exclusive reliance on coercive measures which consequently became increasingly violent and further aggravated the existing difficulties. If some pressure had to be exerted, it could have been accompanied by the social and economic measures proposed by the (future) right wing. Some imports of grain, a rise in the procurement prices, imports of manufactured goods — all of these might have helped to ease the nature and the extent of the pressure, and might perhaps have lessened the impact of the crisis and gone some way to improving relations with the peasantry. But these measures were rejected, or worse still, they were first of all rejected and then adopted (in part) later, in fact *too late.*

b. The decision to collectivize the greatest possible number of peasants, and to dispossess and deport the better-off peasants, which was taken towards the end of 1929, and which certain observers accept as having been inevitable, is equally open to question, at least in respect of its scope and timing. It is true that at that moment, because of the failures of the past, some of which we have already mentioned, there are strong indications that the leadership felt themselves compelled to take exceptional and very dangerous measures. But it is significant that a number of Soviet scholars nowadays express doubts not only about the speed and the excessively administrative nature of the collectivization, but also about the timing of the dekulakization measures undertaken at this stage. They maintain that the mass of the peasants, and particularly the middle peasants, were as yet unprepared for collectivization on such a massive scale, and therefore not ready for liquidation of the kulaks. By making such a statement, they call into question the whole of the spectacular change of policy at the end of 1929.

Our present analysis is not so much concerned with the sudden change as with the long period which led up to it, and we have tried to focus attention on certain factors in this period which have tended to be disregarded by the policy makers, or certain errors which appear particularly blatant. The purpose is not one of speculation about other courses which history might have taken, and so this is not an essay in "if history." It is simply an attempt at isolating a fairly large number of concrete factors which together might have gone to make up a different body of measures, or in other words a different policy, though within the same institutional framework. This might in itself suffice to answer the question: was there any alternative? Let us conclude, however, with a few general observations.

The situation in which Soviet Russia found itself was such that a vigorous campaign of industrialization became a matter of prime necessity, and this could not be achieved without "tribute" from the peasants, the workers, and in fact the entire population. As Preobrazhensky had accurately predicted, this was bound to involve a period of social strain, particularly during the initial phases of the industrial effort. In addition, it may be said that to meet with success in its efforts, the regime had to be a tough one, a resolute dictatorship.

This precondition does not, however, exclude the element of choice in respect of the behavior of such a regime and the policy which it pursued. Granted that tribute was inevitable, its size was still a matter for choice and not a fixed quantity rigidly laid down by some immutable law of history; granted that, in the given situation, some form of dictatorship was necessary, it should not be overlooked that dictatorship, like democracy, can assume many different forms. In this situation, dictatorship would seem to have been a logical necessity, but not necessarily in the autocratic, terroristic, cult-producing guise which it in fact assumed; granted the need for industrialization, the problems of "how much" and "how" were still open to choice. While it is agreed that the process of industrialization was bound to involve sweeping changes in the countryside, it is, in our view, wrong to suppose that these changes could not have been effected otherwise than by collectivization as Russia experienced it. Why the insistence on the kolkhoz as the exclusive form of collective, when village structures suggested several alternatives? Is there any reason why the time-limits which the Politburo chose to set should be accorded the status of immutable historical laws? And what of the wholesale condemnation of any private sector?

Changes in the structures of rural life, necessary as they undoubtedly were, need not have followed a uniform pattern but could have been effected by the setting up of several different sectors, the nucleus of which already existed during the NEP period, and which could have been either sovkhozy, kolkhozy (of which there were several types) or other forms of cooperative or joint association with varying degrees of socialization and varying degrees of integration of private farms and private property, including (why not?) a private peasants' sector.

If we agree that the road which Soviet Russia had to travel left the regime so little room for maneuver that it had to choose between its own destruction and the path which it in fact took, then it would be logical to see in Stalin's policy the direct expression of historical necessity, and to accept all the methods which were used as having been justified, with reservations only in respect of certain errors or excesses; in this case, one might logically argue that what was achieved could only have been achieved by a dictatorship of the most despotic kind, and by one individual — Stalin. . . .

In our view, there are certain weaknesses in this argument. As the present study has shown, there were a series of factors which could have been combined to form an alternative. Again, it is an indisputable fact that Stalin had no foreknowledge of the great leap forward which he was to take, and of all its consequences, and that he had no such ambitions, least of all in 1926 and 1927 when he was concerned with the liquidation of the Left. Doubtless, he was already an "industrializer" . . . , but no more so than his associates at that time, for example Rykov (was the intensification of the industrialization drive in 1926 embarked upon against the wishes of someone like Rykov or Bukharin?). Generalizations about an industrialized Russia, which everybody accepted at the time, are of less account than practical measures. In practical terms, Stalin was a supporter both of industrialization and of NEP (he was simply more cautious in his statements than an unskillful politician like Bukharin) and therefore he moved with prudence and moderation in this domain. For these reasons the theory that the Left, which was enthusiastically pro-industrialization and antikulak, had to be liquidated as an essential prerequisite for future industrialization, and by a Stalin who at that time had still so little thought of what his future policy was to be, is a rather odd theory. It may be accepted, if one accepts another equally odd theory, which presents Stalin as a sort of *deus ex machina*, the only man in the party who was capable of transforming Russia into an industrial country. If this were so, then one would in fact have to accept the elimination of the Left as having been necessary, not because of its "sectarian appeal" to the workers (there is no reason to believe that the Left was incapable of demanding sacrifices from the proletariat) but because anything that might have stood in the way of "the only man who was able to act" and so forth had to be sacrificed for the good of the cause.

As for the elimination of the Right, in order to show that this too was indispensable one would have to prove, first of all, that all of their proposals were basically wrong whereas everything that Stalin proposed, and did, was basically right. This was far from being the case. The sequence of events after 1928, and the results of Stalinist policy, suggest that what the Stalinist administration particularly needed (we leave aside here the eventual need for its own abolition) was precisely the moderating influence which the Right could have exerted. What was called for, therefore, in the case of the Right was not elimination but at most restriction of its responsibilities within the framework of its rights as a minority. The methods which were used by the leaders of the right wing in their struggle against Stalin show that these same leaders were perfectly capable of remaining within the bounds of discipline, and of refraining from carrying on their controversy before the general public, or even the party as a whole, provided they had some assurance that their views would not be rejected out of hand, and that they would be given some opportunity of exerting a restraining influence.

And so events took their course. Historians, and other analysts, record these events and try to interpret them. But an essential precondition for analysis is the ability on the one hand to identify urgent social needs dictated by circumstances, and on the other to judge the practical solutions to these problems which were the result of subjective choice on the part of the leaders. By making this distinction, we are able to appraise the actions of historical personages, and to pass judgment on the quality of the leaders.

Viktor Danilov and N. V. Teptsov

Collectivization: The Results

Dr. Viktor Danilov of the Institute of the History of the USSR in Moscow is the leading Soviet authority on the history of the peasantry since the revolution. N. V. Teptsov is an economist on the staff of the Institute of Marxism-Leninism. Both were interviewed by A. Ilyin in a ground-breaking two-part series in *Pravda* in August and September 1988, reflecting the new openness under Gorbachev about the Soviet past. The interview is reprinted here in a slightly abridged form.

At a New Stage

Q: In our first talk we stopped at the events of August 1930, when the results of the first stage of collectivization were added up. They showed that the "race for tempo" had caused serious harm to the effort, but that at the same time a part of the peasantry (21.4 percent) had by that point tied its fate to the collective farms. I must say that your story has evoked contradictory responses from our readers. For example, some of them note that such negative consequences of the "revolution from above" as the separation of the peasants from the land, from the means of production and the results of their labor, were not emphasized with sufficient clarity.

From "Collectivization: How It Was," part 2, *Pravda*, September 16, 1988, p. 3. Translated by Robert V. Daniels.

Others, on the contrary, complain that the participants in the talk were one-sided in their approach to describing Stalin's role in the collectivization, basically accenting only the negative points. What can you say regarding this?

A: Differences in judgment are inescapable. A considerable amount of published material has recently appeared on collectivization, sharply distinguished from earlier, simplified evaluations and stereotypes. Naturally, not all of this can be accepted without qualification. Besides, in the current publications there are sometimes ambiguous evaluations of certain events, and of their causes and consequences. So, one must get used to this. We have scholarly inquiry and different approaches — this is not harmful but, it seems to us, beneficial, a good basis for creating a full and truthful picture. Besides, we cannot, we must not avoid the painful questions of our history or hush them up. A truthful analysis of the lessons of the past will enable us to solve today's problems, including the upgrading of the rural economy. Today, of course, the main thing is to return to the peasant the position of master of the land that he lost in years past, to stimulate the feeling of love for it and his certainty about tomorrow. And various forms of contract and leasing, and measures of social development of the village, have been invoked to assure success in resolving these tasks, since the renewal of the village is not a simple matter.

As regards Stalin's role, it is best to judge it not by his words — he knew how to represent himself as the unparalleled champion of the good of the people — but by his actual deeds.

Q: Obviously not everyone puts forth completely the difference of principle between the course chosen by the party and Stalinist practice. It was convincingly exposed in the report [by Gorbachev] celebrating the seventieth anniversary of the Great October. It took note of the significance of collectivization in strengthening the position of socialism in the village, for radical change in the whole way of life of the basic mass of the population on socialist foundations; it offered a profound analysis of the causes and consequences of the deformations allowed in those years, and of the abandonment of the Leninist principles of an attentive attitude toward the interests of the toiling peasantry.

A: Socialist reform of agriculture on the basis of radical technical reconstruction and upgrading of the general culture of the village, which would be equivalent to the genuine cultural revolution as Lenin's cooperative plan envisaged it, was historically inevitable. At the end of the twenties and the beginning of the thirties the objective course of socioeconomic development placed these questions on the agenda. Working small patches of land with primitive tools condemned the peasants to heavy manual work, assuring at most the maintenance of their existence and the endless reproduction of all those backward conditions of life and labor. The low level of agricultural production held back the general economic development of the country, and posed serious obstacles to the industrialization that was just getting under way and to the building of socialism as a whole. The country's situation in the world imperatively dictated acceleration of the development of all branches of the economy, especially industry. At the same time this need did not require the implementation of "solid collectivization" in two or three years and by whatever means. No objective conditions could justify the violence against the peasantry that was committed in the Stalinist implementation of collectivization and dekulakization.

Q: So, let's return to August 1930. What conclusions were drawn from the results of the first stage? Wasn't it really beneficial to evaluate the situation, to take account of objective circumstances and real possibilities, and couldn't reform of the village go onward on a healthy basis and achieve more substantial results?

A: Of course. Corrections were made, at least at first. Economic levers were applied more actively. In solving the tasks of collectivization, as before, the basic forces of the party, state, and social organizations were brought together. The scale of technological reconstruction in agriculture expanded, mainly through the creation of state machine-tractor stations (MTS). In the year 1931, 1,040 MTS were created. The level of mechanization of agricultural work notably rose. The process of socializing the peasants' means of production was regularized, although "misunderstandings" with peasant women about their cows continued, as Stalin later admitted. Finally on March 26, 1932, a decision of the CC [Central Committee] came out which obliged local organizations not only to cease compulsory socialization of cattle but to aid collective farmers by providing them with cattle they could use.

In 1930 the state extended great help to the collective farms and offered them substantial tax advantages. In addition, the rates of the agricultural tax were increased for individual peasants, and a one-time tax was imposed on them alone. The quantity of state collections also rose, and they acquired an obligatory character.

The joint plenum of the Central Committee and Central Control Commission of the Communist Party held in December 1930 declared that in the area of agriculture, "In the first two years of the Five-Year Plan we have already managed to achieve double the whole five-year program," and even "basically" to resolve the grain problem (?!) as a result of "the great successes achieved in the area of collective farm and state farm construction, and the liquidation of the kulaks as a class that has been carried out undeviatingly on the basis of solid collectivization." There was no reminder here of the lessons of the previous winter. In the resolution "On the Economic Plan for 1931," control figures were set forth for the collectivization of all regions of the country. For the North Caucasus, the Lower and Middle Volga, and the steppe region of the Ukraine the task was set of bringing together "not less than 80 per cent of peasant households" in collective farms. For the Central Black-Earth region, Siberia, the Urals, the forest-steppe region of the Ukraine and the grain-producing districts of Kazakhstan, the order was "to assure 50 per cent collectivization of peasant households"; "for the [net] consuming regions of grain growing," 20 to 25 per cent; and for the Union as a whole, "not less than half of all peasant households." Further, as was pointed out in Stalin's telegram to the secretary of the Eastern Siberia provincial committee, F. G. Leonov (March 1931), local organizations were "not only not forbidden, but on the contrary, encouraged to overfulfill their assignment." And generally it really was fulfilled and even overfulfilled: for the country as a whole by June 1931, 52.7 percent of peasant households were already included in the collective farms.

The year 1932 was declared to be the "year of completing solid collectivization." At the same time the criterion for completion of collectivization "in principle" was somewhat relaxed: the inclusion of 68 to 70 percent of peasant holdings in the collective farms. By autumn 62.4 percent of peasant holdings were enrolled in the collective farms. The large-scale collective farm thus became one of the foundations of our economy and of the whole social structure.

Relying on the Poor

Q: Collectivization affected the interests and fate of the whole peasantry. But naturally, the different social strata in the village perceived the transition to collective forms of economy in different ways. What did it signify for the mass of the poor peasants and for the middle peasants, a significant portion of whom had entered the collective farms by the autumn of 1932?

A: Obviously we must first define the scale of social differentiation in the village before collectivization. According to the figures of the commission of the USSR Council of People's Commissars on the burden of tax assessments (sometimes called the Rykov Commission), in 1927 among peasant holdings there were 3.9 percent Kulaks, 62.7 middle peasants, 22.1 poor peasants, and 11.3 percent proletarians. The basic mass, as we see, consisted of middle peasants; a third were poor peasants and hired hands. For the latter it was usual to lack a horse, and therefore even if they had land they could not work it independently, but found themselves in the most intimate dependence on the well-to-do strata of the village, especially on the kulaks. Their own experience of "sitting as free owners on free land" showed them that on their own they had no real prospect of escaping from poverty and debt-bondage. This part of the village saw the way out for itself in joining together. So it became the social force that actively supported both solid collectivization and the liquidation of the kulaks.

More complicated and contradictory was the attitude of the middle peasantry. Their circumstances of life and labor were also extremely difficult. A majority of the middle peasants had begun to understand the limited possibilities of small-scale farming. But the transition to collective forms of work meant for them a radical break from their accustomed way of life. Therefore their doubts and vacillations were inevitable. Before deciding on this step, they wanted to see practical, visible proof of the advantages of the collective farms, and to have a chance to construct, by themselves and without compulsion, new forms of life corresponding to their own interests. For this the circumstances of the middle peasant made the choice a voluntary one.

V. I. Lenin taught attentiveness to the interests of the toiling peasantry. In the resolution he wrote in 1919 for the Eighth Party Congress he formulated his most important conclusion: "Only those associations are worthwhile that are implemented by the peasants themselves on their free initiative, and whose benefits are verified by them in practice."

It was also necessary to take into account the fact that during the years after the revolution the peasantry as a class changed in a radical way. The peasant toiler now regarded the Soviet power as his own, and became a real ally of the working class. Reliance on the poor, and consistent implementation of Lenin's line about the alliance with the middle peasantry against the kulak, would have allowed us to avoid the excesses that took place in the late twenties and early thirties. . . .

On December 27, 1929, in a speech to a conference of Marxist agronomists, Stalin announced the transition to a policy of liquidating the kulaks as a class. He announced it as though it were already an accomplished fact. On January 11, 1930, *Pravda* published an editorial, "The Liquidation of the Kulaks as a Class Is on the Agenda." It sounded the call to "declare war to the death on the kulak, and sweep him off the face of the earth for good."

Preparation of the concrete measures and means for accomplishing this policy was entrusted on January 15, 1930, to a special Politburo commission under the chairmanship of V. M. Molotov. On January 30 the Politburo confirmed the decision of the Central Committee of the party, "On measures for the liquidation of kulak holdings in the districts of solid collectivization." It prescribed carrying out confiscation of the kulaks' means of production, cattle, farm and living structures, enterprises for processing agricultural products, and grain supplies. Farm property and structures were turned over to the joint funds of the collective farms as a contribution on behalf of the poor peasants and laborers, while part of the resources went to pay off the debts of kulak farms to the state and the cooperatives.

The dekulakized peasants were divided into three categories. In the first was the "active counterrevolutionary group" —

participants in anti-Soviet and anti-collective-farm manifestations. (They themselves were subject to arrest, while their families were evacuated to remote regions of the country.) In the second category were the "big kulaks and former semi-estate-owners who had actively come out against collectivization." (They were evacuated, together with their families, to remote regions.) Finally, in the third category was the "remaining portions of the kulaks." (They were subject to resettlement in special settlements within the borders of the districts of their previous residence.)

The decision specified that the number of dekulakized peasants, district by district, should not exceed 3 to 5 percent of all peasant households. Still, this was much more than the number of kulak households remaining in the winter of 1930. For the districts of solid collectivization (the North Caucasus, the Lower and Middle Volga, the Central Black-Earth region, the Urals, Siberia, the Ukraine, Belorussia, and Kazakhstan) the decision set figures of "limited contingents" subject to deportation to remote regions of the country: 60,000 households (families) in the first category and 150,000 in the second. On February 25 "limited contingents" were set for dekulakized peasants in the Leningrad, Western, Moscow, and Ivanovo-Industrial regions and in the Nizhny Novgorod Province: 17,000 in the first category, 15,000 in the second.

The rigid allotment of assignments to the districts from above, the prescribed order of implementing large-scale forcible action, the whole tone of the decision, as of the instructions from the central governmental organs and the concrete orders locally, in essence cancelled out warnings they contained against "exaggerations" and "isolation from the masses."

"With the Utmost Urgency" . . .

Extraordinary measures from this time on were turned into a system. They worked like the methods of the time of the Civil War and War Communism, not only against the kulaks, but against the middle peasants.

This found expression in particular in the practice of dekulakization. Thus, in the winter of 1930 a shifting of dekulakized peasants from the third category to the second was widely resorted to. The urge spread everywhere to "overfulfill" the "norms," "control figures," "assignments" sent down from above. Furthermore, we need to keep in mind that beginning in the spring of 1930 the question was essentially the liquidation of former kulak farms, since by an order of the USSR Central Executive Committee and the Council of People's Commissars on February 1, they had already been deprived of the opportunity to lease land and exploit outside labor.

An explosion of peasant indignation compelled the Stalinist leadership to beat a retreat and adopt measures to correct the crudest acts of arbitrariness and violence. Part of the peasants who had been dekulakized or designated for dekulakization were rehabilitated. On the results of the correction of "excesses" in this period there is still only scattered data. In the Kursk Province, for example, of 8,949 dekulakized farms 4,453 were restored, in the Lgovsk Province, 2,390 out of 4,487, i.e., more than half.

Between February and October 1931, there was a new, broader wave of liquidating kulak farms. Its general guidance was handled by a special commission headed by A. A. Andreev. Dekulakization went forward from this time on, even after this commission terminated its existence in March 1932. More and more it took on the character of repression for underfulfillment of grain collection assignments, for misappropriation of collective farm products, for refusal to work.

Not until May 8, 1933, was an instruction distributed to party and governmental organizations finally ordering them to curtail the scale of repressions in the village. This document, signed by Stalin and Molotov, confirmed that in the provinces "Demands still continue to come up about mass deportation from the village and the application of sharp forms of repression. The Central Committee and the Council of People's Commissars have applications for the immediate deportation of approximately 100,000 families from the provinces and regions." The instruction explained that, although "The class struggle in the village will inevitably become more severe" from this time on, nevertheless the old methods "have outlived themselves": "As a result of our successes in the village the

Collective-farm peasants working with a new threshing machine. (Brown Brothers)

time has come when we are not compelled to use mass repressions, which have, as is well known, been directed not only at the kulaks but at individual peasants and part of the collective farmers."

In this connection the decision was made "to cease immediately any mass deportations of peasants." However, in practice it was only a question of restricting the scale of deportations — they were supposed to be carried out "only on an individual and particular basis and affecting only those households whose heads carry on active struggle against the collective farms and organize refusals to plant and deliver produce." The same instruction "allowed" the deportation of 12,000 households, and authorized numbers for each republic and district.

Q: How many families in all were dekulakized? In the press various counts are cited, for instance, a figure "not less than three million" is mentioned, i.e., 11 to 12 percent of all peasant households.

A: It is still hard to specify the number of dekulakized households and of people who suffered under this. Unfortunately, certain authors try to invoke the largest figures possible, without bothering about their reliability and plausibility. They want to shock the reader by saying that 13 or 15 million people perished, as though the figure of 4 or 5 million "in all" were insufficient, in their opinion, for the unreserved condemnation of Stalinist violence against the peasantry.

There are precise data only on the number of families deported to remote regions of the country (i.e., on those who were assigned to the first and second "categories" by the order of January 30, 1930). In 1930, 115,231 families were deported, and in 1931, 265,795. Thus, in two years 381,000 families were sent off to the North, to the Urals, to Siberia and Kazakhstan. Part of the kulak families (200,000 to 250,000) managed to "self-dekulakize," that is, to sell or throw away their belongings and flee to cities or construction sites. From 1932 on campaigns of deportation were no longer conducted. However, the overall number of those deported from the village in this period amounted to not less than 100,000. Approximately 400,000 to 450,000 families who were supposed to be dispersed in individual settlements within the borders of their provinces and regions of previous residence (the third "category"), after the confiscation of their belongings and various hardships, in the main also left the village for construction sites and cities. In sum, there were about one million to 1,100,000 farms that were liquidated in the course of dekulakization.

The Famine of 1932–1933

Q: Yet the most tragic page was the famine that befell the village in 1932–1933. For a long time it was forbidden even to mention it. Besides, the slogan put forth by Stalin, "to make all collective farmers prosperous," was being propagandized to the utmost just at this time.

A: Yes, the famine in the grain-producing districts of the country that broke out in those years was one of the suppressed subjects, and not only in the period of the cult of personality. True, from the works of Mikhail Alekseev and Ivan Stadniuk[1] the Soviet reader of the early sixties learned about villages dying of hunger in the Volga region and in the Ukraine. However, only under the conditions of glasnost did historians have a chance to turn to the study of this tragedy. The very first results of concrete historical analysis have shown that the famine that carried off so many lives was the most terrible crime of Stalin and his entourage. . . .

Let's turn to the facts and figures. Taken together the harvests of 1931 and 1932 were only a little below the average over many years, and in and of themselves did not threaten famine. The trouble came because grain was taken away both from the collective farms and from individual farms by compulsion and in essence "to the last kernel," for the sake of fulfilling the unrealistic goals of industrial development, set arbitrarily by the Stalinist leadership in 1930 contrary to the Five-Year Plan. We may note that they did not succeed in realizing these unlimited goals, as has already been discussed in recent press publications.

For the purchase of industrial equipment foreign exchange was needed. It was possible to get it only in exchange for grain. Meanwhile the crisis in the world economy was intensifying, and the prices of grain had fallen sharply. However, the Stalinist leadership did not think of reconsidering the aim of an industrial "leap" that was beyond the country's strength. The export of grain abroad continued to grow. In 1930, 835 million centners[2] of grain were collected, which permitted the export of 48.4 million centners. In 1931 collections were much lower — 695 million centners of grain — but more grain — 51.8 million centners — was exported to the external market. Many collective farmers had all their grain taken away, including the seed reserve. In Siberia, the Volga region, Kazakhstan, the North Caucasus, and the Ukraine serious provisioning difficulties arose, and in some places famine began. Both

---

[1] Novelists who wrote during the "thaw" under Khrushchev. — Ed.

[2] One centner = 220 lbs. or approximately 4 bushels. — Ed.

collective farmers and individual peasants, sometimes in whole villages, moved out and went to the cities and construction sites. A series of collective farms collapsed. Nevertheless measures were taken that year to normalize conditions in the village (provisioning and seed loans, etc.), which warded off mass famine.

In 1932 the gross grain harvest was 699 million centners, but some of it was left standing. This showed, of course, objective difficulties. However, the main thing was something else. After the bitter experience of 1931 the collective farmers were compelled to search for any earnings on the side and avoided collective work. They remembered well how the grain they had grown that year went onto the "conveyor" — from the field to the threshing machine and then immediately to the collection point, skipping the collective barns.

By the summer of 1932, after a winter of semifamine, the village of the grain-producing zones of Russia and the Ukraine had become physically weakened. On still unripened fields appeared "barbers" — most often women desperate from the sight of their starving children. They cut off spikes of grain with scissors in order to make porridge for their families. (In the collective fields this was usually done surreptitiously, furtively, at night.) When reaping began — and the first threshings were again sent off in their entirety to the collection points — "pilferers" appeared. They carried grain off from the threshing areas in their pockets or in their bosoms.

Now on August 7, 1932, a law was adopted on guarding socialist property, written by Stalin in his own hand. It provided "as a measure of judicial repression for the misappropriation (theft) of collective farm and cooperative property, the highest measure of social defense — shooting, with confiscation of all property, to be commuted under mitigating circumstances to deprivation of freedom for a term of not less than ten years with confiscation of all property." Amnesty in matters of this kind was forbidden. The real meaning of this law — a law introducing lawlessness — was quite clear to contemporaries. "The law of five spikes of grain," they called it in the village. It was even condemned in party circles.

By the beginning of 1933, after less than five months, 54,656 individuals were sentenced under this law. Of them, 2,110 received the supreme penalty. The sentences were carried out in approximately 1,000 cases. The courts declared that it was "out of their hands."

Q: But the terrible famine was already knocking on the peasants' doors. Could you comment on how events unfolded?

A: In 1932, in the North Caucasus, the Lower and Middle Volga, and the Ukraine, the collective farms could not fulfill their assignments for the delivery of grain. When it was reported to Stalin that the leaders of the Orekhovsky district in the Dnepropetrovsk province permitted the collective farms to hold back their seed reserves and to increase their emergency reserves, he fell into a frenzied rage. On December 7, 1932, a circular bearing his signature was sent out to all party organs, in which Stalin declared that these leaders were "deceivers of the party, swindlers, who were skillfully carrying out a kulak policy under the banner of their 'agreement' with the general line of the party." He demanded that they should be "immediately arrested and rewarded according to their deserts, i.e., given 5 to 10 years each of prison confinement."

Repression became the means of carrying out the grain collections. Many collective farms, the initial ones, and not a few district party organizations were declared to be kulak-dominated; secretaries of district committees, chairmen of district executive committees and collective farms, directors of MTS were declared to be saboteurs and degenerates. They were arrested and shot, and reports of this were published in the press. As a result of the purge in the North Caucasus Province, 26,000 persons were expelled from the party, 45 percent of the rural Communists. In the Kuban region the populations of whole villages were deported to northern regions of the country as punishment for nonfulfillment of the grain collection plan.

M. A. Sholokhov [the novelist] wrote to Stalin on April 16, 1933, about the scandalous methods of grain collection activity in Veshensk and other districts. In his letter of reply Stalin accused the collective farmers of carrying out "sabotage" and even "a war of starvation" against the workers and the Red Army. About the disastrous situation in the village itself — not a word.

The village was being flogged to death by a wave of administrative arbitrariness and violence. Later on in their directive of May 8, 1933 . . . , Stalin and Molotov admitted, "Collective farm chairmen and members of the administration of collective farms are being arrested. Chairmen of village soviets and secretaries of party cells are being arrested. District and province officials are being arrested. Anyone who feels like it is making arrests, people who frankly have no right to make arrests. And it is not surprising that in such an outburst of making arrests, the organs of the OGPU, and especially the militia, are losing their sense of measure and often make arrests without any basis, acting on the rule, 'arrest first, and investigate afterwards.' " The directive forbade "arrests made by persons who are not so empowered by law," and also "confinement under guard before trial for crimes of minor importance." However, the "outburst of making arrests," condemned too late, was itself the consequence of the arbitrariness committed by the Stalinist leadership after the villages had been bled white by grain collections during the harvest of 1932.

During the winter of 1932–33 mass famine took hold in the villages of the grain-producing regions of the country — in the Ukraine, the North Caucasus, the Lower and Middle Volga, the Southern Urals, and Kazakhstan. There were cases of the dying off of whole settlements.

It is extremely difficult to establish the number of those who perished as a result of the famine. There is still no scholarly research of Soviet historical demographers, for reasons that we have already spoken about. Foreign Sovietologists ascribe to the solid collectivization of agriculture the annihilation of 13 million peasants, including over 7 million who died in the famine. However, these figures have evoked criticism even in the Anglo-American scholarly literature. It has been quite convincingly shown that some calculations which have been put forth have been based on the use of "shady sources," on "altogether unjustified interpretations," and above all, on the effort to arouse indignation against the Soviet Union, against socialism in general. According to the more objective evaluation of the statistical data in the work of the historians Robert Davies and Stephen Wheatcroft and the demographers Barbara Anderson and Brian Silver, the number of victims of the

famine amounted to 3 to 4 million individuals. It is still up to
Soviet social scientists to carry out extensive research work, in order
to speak their own piece.

To Overcome Alienation . . .

By 1937 collectivization was complete. The total number of collective farms in the country was 243,700, embracing 93 percent of
peasant households.

In speaking of the history of collectivization and its lessons, we
must not forget that we were the first to take this path, and don't
leave the objective difficulties of the quest out of the calculation.
We must not fail to render their due to the collective farm peasantry who did so much for the country to strengthen its economy
and defensive might, which was manifested especially in the years
of the war.

Both our experience, and later on experience abroad, showed
that the large-scale collective farm opens wide possibilities for economic and social progress. But these possibilities are realized to the
full extent only when the labor collective really is its own master,
independent and able to take initiative, when relationships are built
on democratic principles. This is exactly what we are striving for
today.

For a long time these principles were violated. The autonomy
of the collective farms was severely limited from the very beginning, which put the brakes on their initiative and economic
growth. A continuous mobilization of human and material resources left the collective farm village for various needs of the state.
In January 1933, after the failure of the grain collections, obligatory
deliveries of collective farm produce to the state were introduced,
which had the character and force of a tax. Prices for grain and
most other agricultural products were fixed at one-tenth to one-
twelfth of the market prices.

The most important means of production — in practice, all
machinery — and also skilled workers, were concentrated in the
system of state MTS, working the collective farm fields for payment
in kind, the rate of which was set from above.

This also facilitated the alienation of the producer both from the means of production and from the results of his labor. Simultaneously a system of directive planning and bureaucratic command by the apparatus was set up over the collective farms. In addition, the collective farmers did not have passports, which deprived them of the possibility of freely relocating, juridically tied them to the collective farm, and gave their work a forced-labor character. A depeasantification of the village took place.

The bureaucratic command system of running the collective farms, despite the changes accomplished in the late fifties and early sixties, has survived right down to our own day. It became in fact a brake on the development of collective farm production and on the realization of its potential. We must also look to it to explain the causes of the lag of agriculture behind the needs of the country, and also of the flight of peasants from the land and the desolation of the villages.

A Soviet propaganda poster before the Stalin Revolution (1921): "We have beaten the enemy by force of arms, we will earn our bread by labor, everything for our work, comrades!" (© Topham/The Image Works)

PART

III The Counterrevolution from Above

Hélène Carrère d'Encausse

The Return of Inequality

Hélène Carrère d'Encausse is a professor of political science at the University of Paris and a prolific writer on Soviet political and social history. In *Confiscated Power* she analyzed the development and operation of the totalitarian system with its privileged hierarchy and mass manipulation. The selection here describes the revival of special privilege during the Stalin Revolution.

From *Confiscated Power: How Soviet Russia Really Works* by Hélène Carrère d'Encausse, pp. 27–32, 34–37. Copyright © 1982 by Hélène Carrère d'Encausse. Reprinted by permission of Harper & Row, Publisher, Inc.

The industrial revolution of 1929 and collectivization suddenly gave social mobility unprecedented dimensions: geographic mobility, whereby peasants were moved to factories or construction sites and workers displaced as large projects required, and mobility of status, since peasants were excluded from development and considered enemies of progress, forced to participate against their will. Positions of responsibility were closed off to these permanent suspects. Conversely, the workers, leaders of industrial development, became as a result of the war the government declared against the peasantry in 1929, the only laboring class on which Soviet power could rely. Industrialization, collectivization, and the development of the bureaucracy required increasing supervision for all the political, repressive, and technical tasks. The possibilities of acceding to positions of responsibility had never been so great since 1917. But development has its inherent demands, chief among them being competence. From the early thirties on, competence became a central preoccupation of the Soviet government, and in order to stimulate it the government authorized a partial renunciation of the egalitarian ideal that had been maintained until then, at least officially. Stalin spoke clearly on this point as early as 1931, emphasizing that, when a country needs technicians, their usefulness must be taken into account in determining their wages, and he demanded that they be treated differently from common laborers. The consequence of this approach was a growing differentiation of wages which Stalin ratified. There was differentiation of wages between categories and within each category. The position of three groups — political personnel, productive workers, and creative intelligensia — throws light on this evolution.

Little is generally known about the first group, for during Stalin's rule information about its material situation became rare, in contrast to what had been the norm in the twenties. But by juxtaposing various pieces of data, one can estimate that, around 1934, when the average worker's wage was 150 rubles a month, ordinary district or regional officials earned between 250 and 500 rubles a month, while the highest-paid members of this group earned approximately 800 rubles.

Although the earnings gap between average workers and political officials tended to widen, it was nevertheless not substantial and did not really contradict the practice of the preceding years. We can get a better sense of the Stalinist revolution by considering earnings policy in industry. Here the salary scale was constantly changing. While the average worker earned 150 rubles and the lowest-paid laborer earned 63, those at the top of the scale had wages above 1,000 rubles. Still more significant, bonuses granted to particular factories — to reward their efficiency, high levels of output, or the savings they were able to accomplish — were distributed within each factory according to hierarchical position. The highest paid received the largest bonuses, while the lowest wages were barely increased. During the thirties there thus emerged a rigid hierarchy of labor which was consolidated by constantly growing material differences.

In certain areas of activity, the incomes of individuals considered particularly useful to society were still more striking. This was the case in the army; lower-ranked officers were already better paid than workers (approximately twice the average wage), and higher-ranked officers earned nearly 2,000 rubles a month. This was also true for intellectuals who joined the unions created in the early thirties (the Writers' Union, the first of these, was created in 1932) and whose official status as intellectuals guaranteed them an income that could exceed 2,000 rubles a month; but here too there were many inequalities.

A comparison of the incomes of various social categories in the mid-thirties leads to two immediate conclusions. The working class, theoretical holder of power in the U.S.S.R., was the great victim of the policy of income differentiation which was then rapidly developing. At the time, money and material incentives were no longer objects of contempt; quite the contrary, they rewarded competence and usefulness. And workers' wages suggested that their usefulness was evaluated at an infinitely lower price than that of soldiers or industrial managers. A second conclusion that can be drawn is that political cadres remained substantially more modest in their material demands than their equivalents in industry or than the intellectuals. But the truth lies elsewhere. The official documents on incomes policy reveal to those who consult them only one aspect, known monetary income. But the picture is complicated by what these documents leave out, the material or psychological advantages given to certain social categories. These advantages particularly affected the position of those who moved in the circles of power. Although Stalin was in fact inclined to sanction officially the inequalities linked to competence and knowledge in the economic sphere, he was not prepared to do the same for the distance that separated the working class from those who held political power in its place. In the case of the economy, he could invoke the necessities of development to justify his inegalitarian choices. But could he admit that the working class, disfavored by its lack of capacity and education, had been dispossessed of its natural power as well by a ruling group that derived the right to considerable material benefits from its function? To admit that political cadres had exorbitant economic rights could be to admit that nothing remained of the old utopia of justice and equality. This explains the government's remarkable discretion whenever the income of the "political strata" at all levels was at issue. This also explains why the hidden privileges of these strata multiplied and made their nominal wages completely meaningless.

In the thirties, problems of daily survival were crucial. The continuous fall in agricultural production from 1928 to 1934 and the destruction by the peasants, driven to despair by collectivization, of the Soviet stock of cattle had as a consequence a permanent shortage of food products, with particularly tragic episodes like the year of famine 1932–33. But even aside from those exceptional moments when it became absolute famine, the shortage of food was constant, not to mention the chronic shortage of shoes, clothes, apartments, and so on. In spite of strict state price controls, especially on food products, the inhabitants of the U.S.S.R. were daily confronted with price rises and severe shortages.

The government, incapable of providing for the most elementary needs of the whole society, chose on the one hand to carry on a general policy of rationing and, on the other, to reserve access to available goods for certain social categories. Everything in this system was selective. Rationing called upon criteria of utility or timeliness: In the early thirties, foreign specialists had the right to 48 kilos of bread a month, workers to only 24, and office workers and children to 12. For meat, the differences were even greater, the rations ranging from 14 kilos to 4.4 and 2.2. These official rations varied not only in quantity but in reality. In some stores for common mortals, shortages made it impossible to honor customers' coupons. On the other hand, shops reserved for particular categories of Soviet citizens guaranteed their access to indispensable goods. The ordinary, badly paid citizen did not have access to any special shops, which proliferated to supply political cadres, the intelligentsia, the army, and the police. Nadezhda Mandelstam[1] writes in

---

[1] Widow of the purged poet Osip Mandelstam and author of a memoir of the Stalin era, *Hope Against Hope* (New York: Atheneum, 1970). — Ed.

this connection, "In this country, the privileged have always been rewarded not by envelopes containing their wages but by 'extras' — currency placed in sealed envelopes — by special rations, by access to *closed* stores." These stores, established as we have seen during the first years of the regime, multiplied simultaneously with the growth of the bureaucracy. In the thirties they diversified. Sometimes they were stores whose existence was known only to those who could use them, stores hidden from all other eyes — these were known as closed distribution centers (*zakrytye razpredeliteli*) — sometimes there were "special counters" inside stores open to everyone where the privileged could place their orders. They were also served first and thus benefited from the dual advantage of never having to worry about supplies running out and being able to avoid annoying lines, the most typical and permanent characteristic of social life in the U.S.S.R. since 1917. Finally, in 1930, stores were established in which goods were paid for in foreign currency. These stores were supposed to be restricted to foreigners, but they were also open to those whose functions enabled them to travel or placed them in contact with foreigners. It was especially the upper levels of the political system who had access to this last kind of store.

In addition to the possible use of parallel distribution systems, there was at the time another decisive differentiating element, also mentioned by Nadezhda Mandelstam: the "sealed envelopes" whose contents improved the income of their recipient and enabled them to shop in the luxury stores outside the rationing system, stores with exorbitant prices like the Gastronomes, with their piles of goods unobtainable elsewhere. The use of these envelopes, called *pakety* in Russian, grew substantially under Stalin. It appeared in the early twenties as a means of improving, in special circumstances, the income of the leaders, which was still low. But it rapidly spread and became a regular practice, allowing the doubling or tripling of the incomes of principal leaders of the state and the Party without changing their official salaries and without including these extras in the tax system, which, in principle, was supposed to help reduce disparities in income.

Thus the political elite that was established after the revolution enjoyed many privileges, through which it escaped from poverty and attained genuine comfort while hiding behind apparent austerity. But the growing gap between the living conditions of the average Soviet citizen and the conditions of those in power soon made necessary physical segregation in order to conceal the privilege. More and more in the course of the thirties, each category of privileged people was enclosed in its own living quarters, where it enjoyed precise rights connected with its particular status. . . .

From the thirties on, income and social status largely determined the possibilities of later promotion. Indeed, access to education, for which the children of the working classes had priority after 1917, gradually returned to being a social privilege. No doubt the right of everyone in the U.S.S.R. to an education was recognized, and the accelerated development in which Stalin involved the country in 1929 had as a corollary an increased effort to attract masses of adolescents toward higher technical education. During the first five-year plan, the number of students in the U.S.S.R. quintupled, and children of workers entered the universities in large numbers (there were 47 percent in Russian universities in 1932, compared to 30 percent in the late twenties). But in a very few years, university recruitment changed because the rules governing it changed. On June 23, 1936, new principles were adopted for admission. They specified that there was equality of access to the university for all, without consideration of social origin. The primary criterion became the school record and success on the university entrance examination. Children who had been able to follow a ten-year course of study and to work in favorable material conditions were from then on infinitely better prepared for the university than workers' children, who, after a brief course of study, received special preparation in courses designed for workers (Rabfak) and crammed in overpopulated rooms of noisy communal apartments.

If we consider that, beginning on October 2, 1940, the last three years of secondary education involved tuition expenses, and that the cost of a year's study in an institution of higher learning was equivalent to four to six weeks' pay for an average worker, it is easy to understand how promotion through education soon became again a narrow path reserved for those who had the material means. In 1921 the head of the department of professional education in the Commissariat of Education, Preobrazhenski,[2] had said, "At this moment, there is a veritable class war at the gates of institutions of higher learning between the worker-peasant majority of the country that wants to educate specialists

---

[2] The same Eugeny Preobrazhensky who had been a party secretary and was later prominent in the economic controversies, momentarily demoted to this education post. —Ed.

from its ranks, for its own sake, and the ruling classes and the strata connected to them. The proletarian state openly sides with the people." Barely ten years later, Stalin denounced this attitude, which he called "petty-bourgeois egalitarian," and supported a policy that closed higher education to the people on whom Preobrazhenski intended to base the future elites of the country.

Stalin implicitly admitted, by various decisions, that the privileges of political leaders and professional elites included the possibility of perpetuating their extraordinary status. His policies during this period seem at first sight very contradictory. On the one hand, he involved his country in an economic and social revolution of unprecedented magnitude that generated an equally unprecedented social mobility. Because the U.S.S.R. then needed innumerable technical and administrative managers, all active elements of society seemed to be able to benefit from this mobility of structures, jobs, and needs. But at the same time various measures ratified privileges and outlined the contours of a society that already included social differentiation and was quickly becoming stratified. What was new under Stalin was first of all that he accepted and ratified the existence of differences in status. No doubt certain privileges remained concealed, especially those connected with political functions. But in a general sense, Stalinist policies emphasized and gave official status to the privileges of particular categories.

This official status came from the change that was then taking place in the system of values promulgated by the Soviet state. The post-revolutionary years had been dominated by egalitarianism, promotion of the lowly and the working class, and the depersonalization of history, reduced to the history of the popular masses in movement. In the course of the thirties, other values insidiously emerged, values linked to the demands of development. The competence and knowledge that Stalin constantly praised were not characteristic of the lower classes. They belonged to an elite, to those who had studied, who occupied a special place on the ladder of occupations, who did not blend into the mass. Reading what was published in the U.S.S.R. in the years before the Second World War is enough to provide an appreciation of the change that was taking place. Newspapers, literature, painting (all the arts were mobilized to express Stalin's plans through socialist realism) reflected the social and moral hierarchy of these years of the turning point. Out of the mass of the lowly emerged those whom society saluted as its most useful representatives: engineers, managers, experts, leaders. The crowd remained anonymous, but from this anonymous mass emerged individualized heroes. The manager of the factory had a name, a face, a history, abilities. This individualization of talents and exploits extended to the past, and the great figures of history who were restored to their places in books and schools justified by their past services the present privileges enjoyed by their successors.

After having exalted the army of the lowly for ten years, Soviet ideology hierarchized society according to utilitarian criteria. Privileges and high wages were now accepted as rewards for competence and social usefulness. In this way, the judgment of inequality changed. Just as, immediately after the revolution, it was appropriate to conceal privileges in favor of an austerity that placed all Soviet citizens at the level of the worker and made him their model, so after 1930 material success was no longer concealed and everyone dreamed of realizing the new social model, the privileged manager. Egalitarianism had thus given way to a morality of inequality and material success.

This new social model was strengthened by the introduction of titles and rewards that created a new "socialist" hierarchy, but they were oddly reminiscent of the Empire's old "table of ranks." The first title created, Hero of Labor (July 27, 1927), provided substantial material benefits for its recipients: retirement pay, housing, exemption from taxes. But since the requirements for this award were stringent and those who obtained it were generally already privileged, Stalin added the following year the Red Banner of Labor, which was less prestigious, provided fewer concrete benefits, and was frequently awarded to entire factories. After 1930, the system was constantly diversified, ranging from Hero of the Soviet Union and Hero of Socialist Labor to the Order of Lenin and the Red Banner. The army established its own particular order, the Red Star. The benefits tied to these various orders were diversified and hierarchized, but all of them in these difficult years brought their recipients prestige, a certain sum of money, and particular rights. These rights ranged from ease of access to the university to more modest benefits, like more or less free urban or even railroad transportation. Some of the titles — the most prestigious ones, Hero of the Soviet Union and Hero of Socialist Labor, which also provided the greatest benefits — were always reserved for a small number of people. Finally, the war led the government to distribute decorations widely, to multiply titles (especially military titles), ranks (on the model of military hierarchy), and uniforms and insignia.

The Soviet system thus moved steadily away from the directives of Lenin, who had abolished this type of differentiation and condemned the use of traditional titles (like "minister" or "government"). But even before war broke out, Soviet society was strictly hierarchical, divided into categories with clearly defined prestige and rights, even though privileges were less and less public as one approached more closely to the top. What is remarkable in this period was the willingness to ratify officially, to legitimate, these differences.

Sheila Fitzpatrick

Revolution and Counterrevolution in the Schools

Sheila Fitzpatrick, presently a professor of history at the University of Chicago, is an authority on Soviet social history and educational policy in the 1930s. In her first major work she addressed the zigzags in Soviet education before and during the Stalin Revolution and the role of education in the training of the New Class. In the portion excerpted here she describes the contrast between the "Cultural Revolution" of 1929–1931 and the return to the traditional forms of teaching that followed.

The new Commissar of Education for the RSFSR, Andrei Sergeevich Bubnov, was appointed on 12 September 1929. In terms of status

From Sheila Fitzpatrick, *Education and Social Mobility in the Soviet Union, 1921–1934*, © 1979, excerpts from pp. 136–152, 209–227. Reprinted with the permission of Cambridge University Press.

within the party, Bubnov was a relatively high-level appointee for Narkompros [People's commissariat of Education]. He was a member of both the Party Central Committee and the Orgburo [Organizational Bureau], and had previously served as head of the Central Committee agitprop [agitation and propaganda] department and, for the past five years, the political administration (PUR) of the Red Army. He was regarded — in contrast to Lunacharsky [his predecessor] — as a stern, no-nonsense administrator, and he was expected to introduce order and discipline into the commissariat.

This, however, was not Bubnov's only task in Narkompros. The old Narkompros leadership had been accused of "rightist" and "bureaucratic" tendencies, demonstrated above all by its lack of response to the new slogans of class warfare and Cultural Revolution. Bubnov had to show himself to be a true militant revolutionary on the cultural front, and this meant allying himself with the various radical groups which had been criticizing Lunacharsky's "bureaucratic conservatism" over the past two years. But the radicals, unfortunately for Bubnov, had no interest at all in orderly and disciplined procedures.

The call for class-war Cultural Revolution came from above, but it aroused a genuinely enthusiastic response not only among young Communists but among all those with grievances against the "bourgeois" cultural establishment. The response was iconoclastic, and often led to organizational chaos. The radicals produced a real revolution in educational methodology, and they came close to overturning the whole bureaucratic structure of educational administration. Bubnov — hardnosed, practical and unimaginative — found himself presiding over a brief period of wild experimentation with educational methods and organization in which almost all semblance of order and discipline disappeared. . . .

In the realm of pedagogical theory, a radical group had been defining its position and issuing challenges to the "conservative" Narkompros establishment with increasing vehemence during the last eighteen months of Lunacharsky's tenure at the commissariat. The leading radical theorist was Viktor Nikolaevich Shulgin, a young Communist intellectual who had entered Narkompros early in the 1920s on Krupskaya's[1] invitation. In the latter part of the 1920s, he headed a pedagogical research insti-

---

[1] Nadezhda Krupskaya, Lenin's widow. — Ed.

tute (the Institute of Methods of School Work, renamed the Institute of Marxist-Leninist Pedagogy in 1929), belonged to the pedagogical section of Narkompros' Academic Council, and contributed frequently to Krupskaya's journal *Na putyakh k novoi shkole* [On the Way to the New School] and occasionally to the agitprop department's journal *Kommunisticheskaya revolyutsiya* [Communist Revolution].

Epshtein, the sober head of Narkompros' school administration under Lunacharsky, once credited Shulgin with bringing "the Mayakovsky style" into educational theory. During NEP, Shulgin was one of Narkompros' house radicals — a "leftist," or iconoclastic innovator, of the type of Mayakovsky, Meyerhold, Averbakh, Zalkind or Gastev in their various cultural fields.[2] He was a prolific writer, whose style was closer to that of *Komsomol'skaya pravda* or the RAPP[3] journal *Na literaturnom postu* [On the Literary Front] than to that of the scholarly journals. Apart from Krupskaya, Shulgin had no admirers in the old leadership of Narkompros; and his senior professional colleagues — sober and learned Marxist professors like Kalashnikov and Pinkevich of the Moscow Institute of Scientific Pedagogy — saw him as both a lightweight and a troublemaker. . . .

The existing Soviet school, in Shulgin's view, was a largely unfavourable environment. Early in 1928 he noted that the process of socialist construction was forming a new man — that is, a new adult — but not a new child, because children were not directly involved in the construction effort. The child remained in the pre-revolutionary environment of the classroom.

> *You go into the classroom. Everyone stands up. Why do they need to do that? . . . It doesn't happen when you go into a library reading-room for adults or children. There everyone is occupied with their own business, everyone stays sitting, and nobody pays any attention to someone coming in . . . The same thing in a children's laboratory, a room where they are working on the Dalton Plan. Not in the classroom. Why? Well, it is the old residual past; the old dying order; the old type of relationship between adults and children, "bosses" and "subordinates," the "teacher" and the "pupil." An awful fart, a fart of the past . . . It must be driven out of the school, driven out.*

[2] Vladimir Mayakovsky, the poet; Vsevolod Meyerhold, the theater director; Leopold Averbakh, the literary bureaucrat; A. B. Zalkind, the psychologist; A. K. Gastev, director of the trade unions' training institute. — Ed.

[3] Russian Association of Proletarian Writers, under Averbakh. — Ed.

Shulgin's doubts about the existing Soviet school were expressed in more moderate terms by a number of other educationists in 1927 and 1928. Progressives suspected an educational Thermidor in the revived emphasis on academic standards and preparation for VUZ [Higher Educational Institution] entrance examinations. "It was just at that time," one of Shulgin's colleagues later wrote,

> *that the dead started to suffocate the living through the introduction of monitors, grades and examinations; through the liquidation of [student] self-government, the abandonment of the complex system of teaching in order to retain the subject system, renunciation of moral-educational work on the pretext that it was necessary to instill knowledge and skills, and refusal to review the educational system. . . .*

But the real issues, of course, were not those of definition. The theorists were arguing, in the first place, about the future of the Soviet school: Shulgin's broad definition of pedagogy, in the opinion of his opponents, arose from his belief that the school was an essentially bourgeois institution which was destined to wither away under socialism. In the second place, the established leaders of the Marxist pedagogical profession had received a political challenge. Shulgin and his supporters were not only declaring the imminence of Cultural Revolution but also announcing their intention of leading it.

The opportunity to lead came with Bubnov's arrival at Narkompros. He made Shulgin both a collegium member and the head of the department of teacher training within the new Methodological Sector. This was not, as Bubnov later explained, because he really agreed with what Shulgin and his supporters wrote in "their little books," but because of their political orientation and enthusiastic response to the slogan of Cultural Revolution. "I felt a militant political spirit emanating from them; I felt that they were trying to pose the question in accordance with the requirements of our epoch." . . .

While experienced educational administrators like Epshtein and Skrypnik[4] took a gloomy view of the collapse of the upper-level secondary school, the radicals were essentially optimistic rationalizers of events: if the old educational structure began to disintegrate, this was an encouraging sign that a new and better structure would soon emerge. But

---

[4] Mikola Skrypnik, Commissar of Education for the Ukraine, later purged. — Ed.

what would the new structure be like? The educational process would, of course, be closely linked with the processes of production. But for many radicals, including Shulgin, this was not enough. The child must participate in all aspects of adult collective life. Most importantly, he must become a political participant, since Soviet character, Shulgin believed, was formed in the process of class struggle.

"Socially-useful work," the concept which dominated educational thinking during the First Five-Year Plan, meant both practical work in production (or, more broadly, physical labour) and public activism. A child could be socially useful by gathering firewood, working in a factory, teaching peasants to read or distributing antireligious literature. He could not, however, be socially useful by sitting in a classroom reading books or solving mathematical problems. . . .

The project movement was greatly encouraged by a decision of the Congress on Polytechnical Education (which met early in the summer of 1930) to link even primary schools with neighbouring factories, kolkhozy and public utilities. This was a measure which had been long advocated by the Komsomol[5] and doubtfully received by Narkompros. What it meant was that the factory or other enterprise would become the *shef* or patron of the school, giving it material support, introducing the pupils to the processes of production and, in the case of the older children, actually using their labour.

As usual, the greatest attention was concentrated on the schools in industrial districts which were to be linked with factories, and these were henceforth referred to as "factory 7-year schools" or FZS. But the factories did not necessarily share the educationalists' enthusiasm. They did not want the children under foot in the shops, and they were unwilling to let the schools have discarded equipment *gratis* when it could be profitably disposed of elsewhere. A few big enterprises like "Dinamo" in Moscow took up the idea of *shefstvo* [lit. "chiefship"] and incidentally gave support to the radical methodologists. ("The Narkompros programme . . . did not suit us; we had to smash it," reported a spokesman for the Dinamo school. "We had to bury the old Russian language programme, since in practice geography, social studies and Russian language all merged with each other.") The more typical situation was that the factories were prepared to sign a formal contract taking

[5]The Communist Youth League. — Ed.

responsibility for the school, but no more. In Tula, for example, "the pupils had to resort to staging demonstrations, in which they came to the factory gates with slogans, banners and songs, in order to gain access to production." . . .

The policies which came under the general heading of Cultural Revolution — harassment of the old intelligentsia and massive recruitment of workers and Communists to higher education — were introduced in 1928 and reached a peak of intensity in 1930/31. But by the middle of 1931, there were signs that the Cultural Revolution had run its course. The pool of willing and even partially qualified workers and Communist applicants for higher education showed signs of drying up. The industrial enterprises were resisting further inroads on their skilled labour force; and the industrial leadership was actively campaigning for an end to the persecution of the old engineers. In the summer of 1931, the "bourgeois intelligentsia" was formally rehabilitated in a speech by Stalin. In the autumn, the organized recruitment of workers to full-time study in the VTUZy [Higher Technical Educational Institutions] was quietly abandoned.

Cultural Revolution, however, had meant more than proletarian *vydvizhenie* [promotion] and the harassment of bourgeois specialists; and the restoration of order in education and cultural life was consequently a complex and many-faceted process. It is likely, indeed, that the party leadership only became fully aware of the dimensions of the cultural upheaval it had sponsored when the time came to reverse the policy.

Cultural Revolution had meant, in the first place, the establishment of "proletarian hegemony" in the cultural professions by groups of militant Communist intellectuals. These activists, who were greatly disliked in their professions, had dispatched the "bourgeois" and "rightist" enemies by 1931, and were in the process of splitting into warring factions. They had ignored a number of warning signals from the leadership, and failed altogether to respond to its pleas for *practical* support of the industrialization and collectivization effort. To an impartial eye, as well as to Stalin's, they were serving no useful function; and their political and professional enemies were legion.

In the second place, the cultural upheaval had produced a complete, and in many ways remarkable, structural and financial reorganization of the education system. Industry was maintaining the greater

A Soviet propaganda poster after the Stalin Revolution (1934): "Hold high the banner of Lenin—it is leading us to victory!" (Art Resource)

part of all secondary and higher education. The senior grades of general secondary school were gone, and there was no direct path from the 7-year school to VUZ. The enormously expanded FZU apprenticeship school was providing more candidates for further education than apprentices. The old VUZy had been split up into highly specialized institutes, subordinate to a bewildering variety of state and economic agencies. The old universities retained only a marginal existence, with the teaching of pure science restored only after protest from the scientific community, and the humanities and social sciences apparently heading for complete extinction. The situation was scarcely compatible with a rapprochement between the regime and the scientific and professional community, and probably intolerable for industry on any long-term basis.

The third aspect of Cultural Revolution was methodological "harebrained scheming" in education. For some years, this apparently passed unnoticed by the party leadership. But it was a cause of disorder and indiscipline in the schools, and contributed to the general lowering of education standards. Protests came from teachers, parents, and the admissions boards of technicums and VUZy. The radicals responded only by moving further to the left. With the rehabilitation of bourgeois specialists, the professors added their voices to the chorus of criticism. When the party leadership finally became aware of the situation, it had no reason to support the educational radicals and many reasons to repudiate them.

The process of restoring order followed two distinct lines, parallel to a great extent but separate. Industry — led by Vesenkha [Supreme Economic Council] and (from 1932) its successor, the Commissariat of Heavy Industry — initiated the rehabilitation of the bourgeois specialist and subsequently supervised the reorganization of higher technical education, which served as a model for other professional schools. It also reorganized the system of factory apprenticeship schools. The development of pure science was fostered by an informal alliance of the industrial leadership and the scientific community; in institutional terms, this was expressed in the cooperation between the Commissariat of Heavy Industry, the Committee on Higher Technical Education under TsIK[6] and the Academy of Sciences.

---

[6]Central Executive Committee, the nominal government. — Ed.

The party Central Committee organized the reform of primary and secondary education and the purging of the Communist cultural militants. Until 1936, it remained aloof from questions of higher education, with the one notable exception of history. Stalin, who was the driving force behind the Central Committee's involvement in education, took a strong personal interest in the revival of history teaching in schools and universities; and in history, as in the industrial reorganization, "bourgeois specialists" were co-opted. But in contrast to the industrial leaders, whose role was almost that of patrons of the old intelligentsia, Stalin and the officials of the Central Committee secretariat acted as stern ideological overseers of both "bourgeois" and Marxist historians. . . .

Even before industry became concerned about the VTUZy, the Central Committee had started to undo the effects of Cultural Revolution in the schools. The reason for the Central Committee's involvement was, apparently, Stalin's personal interest and his lack of confidence in Narkompros. Stalin's interest, according to Kaganovich,[7] was aroused almost by chance. Somebody called his attention to the fact that "teaching in one school was going badly and the training of the children was poorly organized." He discovered that there was no discipline in the school, very little formal teaching by subject and no regular textbooks. He also presumably became aware of Shulgin's theory of the "withering away of the school," a close relative to the theory of the imminent "withering away of the state" which Stalin had condemned a year earlier. Out of these discoveries, Kaganovich said, "emerged the whole complex of questions about the school; and a decision about the school — which later the educational workers themselves justly called a historic decision — was made."

There was, of course, a somewhat broader context in which the decision was made. Others beside Stalin were disturbed by the disorganization of school life and the fact that pupils were not receiving a systematic general education. The enterprises disliked their new role as school guardians, and the VTUZy and technicums were complaining of the inadequate preparation of entering students. By the summer of 1931, there was talk of the need to re-establish the old grades VIII–X of the general secondary school. Bubnov rejected any idea of returning to

---

[7] Lazar Kaganovich, key Politburo member during the Stalin Revolution. — Ed.

the "old academic school" but acknowledged the deficiencies of the new one: . . .

> *It must be said with the greatest severity that the 7-year school is not giving an adequate educational preparation for the technicums. . . .*

Bubnov may have had a hand in framing the Central Committee's resolution of 25 August 1931 "On the elementary and middle school," but his role was minor. The resolution was far more outspoken than any earlier criticism from Bubnov. On the theoretical level, it repudiated the theory of "withering away of the school" and denounced the project method. On the practical level, it found that the school's "basic failing" was that it "does not give a sufficient amount of general knowledge, and does not adequately solve the problem of training fully literate persons with a good grasp of the bases of the sciences (physics, chemistry, mathematics, native language, geography and so on) for entrance to technicums and higher schools."

The core recommendation was that the teaching of physics, chemistry and mathematics, in particular, "must be based on strictly delineated and carefully worked-out programmes and study plans," and classes should be organized on a firm timetable. Narkompros was to work out systematic programmes in the basic subjects and see that the schools followed them.

Many people welcomed the Central Committee resolution as a return to the "old school." This interpretation, though not far from the truth, was too much for Narkompros and the progressive educationalists to swallow. Editorialists in the educational press struggled to work out the Central Committee's real meaning. Surely it was not endorsing old-fashioned classroom teaching of individual subjects? It could not mean "that our school must return to the work methods of the old, scholastic, academic school," concluded one of the educational journals. It *must* mean, despite the condemnation of the project method, that "our school should apply all the variety of activity methods already proved in practice (research, laboratory and excursion methods)." . . .

In the early months of 1931, Bubnov initiated a discussion on pedagogical theory. Like other theoretical discussions of the period, it amounted to a condemnation of the "right" and the "left" deviation. Attacks against "leftism" were at first directed at the political Oppositionist Vaganyan, although Shulgin's theory of the withering away of the school was sometimes included. Krupskaya's journal *Na putyakh* did not participate in the discussion since, as she bluntly stated, she found it "very scholastic and boring."

In April, Bubnov provoked a confrontation with Shulgin and Krupskaya. Shulgin, he said, was insubordinate, showed "theoretical arrogance" and refused to give his mistakes "the correct political evaluation." Yet Bubnov's attitude to Shulgin still seems to have been basically friendly (he remarked that he was "very sad" to see someone with "a fine past" heading for trouble). Krupskaya concluded, probably correctly, that the attack was really directed against her. She responded with a very indignant written protest invoking Lenin's authority on the side of the "leftists."

> All my life I have fought rightists, and will go on fighting them. For me, the words "the greatest danger is from the right" are not simply words: they are filled with living content . . . As for the leftists, in particular Shulgin and Krupenina, Ilyich wrote that one must do everything to welcome those who fight against the old school. And I must say that in the struggle against the old school I did form a `bloc with . . . Shulgin.

By August, Bubnov had proposed liquidating Shulgin's Institute, a suggestion which Krupskaya and Shulgin took rather badly. He presumably already knew the contents of the resolution on the schools in preparation in the Central Committee; and, while he was not prepared to condemn the educational revolution of the past three years *in toto*, he conceded that Shulgin's ideas had done considerable damage. "The theory of 'the withering away of the school' has a very nimble nature," he said. "It gets in everywhere. It gets into the question of activity methods, including the 'project method.' It also gets into the question of self-government in the school, the role of the Pioneers, and so on."

After the publication of the Central Committee resolution, Shulgin's Institute was dissolved; and Shulgin was removed from the Narkompros collegium and persuaded "under very great pressure" to repudiate the theory of "the withering away of the school." He then departed, probably under the auspices of the association of proletarian writers, RAPP, to write a novel about the Stalingrad Tractor Factory, and took no further part in educational life.

Katerina Clark

The Remaking
of Literature

Katerina Clark is a professor of Russian literature at Indiana University and
a specialist on Soviet fiction. Her major works include *The Soviet Novel:
History as Ritual* (1981). The selection here is from her contribution to the
symposium edited by Sheila Fitzpatrick on Soviet culture during the time
of the First Five-Year Plan.

Most Western commentators have seen literature under the Five-Year
Plan as moving toward a disastrous culmination: the end of literature as
an autonomous activity and the drastic lowering of literary standards in
the Stalinist thirties. However, the opposite could be argued: it was
precisely in the aftermath of the First Five-Year Plan that writers and
literary critics showed a renewed concern about literary quality. In
literature, as in so many other spheres, the First Five-Year Plan period
represented the high point of a radical utopianism that threatened traditional literary values. Utopian tendencies were already noticeable in the
literary debates of the twenties, but it was only under the peculiar
conditions of the Five-Year Plan that they received widespread application. The change of policy in 1932–34, however, checked rather than
further institutionalized this radical movement.

As we know, under the First Five-Year Plan the Soviet Union
underwent rapid planned industrialization and collectivization. But
that general description cannot convey the period's peculiar flavor. It
was a time of extremism, of dramatic gestures, of contrasts and
paradoxes. On construction sites, for example, teams of self-sacrificing
volunteers rubbed elbows with gangs of forced laborers and illiterate
peasant recruits. But the singularity of the period lay in the fact that —

From Katerina Clark, "Little Heroes and Big Deeds: Literature Responds to the First Five-
Year Plan," in Sheila Fitzpatrick, ed., *Cultural Revolution in Russia*, excerpts from
pp. 189–206. Copyright © Indiana University Press, 1978, reprinted by permission.

as in Akhenaton's Egypt, Peter the Great's Russia, or France in the Great Revolution — utopian striving was the prerogative not of dreamers in garrets or holy men in the desert, but of the government itself.

The focus of this utopian striving was not just the industrial revolution, but a "cultural revolution" as well. However, the key myths of the age were so colored by a fervor for industrialization that they were usually expressed in terms of the factory model. Society itself was conceived as a machine, whose separate parts were harmoniously interrelated and regulated. In Five-Year Plan novels, even those dealing with the kolkhoz, one can find countless uses of the machine metaphor for society. For instance, in a novel by Ia. Ilin, Soviet society is likened to a large factory in which the work of every department contributes to the running of the "Great Conveyor Belt" (*Bol'shoi konveier*, 1934). Some writers were so carried away by the Five-Year Plan cult of technology that they depicted industrial machines as actually impressing their own rhythms and harmonies on the psyche of the workers who operated them. . . .

In literature, the First Five-Year Plan was an age of the minor parts, the masses or, in Gorkii's[1] phrase, the "little men." Gone was the age of Gogol and Chekhov, when little men were represented in literature as pathetic creatures. They were now, as Gorkii put it, raised to their full "human dignity," to a "realization of the importance of the 'little men' in the world," and to a position in which they could fulfill their "creative" potential. They were valuable, however, not in themselves but as the bolts and whistles of the great train of society. The nearest, although decidedly more primitive, analogy Gorkii could find for them was the millions of molluscs whose creative work over time built up great coral reefs. But, "little men" though they were, they shared in the great achievements of the age; and for this reason their deeds were also "great."

In Gorkii's essay, the society in which "little men" accomplish "great deeds" is contrasted with the old oppressive bourgeois society dominated by "great men." His views here are typical of the First Five-Year Plan rhetoric, which celebrated the achievements of the masses rather than those of exceptional individuals.

---

[1] Maxim Gorky, the Russian novelist who returned from the emigration to serve Stalin until his death, under suspicious circumstances, in 1936. — Ed.

A second characteristic was the emphasis on rapid and radical change. "We are fifty to one-hundred years behind the most advanced countries," Stalin told a meeting of Soviet managers in February 1931. "We must cover that distance in ten years." The writers took their cue to collapse time, and the *topos* of literature in the period became the observation of millennial change. In Ilin's *The Great Conveyer Belt*, the construction site is transformed in a mere two weeks, while in V. Kataev's novel *Time, Forward!* the hero finds that the terrain changes so radically every *day* that he has to change his route to work. Some writers were not content to deal with days, months, or years, but preferred to invoke centuries and epochs. In the collectively written *People of the Stalingrad Tractor Factory*, the authors embellished Stalin's time model and claimed that in one year "we have advanced 200 years." The hero of Leonov's *Sot'* perceives the leap (in a local context) as from the sixteenth century to the twentieth; while in another example of collective authorship, *The History of the Construction of the White Sea–Baltic Canal*, the Five-Year Plan advance is described as a movement not from one century to another but from one epoch to another — from the "wooden age" to the "iron age."

With the great leap forward of industrialization and collectivization, society had to be remade. Verbs expressing remaking and redoing (*perestraivat'*, *perekovat'*, *peredelat'*, *pererozhdat'*, *perelozhit'*, *perevospitat'*, and so on) are characteristic of the language of the period. However, the list of things to be changed included not just the terrain, but also man himself. In keeping with the dominant industrial imagery, social institutions were seen as a sort of assembly line for retooling a human product and turning out the new Soviet man.

The main instrument for this retooling was labor — in factories, on construction sites, or in collective farms. Indeed it was widely believed that the experience of production could transform not only the masses of society, but individual deviants — the "alien elements" inherited from capitalism, "wreckers," hooligans, and criminals.

One of literature's functions in these years was to provide illustrations of these human transformations. And so in a book about a new tractor factory, for instance, the author is delighted to note that as a result of the workers' participation in socialist labor they no longer drink or swear in their leisure time. The most dramatic illustrations can be found in books about "alien elements." One such source, and a particularly rich one, is the book commissioned to celebrate the White Sea–

Baltic Canal project, an undertaking that used thousands of convict laborers. On almost every page the authors describe how the "human raw materials" were "reworked" (largely through hard labor and exposure to "culture" — libraries, lectures, classes in basic literacy and technical skills, and so on). . . .

The radical mood and industrial orientation of the Five-Year Plan period affected not only literary themes but the prevailing concepts of literature itself. Many of those involved believed that literature should be put at the service of the Five-Year Plan, and that it should be organized by analogy with industrial production. The most zealous of them attempted to find literary equivalents for each new official policy in the economic or political sphere: when the government launched a campaign to encourage "shock workers" in industry, many critics declared that literature should have them too; and when *Pravda* urged all industrial plants to fulfill the "Promfinplan," [industrial finance plan] then *Literaturnaia gazeta* asked writers to do likewise.

These responses on the part of the writers to the demands of the age can be interpreted in different ways. Perhaps the millennial sentiment of the period was infectious; perhaps the pressures of class war obliged writers to offer palpable proof of their Five-Year Plan zeal; perhaps they were merely acting as seemed expedient. They were not, whatever else was the case, following a central "Party line" on literature, since the Party never gave any explicit instructions for the writers to follow.

In Western commentary, the literary extremism of these years is usually ascribed to the infamous "proletarian" literary association RAPP [Russian Association of Proletarian Writers] . . . which was responsible for many of the Five-Year Plan slogans for literature and took a bullying role toward other literary groups. Our contention, however, is that RAPP's power was not a cause but a symptom of the prevailing atmosphere of extremism. The salient features of RAPP's stance throughout the twenties — its crusade against the torchbearers of traditional intellectualism and "nonproletarian" elements, its xenophobia, and its insistence that literary activity should be subordinated to the interests of the whole society — all made the organization a natural leader of cultural revolution. But the radical policies it advanced for literature during the Five-Year Plan were hardly exclusive or original to RAPP, nor were they the most iconoclastic of the day. In short, the narrow focus of literary factionalism does not provide the only, or even necessarily the best, context in which to view the literary dynamic of these years. . . .

Soviet architecture before the Stalin Revolution: The *Pravda* building, built in the 1920s. (Wide World Photos)

As Five-Year Plan fever took hold, critics interpreted the demand that literature "should not be a single step away from socialist construction" to mean that it should imitate the accelerated tempos of the industrialization effort. They suggested that writers should try to finish each work as rapidly as possible: after all, they said, it was necessary to "catch up and surpass" the capitalist West in book production as well as industry. Writers should overcome the old prejudices about "nurturing" the material and striving for a polished product, for with that approach the product would be obsolete before it was finished.

It was even argued that books should have a direct effect on production itself. Occasional slogans in the literary press reminded writers that "The Book Is An Instrument of Production," and "In Order to Conduct a Successful Spring Sowing Campaign We Must Arm Each Kolkhoz Member With A Book, and Likewise Every Sovkhoz Worker and Each Poor- and Middle-Peasant Household." At a rather higher level of sophistication, a joint appeal of the Education Commissariat and the Federation of Soviet Writers described the writer's function as "raising the morale high, inspiring the masses for the struggle, ruthlessly exposing indifference, stagnation and desertion, all of which undermine the plan."

The literary press placed great emphasis on the writers' part in the

Soviet architecture after the Stalin revolution: The University of Moscow, built in the 1940s. (Sovfoto)

national campaign to raise the cultural and educational level of the masses. To this end, it was held, writers should provide a literature that was within the price range and intellectual reach of the newly literate. Publishing houses began putting out series of cheap mass editions. Journals undertook campaigns to increase their readership.

The masses were not only important to the literary profession as readers, but as potential writers as well. Overnight, as it seemed, the ranks of the profession were swelled by an influx of workers and peasants. RAPP regarded the training of these novices as the most important of its current tasks, and was so zealous in prosecuting it that in 1931 it was able to report an 80 percent increase in membership over the past year, bringing its numbers to ten thousand. . . .

For the militants of the literary world, the ultimate goal of this mass recruitment was to abolish traditional literature and supplant the old-style professional writers. This view was to some extent influenced by the strident anti-intellectualism that accompanied the campaign against the bourgeois intelligentsia. The demand that a literature should be provided for the masses became a demand that *all* literature should be mass literature, or even that all literature should be accessible to the semiliterate! Groups vied with each other to prove their greater commitment to the masses. Even RAPP, the traditional stronghold of opposition to bourgeois intellectualism, was reproached for the fact that articles in its journal *On the Literary Front* were too abstruse to be understood by the mass reader.

The mass reader was called to sit in judgment on the professional writer's efforts. Many theorists suggested that the mass reader's response should be the ultimate test of a work's worth — and therefore of whether a given writer should be published, or his works given wide circulation. Workers assumed *shefstvo* or supervision over the activities of literary groups. No doubt a good part of this was window-dressing. But it raises an interesting question about the *kto-kogo*[2] of ideological influence: were the writers supposed to be molding the masses, or to be molded by them?

The literary journals abounded with triumphant and extravagant progress reports on the battle between "mass-ism" (*massovost'*) and the traditional prejudices of the profession. "This is a struggle against those

___

[2] "Who-whom" —, "Who does it to whom." — Ed.

illusions of grandeur which still persist in our literary community," declared the RAPP critic Ermilov in 1930. In the same year, M. Kozakov claimed that the effects of the campaign against traditional literature had been so far-reaching that the very "contours of the writer's psyche have changed." A common refrain of these years was expressed in the slogan "We must break the writer's individualism!"

While the writer was urged to abandon the position of "independent observer" and become a "writer-fighter" (*pisatel'-boets*), the new conception of his role in fact incorporated a number of specific and fairly mundane tasks — organizing libraries in the enterprises, running the literary circles, helping with the wall-newspapers, lecturing, arranging public debates and exhibitions, composing slogans and appeals to the workers, and finding worker representatives for the major literary committees.

The writer, in other words, was to be "remade" as a journalist, technical expert, cultural worker, teacher, librarian, and public relations officer. Often, the articles on his new role neglected even to mention the possibility that he should be writing his own works — and when, after all, would he find time to do so? Self-effacement on the part of the established writers was considered essential for their reconstruction. But, with such a degree of self-effacement, literature as traditionally understood seemed to be withering away.

It should not be glibly assumed that this "withering away" was a purely artificial process generated from above. There was a genuine, if very diffuse, desire on the part of many writers to transform their own status in some way, to participate in the construction of the new society and to achieve a more direct link with the masses. Russian history provides precedents for this: the dispatch of the writers to Soviet enterprises during the Five-Year Plan can be seen as an industrial version of *narodnichestvo* [Populism], a resurgence of the impulse that sent the intelligentsia to the people in the 1870s. In both cases, the educated went "to the people" to bring them enlightenment and to teach. But they also went to learn, to dissolve their own class prejudices, and to establish contact with those whom they perceived to be the crucial element in contemporary society. . . .

From the end of 1930, the literary press shows a progressive retreat from the extreme positions adopted by the literary militants over the past three years. New slogans appeared: "Let Us Turn Our Attention To

Creative Writing!" "For Artistic Quality!" "For the *Big* [italics mine] Art of Bolshevism!" and "Show the Country Its Heroes!" There were critical appraisals of the literature of novice writers. An article of February 1931, for example, described their works as "overrated," "in general rather primitive," and "schematic." Critics complained that, in the Five-Year Plan literature in general, there was too much "glossing-over of reality," and that it was often shoddy and hastily written. It was said that topicality and the cult of technology had excluded not only human interest from literature but even ideology (!). In May 1931 RAPP called on the writers to depict the "heroes" of the Five-Year Plan in their works. And, from the beginning of 1931, the literary journals broke out of their previous isolationism and began to take an interest in developments in contemporary Western literature.

These changes can be explained in various ways. In the first place, Maksim Gorkii was to return permanently to the USSR in the spring of 1931, and it is clear from the comments in the literary journals that the writers were expecting him to play a leading role in literature. By April the strains of deference to Gorkii had built up to the slogan "Work Gorkii Style!" This probably meant, in effect: pay more attention to literary craftsmanship. In a programmatic article "On literature" published that January, Gorkii declared:

> It is not always the subject-matter which plays a decisive role in a work, but real mastery of the art always plays that role. . . . It is my opinion that one should learn not only from the classics, but even from the enemy if he has wit. To learn is not just to imitate, but to command the techniques of literary mastery.

In other words, ideas that less than a year ago had been considered heretical were coming back into currency.

In the second place, literature was affected by developments in the broader political sphere. In June 1931 Stalin rejected "vulgar egalitarianism" (*uravnilovka*) in favor of wage differentials, and announced a new policy of "encouragement and concern" toward the old intelligentsia. Under these circumstances, the "proletarian hegemony" of RAPP was no longer appropriate, and neither was a literary preoccupation with the undifferentiated working-class masses.

In literature, the slogan arising out of Stalin's speech was "Let Us Turn Our Attention to Literary Technique!" This was to some extent ambiguous because of the two meanings of the Russian word "*tekh-*

nika": a year earlier, one suspects, the slogan might have been interpreted as a reference to *industrial* technology. There were, indeed,
important elements of continuity between the literary orientation of the
First Five-Year Plan and the Second. The pathos of industrialization
continued to engage much of the writers' attention. Literary organizations continued to send "brigades" of "shock-worker" writers to the
factories, and writers were still periodically enjoined to look to their
"tempos" of literary production. But after 1931 these latter activities
were conducted on a very much reduced scale and with little fanfare.

The major upheaval in literary life, which occurred only in 1932,
was the dissolution of RAPP and other independent literary organizations
and the founding of a single Union of Soviet Writers. Western commentators have seen these events as a final nail in the coffin of literary
autonomy. There is, however, a good deal of evidence to suggest that
the Party's action in dissolving RAPP was prompted by a desire to halt
RAPP's persecution of independent writers' groups and of non-Party writers in particular; and that the intention was not to oppress the literary
profession but to rid it of ugly and counterproductive faction fighting.
Certainly the relatively broad composition of the initial Writers' Union
committees lends support to such an interpretation.

This is not to deny that the post-1932 reorganization was designed
to provide an institutional framework for literature that would guarantee
a high degree of ideological conformity. But it must also be recognized
that the excesses of the First Five-Year Plan period had damaged literature, and that some aspects of the damage were of particular concern to
the Party leadership. Among the deficiencies of the Five-Year Plan
literature was its low degree of acceptability in the world outside the
Soviet Union. With Gorkii's return, the Party leadership clearly wanted
international recognition of Soviet accomplishments in the cultural
field. It achieved this in some measure through the presence of a number of non-Communist foreign writers of international fame at the First
Congress of Soviet Writers, held in 1934 in a spirit of conciliation and
respect for the literary tradition.

We can chart the changing orientation of literature through a series
of critical responses to a major RAPP novel of socialist construction
mentioned earlier in this article — Ilenkov's *The Driving Axle*. The
novel was originally hailed as model for proletarian writers by
Serafimovich, the grand old man of proletarian literature, writing in
Pravda early in 1932. But by mid-March of that year it was under attack

at a meeting organized for the purpose at the House of Proletarian Literature. Just as the criticisms of Gladkov's *Cement* in 1929 were part of a campaign against heroization in the novel, so were these attacks on *The Driving Axle* indications that the literary reign of the "little man" of socialist construction was coming to an end. Of the various criticisms of the novel published at this time, Gorkii's is probably the most indicative of the general change — especially if one compares it with his earlier essay on the literary role of "little men." Gorkii wrote:

> *The tempos of our life will not allow rushed work and writing tossed off anyhow in the hope of getting it done as soon as possible. . . . Among the proletarians, you still find ideas which are harmful to their interests. For instance, we came up with the doctrine of the necessity for an "organized lowering of culture." Echoes of this theory have not yet died in the noise of construction, and the impulse to simplify in literature is one such echo of the anti-proletarian, anti-culture heresy. . . .*
>
> *The Soviet day sings out loudly and to the whole world of the gigantic, heroic and talented work of your class. It sings of the human hero, who gives birth to the collective heroism of the class. This grandiose work and this hero is still not being described in literature.*

In Ilenkov's novel, Gorkii wrote, "the mechanical role of the 'driving axle' as a part of the train obscured . . . the work of the political axle." This was not to be a fault of future Soviet literature, in which the guiding role of the "political axle" — the Party, and especially its leadership — becomes abundantly clear. On the other hand (and leaving aside the quality of the literature itself), it would also be impossible in the future for Soviet critics to ignore the question of literary quality, and — as at least one critic did in the Five-Year Plan years — to give wholehearted endorsement to a work that was acknowledged to contain *major* compositional and stylistic defects.

Reading Zhdanov's[3] famous address to the 1934 Writers' Congress with the immediate historical context in mind, it seems inappropriate to put too much stress on his frequently quoted formula that writers should be "engineers of human souls." The thought, if not the precise words, was extremely familiar to writers who had lived through the First Five-Year Plan period; and it must have sounded less like a threat than a slight anachronism.

---

[3] Andrei Zhdanov, Party secretary for ideology and culture under Stalin, from 1934 until his death in 1948. — Ed.

What was perhaps more significant was his emphasis on the crucial importance of literary technique for the Soviet writer, and his view of the place of heroes in Soviet literature. It was in the decaying West, Zhdanov argued, that one found a preference for little heroes, minor writers, and modest themes. Soviet literature, in contrast, reflected the great themes and heroism of the Soviet construction achievement. The hallmark of the new Soviet literature, Zhdanov said, was to be "heroization."

This indeed turned out to be the case. The "little man" as a central concern of Soviet writers disappeared along with other manifestations of the First Five-Year Plan cultural revolution. It was the turn toward the hero that would define Soviet literature for decades to come.

J. Arch Getty

Forging the Totalitarian Party

J. Arch Getty is a professor of history at the University of California at Riverside. His exhaustive research on Soviet politics in the 1930s has earned him a prominent place among "revisionist" historians who find the Soviet scene in those years much more chaotic and much less coordinated than is usually thought. In the selection that follows he examines the inner discord in the Communist party that led to the Great Purge of 1936–1938.

Reflection on the Soviet Communist Party in the 1930s has often produced the image of a closed, monolithic, disciplined organization that functioned without dissent and with a high level of centralized control. With Stalin's assumption of supreme leadership, the era of the 1920s with its freewheeling disputes on culture, its heroic personal

From J. Arch Getty, *The Origins of the Great Purges*, 1985, pp. 10–11, 12–14, 198–200, 203–206. Reprinted with the permission of Cambridge University Press.

struggles, and its debates on society and economics seemed finished. Stalin's control appears to have frozen the party into a mold of obedience rather than discussion, centrally initiated terror rather than freedom, and petrification rather than evolution.

Yet it would be naive to be taken in by Stalin's cult of personality and to accept Stalinist protestations of unity. It would be unrealistic to assume that differences of opinion in the party simply disappeared after 1929. The discussions surrounding the rate and character of industrialization, the nature of centralized decision making, the peasant question, and the parameters of political dissent certainly were muted after 1929, but they did continue.

A good deal is now known about the internal party debates on the nature and extent of collectivization that took place in 1929–31. One also knows something about the disagreements and uncertainties surrounding the treatment of "bourgeois specialists" and the changes in educational and social policy. Even later in the 1930s, writers have long suspected the existence of debates on the nature and extent of the Great Purges. Despite the efforts of the Stalinist leadership to avoid "going public" on these debates, the outlines of controversy spilled over into the press and can be studied by careful scholars. Interest groups in the bureaucracy usually could not oppose the established line, but in cases where there was no firmly fixed policy, debate, negotiation, and lobbying were possible even in the Stalin years.

The constant shifts in official policy on certain issues strongly suggest debate and disagreement. The Stalinist press was constantly affirming the correctness of the leadership's policies and never stopped trying to rally the country around the "General Line." But what was the "General Line"? Was it the "destruction of the kulaks as a class" of 1930 or the slower collectivization of the following year? Was it embodied in the fantastic rates prescribed for industrial growth in the First Five Year Plan or the more modest projections of the second? Was it the expulsion and degradation of the party opposition or the welcoming of former oppositionists at the Seventeenth Party Congress in 1934? Was it represented by tight central control over personnel appointments or the relative autonomy of local party leaders in the regions?

In fact, the relentless calls to heed the teachings of the "Great and Wise Teacher" Comrade Stalin, and the constant proofs adduced in the press to the effect that the country and party were solidly united around the leader, take on a tone of desperation to scholars who read them years later. Why was it necessary to attribute every initiative and policy to the Great Teacher? Why was it politically desirable for the bureaucracy to mask the real political process behind a puerile facade of revealed truth from the Master? Could there be a political use for Stalin's cult of personality over and above his supposed need for adulation? It may well be that where one finds the loudest affirmations of unity are the places where unity is most lacking. . . .

The Seventeenth Party Congress, which took place between January 26 and February 10, 1934, went down in party history as the "Congress of Victors" and met in an atmosphere of triumph. The optimistic atmosphere was inspired by the successful harvest of 1933. This event was generally regarded as the first concrete proof of the "correctness" of the General Line of the party: collectivization of agriculture accompanied by rapid industrial growth. Until then the General Line had in no way proved itself, and its permanence had not been ensured.

The apparent unanimity of the Congress of Victors was an illusion. It seems, for example, that a number of delegates to the congress discussed removing Stalin or reducing his power. Rumors suggest that this anti-Stalin bloc was led by dissident regional party secretaries, but it is not currently possible to document or even elaborate upon this shadowy incident. The minutes of the congress do, however, reveal another conflict among the assembled party leaders. An unusual floor fight developed between premier V. M. Molotov and commissar of heavy industry G. K. Ordzhonikidze over the rate of economic planning.

The First Five Year Plan (1929–32) has been described as a period of "cultural revolution" during which radicals and activists within the Communist Party (and in society) criticized capitalism and "bourgeois values" in everything from art and education to economic planning. The movement was diffuse and contained many aspects — radicals criticized conservative professors, proposed visionary utopian schemes, championed "proletarian culture," and criticized "bourgeois artists." Coinciding with the political defeat of Bukharin and the Right Opposition, the cultural-revolution period also saw radicals establish very high production targets in industry (the "maximum variant" of the First Five Year Plan). Based on the "revolutionary-heroic" tradition in the party, which held that Bolsheviks could "storm any fortresses," radicals believed that enthusiasm was necessary and sufficient for economic success. For them, advocating the lowering of plan targets ("slowing the tempo") was tantamount to counterrevolution, and the violent and chaotic early stages of rural collectivization took place under radical control. Radicals also sought to annihilate the prerevolutionary technical specialists and replace them with newly promoted workers "from the bench." Radical strength was greatest in the Komsomol, among young technical students, and among the enthusiastic party activists who carried out collectivization and led the "class war" against the New Economic Policy (NEP) and all it stood for.

The other point of view might be called moderate and included those leaders, officials, and economic planners who, although not joining Bukharin's Right Opposition, nevertheless made many of the same gradualist assumptions about economic growth and agricultural collectivization. The Stalinist, or pro-Stalin, moderates were opposed to the "adventurist," voluntarist approach of the radicals and argued for "realistic" or "rational" — meaning lower — planning targets. Moderates valued professionalism and expertise more than enthusiasm and sought to protect the "bourgeois specialists" from radical attack. Consisting of more traditionally trained graduate engineers, professional economists, and establishment planners, this group argued that the fantastically high industrial tempos of the radicals violated "technical norms," in that the machinery would not stand the abuse of speeded-up production at the hands of the enthusiasts. Moderates further pointed out that the emphasis on quantity and speed would certainly decrease the quality of goods produced.

Both the radical and moderate point of view existed *within* a Stalinist bloc that contained elements inclined toward both extremes. The radical-moderate dichotomy simply reproduced the wider political spectrum of which the Left and Right oppositions had been only the extremes. The apparent defeats of these two officially recognized oppositional groups only ostracized the more strident partisans who had been willing to force the issues and who were branded leaders of "factions." Unlike the Left and Right oppositions, the Stalinist radicals and moderates both supported the General Line, although with differing emphases. . . .

[T]he Bolshevik Party was not the monolithic and homogeneous machine both totalitarian theorists and Stalinists would have us believe. Administration was so chaotic, irregular, and confused that even Merle

Fainsod's characterization of the system [in *Soviet Rule in Smolensk*] as "inefficient totalitarianism" seems to overstate the case.

Although the Soviet government was certainly dictatorial (or tried to be), it was not totalitarian. The technical and technological sophistication that separates totalitarianism from dictatorship was lacking in the thirties. The primitive texture of the Smolensk Archive, the real weakness of the central government in key areas, and a certain degree of political pluralism argue strongly against any totalitarian characterization. On a local level (where most of the population interacts with the government), political administration was marked by incompetence, sloth, inertia, and real cultural backwardness. The system had the disadvantages of bureaucratism without the corresponding benefits of efficient bureaucracy. Administration on a local level often resembled a popular peasant culture that was trying clumsily and sometimes halfheartedly to be a modern bureaucracy.

This chaos, although historically important in its own right, has implications for political conflicts. The confusion and disorder in local party membership files and the inefficient fulfillment of central directives served to augment and protect the powers of local officials. The less the center knew about local affairs, the less it could intervene and control them, and Moscow party leaders spent much of their time trying to find out what was happening in the provinces. Conflict erupted as the center tried to streamline, regularize, and ultimately control local political organizations.

An inefficient and clumsy bureaucracy also meant that the effects of campaigns and orders from Moscow could be either minimized or exaggerated as they reverberated down the chain of command. Because chaos implied a certain local autonomy, some tasks (like the *proverka* [review of party membership] of 1935) died a bureaucratic death without being completed. Inefficiency, confusion, and local self-protection also meant that other campaigns . . . could easily run out of control.

In addition to the ramshackle and unresponsive nature of its bureaucracy, the party was also split by conflicts between factions, strata, and key personalities. There were local frictions between leaders and led, middle-level struggles between regional and district committees, and higher-order battles between provincial bodies and the Moscow center. At the summit, personal fights among key leaders were so bitter that they leaked into the staid and usually restrained Stalinist press. The competitions between Molotov and Ordzhonikidze and between

Sergei Kirov, Leningrad Soviet Secretary and Stalin's rival in the early 1930s, as he appeared in 1932. (Sovfoto)

Zhdanov and Ezhov were only the most obvious struggles — future researches will uncover others. Such struggles among courtiers (who were themselves powerful political actors) are not new to historians and should not surprise students of even the Stalin period. As Timothy Dunmore recently noted,[1] "Few are now prepared to accept too literally

[1] In *The Stalinist Command Economy* (New York: St. Martin's, 1980), p. 2, referring to *Conversations with Stalin* (New York: Harcourt, Brace & World, 1962), by the former vice-president of Yugoslavia. — Ed.

Milovan Djilas's picture of senior Politburo members obsequiously following Stalin about and taking his orders down on a convenient note pad."

There was a lively politics in the party during the 1930s. Indeed, open controversies on broad policy options were forbidden, and no alternative grand strategies could be proposed in public. But although there were no more open arguments about what to do, there were many options and disagreements about how to do it. The strategy (the General Line) had been set, but the tactics of implementation were undecided; this, too, was politics. Anyone who has worked in a large organization knows that the politics of implementation is at least as important (and personally bitter) as the politics of grand strategy. It was easy to forge broad public agreement on general strategy and even on the nature of the problems facing the apparatus, but it was next to impossible for various factions and strata to agree on or coordinate solutions.

Although the inner politics of the Kremlin still eludes us, it is clear that in the thirties Stalin's lieutenants represented policy alternatives and options. It is surely significant, for example, that V. M. Molotov always advocated fast industrial growth and the need to destroy "underestimators," oppositionists, and other "enemies." It is just as clear that Sergo Ordzhonikidze represented opposite policies.

As far as the struggles within the party apparatus proper are concerned, the views and policies of A. A. Zhdanov are important. He believed that most of the party's problems could be solved through indoctrination, propaganda, and the sound political education of new cadres. Zhdanov always defended the rights of rank-and-file activists and was a consistent advocate of *samokritika* [self-criticism] and criticism from below. He wanted to involve the activists in the work of party committees, to protect them from abuse and expulsion by local secretaries, and to promote them to leadership work. Even passive and peripheral members were to be salvaged.

Zhdanov's advocacy of a "new, more flexible dictatorship" and his conception of the party as an educational institution and vehicle for indoctrination put him in conflict with those party security specialists who traditionally controlled personnel assignments. He clashed with cadre chiefs Ezhov (1934–9) and Malenkov (1939–48) over party tactics and strategy. Whereas Zhdanov believed that reeducation and reclamation of party members could solve every problem from bureaucratization to continued political opposition, Ezhov, the mandate checker turned personnel specialist, advocated more stringent selection and security measures. He favored pruning the party through purges and expulsions that inevitably removed the passive and "ballast" elements that Zhdanov the ideologist sought to preserve and educate. . . .

Some will feel that this study has taken a naive view of Stalin's role as planner and perpetrator. There is no doubt that he had chief responsibility for political leadership, but the present account has more than once failed to conclude that the events were part of a coherent plan. Evidence of high-level confusion, counterproductive initiatives, and lack of control over events has not supported the notion of a grand design. Careful analysis of archival, documentary, press, and creditable memoir sources neither supports nor disproves the existence of a plan. It is still possible that the events of 1933–9 were parts of a devilish and devious strategy, but the evidence indicates that a master Stalin plan must remain an a priori assumption, an intuitive guess, or a hypothesis. It can be suspected but not established on the basis of the presently available classes of evidence.

Stalin did not initiate or control everything that happened in the party and country. The number of hours in the day, divided by the number of things for which he was responsible, suggests that his role in many areas could have been little more than occasional intervention, prodding, threatening, or correcting. In the course of a day, Stalin made decisions on everything from hog breeding to subways to national defense. He met with scores of experts, heard dozens of reports, and settled various disputes between contending factions for budgetary or personnel allocations. He was an executive, and reality forced him to delegate most authority to his subordinates, each of whom had his own opinions, client groups, and interests.

It is certainly dangerous to take the speeches of Soviet leaders at face value. All politicians dissimulate about their roles and plans. Yet it is not naive to assume that the speeches and articles of Soviet politicians reflect real conflicts, struggles, and policies. After all, in the political culture of the thirties, Stalin's speeches were taken as revealed truth. They were widely publicized, memorized, discussed, and taken as directives by local party committees. Stalin's word was law, and for this reason alone his pronouncements are worth studying as a certain reflection of political reality.

The problem is to separate Stalin's "real thoughts" from the needs of the "cult of personality." A look at his theoretical pronouncements shows that, like all skilled politicians, he spoke out of both sides of his mouth. Throughout the thirties, Stalin publicly tried to synthesize several points of view. Diametrically opposed moderate sentiments (the period of struggle and repression is over) and radical prescriptions (class struggle and vigilance should increase) were both incorporated into Stalin's public statements.

For example, in his 1934 speech to the Seventeenth Congress, Stalin defended the theory that "intensifying the class struggle" was necessary to build a classless society. In the same speech, though, he proclaimed the "complete victory of Leninism" and observed that opposition in the party had been "utterly demoralized and smashed." "There is nothing to prove and, it seems, no one to fight." The only remaining problem was that "remnants of their [oppositionists'] ideology still live in the minds of individual members," producing "confusion on a number of questions of Leninism." Despite the intensification of struggle, Stalin said that the only necessary measures were those designed to raise the ideological level of the party.

Even in 1937, when he said that "the further forward we advance . . . the greater will be the fury of the remnants of the broken exploiting classes, the sooner they will resort to sharper forms of struggle . . . and . . . clutch at the most desperate means . . . as the last resort of doomed people," he was not technically contradicting his previous assertions on the victory of socialism. The enemy was "broken," "desperate," and "doomed." The means of struggle (assassination) became sharper, but the *level* of class struggle (mass violence and class conflict) was being lowered in the country.

Stalin's facile theoretical combination of the radical and moderate points of view was, to say the least, a flexible one. The synthesis was plausible, appropriate, and optimistic in 1934; but by 1937, after Stalin's gradual swing from moderation to radicalism, it could be used as a theoretical justification for terror.

His vague, Olympian pronouncements demonstrate one use of the "cult of personality": to downplay conflict at higher levels. All Bolshevik politicians conjured up Stalin's approval in support of their particular views. Zhdanov could press for the primacy of party work; Ezhov could call for more vigilance; Molotov could demand faster industrial tempos; Ordzhonikidze could call for moderation; and all of them could invoke quotations from the great Stalin in support. This arrangement not only tended to cover up political disputes but also maximized the dictator's freedom to maneuver. . . .

Western scholars have remained hypnotized by Stalin's cult of personality, and their obsession with him has led to studies of the Great Purges period that provide no detailed investigation of the political, institutional, and structural milieu of the phenomena. Rather than placing events in these contexts, scholars have often discussed the Great Purges only against the background of Stalin's personality and categorized Stalinism simply as the undisputed rule of an omniscient and omnipotent dictator. Contradictions and confusion are seen as manifestations of Stalin's caprice, and too often the political history of the Stalin period has merely been the story of Stalin's supposed activities. An understanding of the thirties based on Stalin's personality is as limiting and incomplete as an explanation of Nazism derived primarily from Hitler's psyche.

It is not necessary for us to put Stalin in day-to-day control of events to judge him. A chaotic local bureaucracy, a quasi-feudal network of politicians accustomed to arresting people, and a set of perhaps insoluble political and social problems created an atmosphere conducive to violence. All it took from Stalin were catalytic and probably ad hoc interventions at three pivotal points — early 1936 (to reopen the Kirov investigation), June 1937 (to unleash Ezhov), and November 1937 (to condemn Piatakov [industrial leader and former Trotskyist]) — to spark an uncontrolled explosion. That he did so intervene speaks for itself.

Actually, the question of Stalin's role as planner was — or should have been — a secondary one in this analysis, which has, rather, tried to show that the party before World War II was a certain type of disorganized and cumbersome machine. The existence of high-level personal rivalries, disputes over development or modernization plans, powerful and conflicting centrifugal and centripetal forces, and local conflicts made large-scale political violence possible and even likely.

The evidence suggests that the Ezhovshchina [the "Ezhov business," when N. I. Ezhov (Yezhov) headed the secret police] — which is what most people really mean by the "Great Purges" — should be redefined. It was not the result of a petrified bureaucracy's stamping out dissent and annihilating old radical revolutionaries. In fact, it may have been just the opposite. It is not inconsistent with the evidence to argue that the Ezhovshchina was rather a radical, even hysterical, *reaction* to bureaucracy. The entrenched officeholders were destroyed from above and below in a chaotic wave of voluntarism and revolutionary puritanism.

The radicalism of the thirties did not last. Although ritualized

kritika/samokritika became a regular part of party pra
never again have the impact it did in 1937. Although
thirties was often populist and even subversive, the
World War II combined with the practical demands of r
creasingly complicated economy meant that radicalism ᵤ ₐₙₜibu-
reaucratism would fade into the past and be replaced by a new respect
for authority. In the thirties, Stalin was often a populist muckraker, and
his image, as Avtorkhanov remembered, was of someone who hated
neckties. The real petrification of the Stalinist system set in during and
after the war, when commissariats became ministries, when the party
leader became premier, and when the man who hated neckties became
the generalissimo.

Nikita S. Khrushchev

The Cult of Personality

The ultimate step of the Stalin Revolution, climaxing the Soviet dictator's
accumulation of personal power, was the Great Purge of 1936–1938. Its
magnitude was officially revealed, along with an attempt to explain its
motives, by Nikita Khrushchev (1898–1971) in his celebrated "Secret
Speech" to the Twentieth Congress of the CPSU in 1956, shortly after he
had succeeded to Stalin's position as party leader. That speech is excerpted here.

When we analyze the practice of Stalin in regard to the direction of the
party and of the country, when we pause to consider everything which
Stalin perpetrated, we must be convinced that Lenin's fears were justified. The negative characteristics of Stalin, which, in Lenin's time,
were only incipient, transformed themselves during the last years into a
grave abuse of power by Stalin, which caused untold harm to our party.

We have to consider seriously and analyze correctly this matter in
order that we may preclude any possibility of a repetition in any form

Excerpts reprinted from the translated text issued by the United States Department of
State, June 4, 1956 (eventually published in the Soviet Union in the official journal
Izvestiya TsK, March 1989).

whatever of what took place during the life of Stalin, who absolutely did not tolerate collegiality in leadership and in work, and who practiced brutal violence, not only toward everything which opposed him, but also toward that which seemed to his capricious and despotic character, contrary to his concepts.

Stalin acted not through persuasion, explanation, and patient cooperation with people, but by imposing his concepts and demanding absolute submission to his opinion. Whoever opposed this concept or tried to prove his viewpoint, and the correctness of his position, was doomed to removal from the leading collective and to subsequent moral and physical annihilation. This was especially true during the period following the Seventeenth Party Congress, when many prominent party leaders and rank-and-file party workers, honest and dedicated to the cause of Communism, fell victim to Stalin's despotism.

We must affirm that the party had fought a serious fight against the Trotskyites, rightists and bourgeois nationalists, and that it disarmed ideologically all the enemies of Leninism. This ideological fight was carried on successfully, as a result of which the party became strengthened and tempered. Here Stalin played a positive role.

The party led a great political ideological struggle against those in its own ranks who proposed anti-Leninist theses, who represented a political line hostile to the party and to the cause of socialism. This was a stubborn and a difficult fight but a necessary one, because the political line of both the Trotskyite-Zinovievite bloc and of the Bukharinites led actually toward the restoration of capitalism and capitulation to the world bourgeoisie. Let us consider for a moment what would have happened if in 1928–1929 the political line of right deviation had prevailed among us, or orientation toward "cotton-dress industrialization," or toward the kulak, etc. We would not now have a powerful heavy industry, we would not have the kolkhozes, we would find ourselves disarmed and weak in a capitalist encirclement.

It was for this reason that the party led an inexorable ideological fight and explained to all party members and to the nonparty masses the harm and the danger of the anti-Leninist proposals of the Trotskyite Opposition and the rightist opportunists. And this great work of explaining the party line bore fruit; both the Trotskyites and the rightist opportunists were politically isolated; the overwhelming party majority supported the Leninist line and the party was able to awaken and organize the working masses to apply the Leninist party line and to build socialism.

Worth noting is the fact that even during the progress of the furious ideological fight against the Trotskyites, the Zinovievites, the Bukharinites and others, extreme repressive measures were not used against them. The fight was on ideological grounds. But some years later when socialism in our country was fundamentally constructed, when the exploiting classes were generally liquidated, when the Soviet social structure had radically changed, when the social basis for political movements and groups hostile to the party had violently contracted, when the ideological opponents of the party were long since defeated politically — then the repression directed against them began.

It was precisely during this period (1935–1937–1938) that the practice of mass repression through the government apparatus was born, first against the enemies of Leninism — Trotskyites, Zinovievites, Bukharinites, long since politically defeated by the party, and subsequently also against many honest Communists, against those party cadres who had borne the heavy load of the Civil War and the first and most difficult years of industrialization and collectivization, who actively fought against the Trotskyites and the rightists for the Leninist party line.

Stalin originated the concept "enemy of the people." This term automatically rendered it unnecessary that the ideological errors of a man or men engaged in a controversy be proven; this term made possible the usage of the most cruel repression, violating all norms of revolutionary legality, against anyone who in any way disagreed with Stalin, against those who were only suspected of hostile intent, against those who had bad reputations. This concept, "enemy of the people," actually eliminated the possibility of any kind of ideological fight or the making of one's views known on this or that issue, even those of a practical character. In the main, and in actuality, the only proof of guilt used, against all norms of current legal science, was the "confession" of the accused himself; and, as subsequent probing proved, confessions were acquired through physical pressures against the accused.

This led to glaring violations of revolutionary legality, and to the fact that many entirely innocent persons, who in the past had defended the party line, became victims.

We must assert that in regard to those persons who in their time had opposed the party line, there were often no sufficiently serious reasons for their physical annihilation. The formula, "enemy of the people," was specifically introduced for the purpose of physically annihilating such individuals.

It is a fact that many persons, who were later annihilated as enemies of the party and people, had worked with Lenin during his life. Some of these persons had made errors during Lenin's life, but, despite this, Lenin benefited by their work, he corrected them and he did everything possible to retain them in the ranks of the party; he induced them to follow him. . . .

Lenin used severe methods only in the most necessary cases, when the exploiting classes were still in existence and were vigorously opposing the revolution, when the struggle for survival was decidedly assuming the sharpest forms, even including a civil war.

Stalin, on the other hand, used extreme methods and mass repressions at a time when the revolution was already victorious, when the Soviet state was strengthened, when the exploiting classes were already liquidated and socialist relations were rooted solidly in all phases of national economy, when our party was politically consolidated and had strengthened itself both numerically and ideologically. It is clear that here Stalin showed in a whole series of cases his intolerance, his brutality and his abuse of power. Instead of proving his political correctness and mobilizing the masses, he often chose the path of repression and physical annihilation, not only against actual enemies, but also against individuals who had not committed any crimes against the party and the Soviet government. Here we see no wisdom but only a demonstration of the brutal force which had once so alarmed V. I. Lenin.

Lately, especially after the unmasking of the Beria[1] gang, the Central Committee has looked into a series of matters fabricated by this gang. This revealed a very ugly picture of brutal willfulness connected with the incorrect behavior of Stalin. As facts prove, Stalin, using his unlimited power, allowed himself many abuses, acting in the name of the Central Committee, not asking for the opinion of the committee members nor even of the members of the Central Committee's Political Bureau; often he did not inform them about his personal decisions concerning very important party and government matters. . . .

In practice Stalin ignored the norms of party life and trampled on the Leninist principle of collective party leadership.

Stalin's willfulness vis-à-vis the party and its Central Committee became fully evident after the Seventeenth Party Congress which took place in 1934.

---

[1] Lavrenty Beria, head of the secret police, 1938–1953; executed after Stalin's death. — Ed.

Having at its disposal numerous data showing brutal willfulness toward party cadres, the Central Committee has created a Party Commission under the control of the Central Committee Presidium; it was charged with investigating what made possible the mass repressions against the majority of the Central Committee members and candidates elected at the Seventeenth Congress of the All-Union Communist Party (Bolsheviks).

The commission has become acquainted with a large quantity of materials in the NKVD[2] archives and with other documents and has established many facts pertaining to the fabrication of cases against Communists, to false accusations, to glaring abuses of socialist legality — which resulted in the death of innocent people. It became apparent that many party, Soviet and economic activists who were branded in 1937–1938 as "enemies" were actually never enemies, spies, wreckers, and so forth, but were always honest Communists; they were only so stigmatized, and often, no longer able to bear barbaric tortures, they charged themselves (at the order of the investigative judges-falsifiers) with all kinds of grave and unlikely crimes. The commission has presented to the Central Committee Presidium lengthy and documented materials pertaining to mass repressions against the delegates to the Seventeenth Party Congress and against members of the Central Committee elected at that Congress. These materials have been studied by the Presidium of the Central Committee.

It was determined that of the 139 members and candidates of the party's Central Committee who were elected at the Seventeenth Congress, 98 persons, that is, 70 percent, were arrested and shot (mostly in 1937–1938). (*Indignation in the hall.*)

What was the composition of the delegates to the Seventeenth Congress? It is known that 80 percent of the voting participants of the Seventeenth Congress joined the party during the years of conspiracy before the revolution and during the Civil War; this means before 1921. By social origin the basic mass of the delegates to the congress were workers (60 percent of the voting members).

For this reason, it was inconceivable that a congress so composed would have elected a Central Committee, a majority of which would prove to be enemies of the party. The only reason why 70 percent of the Central Committee members and candidates elected at the Seventeenth

---

[2] People's Commissariat of Internal Affairs, which included the secret police after 1934. — Ed.

Nikita Khrushchev at the Twentieth Party Congress, 1956, where he delivered his "Secret Speech." (Sovfoto)

Congress were branded as enemies of the party and of the people was that honest Communists were slandered, accusations against them were fabricated, and revolutionary legality was gravely undermined.

The same fate met not only the Central Committee members but also the majority of the delegates to the Seventeenth Party Congress. Of 1,966 delegates with either voting or advisory rights, 1,108 persons were arrested on charges of antirevolutionary crimes, that is, decidedly more than a majority. This very fact shows how absurd, wild and contrary to common sense were the charges of counterrevolutionary crimes made out, as we now see, against a majority of participants at the Seventeenth Party Congress. (*Indignation in the hall.*)

We should recall that the Seventeenth Party Congress is historically known as the Congress of Victors. Delegates to the congress were active participants in the building of our socialist state; many of them suffered and fought for party interests during the prerevolutionary years in the conspiracy and at the Civil War fronts; they fought their enemies valiantly and often nervelessly looked into the face of death. How then can we believe that such people could prove to be "two-faced" and had joined the camps of the enemies of socialism during the era after the political liquidation of Zinovievites, Trotskyites and rightists and after the great accomplishments of socialist construction?

This was the result of the abuse of power by Stalin, who began to use mass terror against the party cadres.

What is the reason that mass repressions against activists increased more and more after the Seventeenth Party Congress? It was because at that time Stalin had so elevated himself above the party and above the nation that he ceased to consider either the Central Committee or the party. While he still reckoned with the opinion of the collective before the Seventeenth Congress, after the complete political liquidation of the Trotskyites, Zinovievites and Bukharinites, when as a result of that fight and socialist victories the party achieved unity, Stalin ceased to an ever greater degree to consider the members of the party's Central Committee and even the members of the Political Bureau. Stalin thought that now he could decide all things alone and all he needed were statisticians; he treated all others in such a way that they could only listen to and praise him.

After the criminal murder of S. M. Kirov, mass repressions and brutal acts of violation of socialist legality began. On the evening of December 1, 1934, on Stalin's initiative (without the approval of the Political Bureau — which was passed two days later, casually) the secretary of the Presidium of the Central Executive Committee, Yenukidze, signed the following directive.

  I. *Investigative agencies are directed to speed up the cases of those accused of the preparation or execution of acts of terror.*

 II. *Judicial organs are directed not to hold up the execution of death sentences pertaining to crimes of this category in order to consider the possibility of pardon, because the Presidium of the Central Executive Committee [of the] USSR does not consider as possible the receiving of petitions of this sort.*

III. *The organs of the Commissariat of Internal Affairs [NKVD] are directed to execute death sentences against criminals of the above-mentioned category immediately after the passage of sentences.*

This directive became the basis for mass acts of abuse against socialist legality. During many of the fabricated court cases the accused were charged with "the preparation" of terroristic acts; this deprived them of any possibility that their cases might be reexamined, even when they stated before the court that their "confessions" were secured by force, and when, in a convincing manner, they disproved the accusations against them.

It must be asserted that to this day the circumstances surrounding Kirov's murder hide many things which are inexplicable and mysterious and demand a most careful examination. There are reasons for the suspicion that the killer of Kirov, Nikolayev, was assisted by someone from among the people whose duty it was to protect the person of Kirov. A month and a half before the killing, Nikolayev was arrested on the grounds of suspicious behavior, but he was released and not even searched. It is an unusually suspicious circumstance that when the Chekist[3] assigned to protect Kirov was being brought for an interrogation, on December 2, 1934, he was killed in a car "accident" in which no other occupants of the car were harmed. After the murder of Kirov, top functionaries of the Leningrad NKVD were given very light sentences, but in 1937 they were shot. We can assume that they were shot in order to cover the traces of the organizers of Kirov's killing. (*Movement in the hall.*)

Mass repressions grew tremendously from the end of 1936 after a telegram from Stalin and Zhdanov, dated from Sochi on September 25, 1936, was addressed to Kaganovich, Molotov and other members of the Political Bureau. The content of the telegram was as follows:

> *We deem it absolutely necessary and urgent that Comrade Yezhov be nominated to the post of people's commissar for internal affairs. Yagoda has definitely proved himself to be incapable of unmasking the Trotsky-ite-Zinovievite block. The OGPU [secret police; same as GPU] is four years behind in this matter. This is noted by all party workers and by the majority of the representatives of the NKVD.*

Strictly speaking we should stress that Stalin did not meet with and therefore could not know the opinion of party workers.

This Stalinist formulation that the "NKVD is four years behind" in applying mass repression and that there is a necessity for "catching up" with the neglected work directly pushed the NKVD workers on the path of mass arrests and executions.

We should state that this formulation was also forced on the February–March plenary session of the Central Committee of the All-Union Communist Party (Bolsheviks) in 1937. The plenary resolution ap-

---

[3] "Chekist" — familiar term for a member of the secret police, from "Cheka," the name of the secret police, 1917–1922. — Ed.

proved it on the basis of Yezhov's report, "Lessons flowing from the harmful activity, diversion and espionage of the Japanese-German-Trotskyite agents," stating:

> *The plenum of the Central Committee of the All-Union Communist Party (Bolsheviks) considers that all facts revealed during the investigation into the matter of an anti-Soviet Trotskyite center and of its followers in the provinces show that the People's Commissariat of Internal Affairs has fallen behind at least four years in the attempt to unmask these most inexorable enemies of the people.*

The mass repressions at this time were made under the slogan of a fight against the Trotskyites. Did the Trotskyites at this time actually constitute such a danger to our party and to the Soviet state? We should recall that in 1927 on the eve of the Fifteenth Party Congress only some 4,000 votes were cast for the Trotskyite-Zinovievite Opposition, while there were 724,000 for the party line. During the ten years which passed between the Fifteenth Party Congress and the February–March Central Committee plenum Trotskyism was completely disarmed; many former Trotskyites had changed their former views and worked in the various sectors building socialism. It is clear that in the situation of socialist victory there was no basis for mass terror in the country.

Stalin's report at the February-March Central Committee plenum in 1937, "Deficiencies of party work and methods for the liquidation of the Trotskyites and of other two-facers," contained an attempt at theoretical justification of the mass terror policy under the pretext that as we march forward toward socialism, class war must allegedly sharpen. Stalin asserted that both history and Lenin taught him this.

Actually Lenin taught that the application of revolutionary violence is necessitated by the resistance of the exploiting classes, and this referred to the era when the exploiting classes existed and were powerful. As soon as the nation's political situation had improved, when in January 1920 the Red Army took Rostov and thus won a most important victory over Denikin [the top "white" general], Lenin instructed Dzerzhinsky [the head of the Cheka] to stop mass terror and to abolish the death penalty. Lenin justified this important political move of the Soviet state in the following manner in his report at the session of the All-Union Central Executive Committee on February 2, 1920:

> *We were forced to use terror because of the terror practiced by the Entente, when strong world powers threw their hordes against us, not avoiding any type of combat. We would not have lasted two days had*

> *we not answered these attempts of officers and White Guardists in a*
> *merciless fashion; this meant the use of terror, but this was forced upon*
> *us by the terrorist methods of the Entente.*
>
> *But as soon as we attained a decisive victory, even before the end of*
> *the war, immediately after taking Rostov, we gave up the use of the*
> *death penalty and thus proved that we intend to execute our own*
> *program in the manner that we promised. We say that the application*
> *of violence flows out of the decision to smother the exploiters, the big*
> *landowners and the capitalists; as soon as this was accomplished we*
> *gave up the use of all extraordinary methods. We have proved this in*
> *practice.*

Stalin deviated from these clear and plain precepts of Lenin. Stalin put the party and the NKVD up to the use of mass terror when the exploiting classes had been liquidated in our country and when there were no serious reasons for the use of extraordinary mass terror.

This terror was actually directed not at the remnants of the defeated exploiting classes but against the honest workers of the party and of the Soviet state; against them were made lying, slanderous and absurd accusations concerning "two-facedness," "espionage," "sabotage," preparation of fictitious "plots," and so forth.

At the February–March Central Committee plenum in 1937 many members actually questioned the rightness of the established course regarding mass repressions under the pretext of combating "two-facedness."

Comrade Postyshev[4] most ably expressed these doubts. He said:

> *I have philosophized that the severe years of fighting have passed; party*
> *members who have lost their backbones have broken down or have joined*
> *the camp of the enemy; healthy elements have fought for the party.*
> *These were the years of industrialization and collectivization. I never*
> *thought it possible that after this severe era had passed Karpov and*
> *people like him would find themselves in the camp of the enemy. (Kar-*
> *pov was a worker in the Ukrainian Central Committee whom Postyshev*
> *knew well.) And now, according to the testimony, it appears that*
> *Karpov was recruited in 1934 by the Trotskyites. I personally do not*
> *believe that in 1934 an honest party member who had trod the long road*
> *of unrelenting fight against enemies, for the party and for socialism,*
> *would now be in the camp of the enemies. I do not believe it . . . I can-*
> *not imagine how it would be possible to travel with the party during the*
> *difficult years and then, in 1934, join the Trotskyites. It is an odd thing.*

---

[4]At the time, second secretary for the Ukraine; later purged. — Ed.

(*Movement in the hall.*)

Using Stalin's formulation, namely that the closer we are to socialism, the more enemies we will have, and using the resolution of the February–March Central Committee plenum passed on the basis of Yezhov's report — the provocateurs who had infiltrated the state security organs together with conscienceless careerists began to protect with the party name the mass terror against party cadres, cadres of the Soviet state and the ordinary Soviet citizens. It should suffice to say that the number of arrests based on charges of counterrevolutionary crimes had grown ten times between 1936 and 1937.

It is known that brutal willfulness was practiced against leading party workers. The Party Statute, approved at the Seventeenth Party Congress, was based on Leninist principles expressed at the Tenth Party Congress. It stated that in order to apply an extreme method such as exclusion from the party against a Central Committee member, against a Central Committee candidate, and against a member of the Party Control Commission, "It is necessary to call a Central Committee plenum and to invite to the plenum all Central Committee candidate members and all members of the Party Control Commission"; only if two thirds of the members of such a general assembly of responsible party leaders find it necessary, only then can a Central Committee member or candidate be expelled.

The majority of the Central Committee members and candidates elected at the Seventeenth Congress and arrested in 1937–1938 were expelled from the party illegally through the brutal abuse of the Party Statute, because the question of their expulsion was never studied at the Central Committee plenum.

Now when the cases of some of these so-called "spies" and "saboteurs" were examined it was found that all their cases were fabricated. Confessions of guilt of many arrested and charged with enemy activity were gained with the help of cruel and inhuman tortures.

At the same time Stalin, as we have been informed by members of the Political Bureau of that time, did not show them the statements of many accused political activists when they retracted their confessions before the military tribunal and asked for an objective examination of their cases. There were many such declarations, and Stalin doubtlessly knew of them.

The Central Committee considers it absolutely necessary to inform the congress of many such fabricated "cases" against the members of the party's Central Committee elected at the Seventeenth Party Congress.

Leon Trotsky in exile in Mexico, 1937, denouncing the Moscow purge trials. (UPI/ Bettmann Newsphotos)

Interpretations
and Perspectives

James H. Billington

The Legacy of
Russian History

From the standpoint of the historian of Russian culture there is much that
is familiar in the method and spirit of Stalin's rule, harking back more to
the tone of old Muscovy than to the westernizing currents of the immediate
prerevolutionary and postrevolutionary eras. James Billington, formerly a
professor of history at Princeton University and now the Librarian of Congress, in this selection from his monumental account of the development of
the Russian mind, *The Icon and the Axe*, sets Stalin squarely in the old
tradition.

From *The Icon and the Axe: An Interpretive History of Russian Culture*, by James H.
Billington, pp. 532–540, 544–545. Copyright © 1966 by James H. Billington. Reprinted
by permission of Alfred A. Knopf, Inc.

For the historian of culture, Lenin's brief rule was still something of a chaotic interregnum; and it is the age of blood and iron under Stalin that marks the real watershed. Once his dictatorial power was securely established in the late twenties, Stalin systematically imposed on Russia a new monolithic culture that represented the antithesis of the varied, cosmopolitan, and experimental culture that had continued on into the twenties from prerevolutionary days. During the quarter of a century that stretched from the beginning of his First Five-Year Plan in 1928 to his death in 1953, Stalin sought to convert all creative thinkers into "engineers of the human soul." They were to be cheerleaders along his assembly lines — deliberately kept uncertain of what cheer was required of them and denied that last refuge of human integrity in most earlier tyrannies: the freedom to be silent. . . .

The qualities that Stalin professed to admire in Lenin — "hatred for sniveling intellectuals, confidence in one's own strength, confidence in victory" — were those which he attempted to instill in himself. To these were added the compulsive chauvinism of the provincial parvenu, the scholastic dogmatism of the half-educated seminarian, and a preoccupation with organizational intrigue already noticeable during his revolutionary apprenticeship in the world's largest oil fields in Baku.

Stalin's only god was Lenin; yet in Stalin's depiction the god acquires a bestial if not satanic form. Stalin compared Lenin's arguments to "a mighty tentacle which twines all around you and holds you as a vice"; Lenin was said to have been obsessively concerned that the enemy "has been beaten but by no means crushed" and to have rebuked his friends "bitingly through clenched teeth: 'Don't whine, comrades. . . .'"

Stalin's formula for authoritarian rule was experimental and eclectic. It might be described as Bolshevism with teeth or Leninism minus Lenin's broad Russian nature and ranging mind. Lenin, for all his preoccupation with power and organization, had remained, in part, a child of the Volga. He had a revolutionary mission thrust upon him and took his revolutionary name from one of the great rivers of the Russian interior: the Lena.

Stalin, by contrast, was an outsider from the hills, devoid of all personal magnetism, who properly derived his revolutionary name from *stal'*, the Russian word for "steel." His closest comrade — and the man he picked to succeed him as formal head of state throughout the 1930s went even further — shed his family name of Scriabin, so rich in cultural association, for Molotov, a name derived from the Russian word for "hammer." No figure better illustrates the unfeeling bluntness and technological preoccupations of the new Soviet culture than this expressionless bureaucratic hammer of the Stalin era, who was generally known as "stone bottom" (from "the stone backside of the hammer" — *kamenny zad molotova*).

Yet for all the grotesqueness, gigantomania, and Caucasian intrigue of the Stalin era, it may in some way have had roots in Russian culture deeper than those of the brief age of Lenin. Lenin benefited from the St. Petersburg tradition of the radical intelligentsia, studied briefly in St. Petersburg, began his revolution there, and was to give his name to the city. When Lenin moved the capital from St. Petersburg and entered the Moscow Kremlin for the first time on March 12, 1918, he was uncharacteristically agitated, remarking to his secretary and companion that "worker-peasant power should be completely consolidated here." Little did he imagine how permanent the change of capital was to prove and how extensive the consolidation of power in the Kremlin. The year of Lenin's death brought a flood to the former capital, newly rebaptized as Leningrad. It was an omen perhaps of the traditionalist flood that was about to sweep the revolutionary spirit out of the Leninist party. With Stalin in the Kremlin, Moscow at last wreaked its revenge on St. Petersburg, seeking to wipe out the restless reformism and critical cosmopolitanism which this "window to the West" had always symbolized.

Stalin had many roots in the Russian past. His addiction to mass armies overbalanced with artillery follows a long tradition leading back to Ivan the Terrible; his xenophobic and disciplinarian conception of education is reminiscent of Magnitsky, Nicholas I, and Pobedonostsev,[1] his passion for material innovation and war-supporting technology echoes Peter the Great and a number of nineteenth-century Russian industrialists. But Stalinism in the full sense of the word seems to have its deepest roots in two earlier periods of Russian history: the nihilistic 1860s and the pre-Petrine era.

First of all, Stalinism appears as a conscious throwback to the

---

[1] Mikhail Magnitsky, conservative education official under Tsar Alexander I; Nicholas I, Tsar 1825–1855; Konstantin Pobedonostsev, conservative chief of religious affairs under Alexander III and Nicholas II, and tutor to the latter. — Ed.

militant materialism of the 1860s. Insofar as there was a positive content to Stalinist culture, it was rooted in the ascetic dedication to progress of the materialistic sixties rather than the idealistic spirit of the populist age. Stalin and some of his close associates — Molotov, Khrushchev, and Mikoyan — were like Chernyshevsky[2] and so many other men of the sixties largely educated by priests, and had merely changed catechisms in midstream. Stalin's belief in physiological and environmental determinism — evidenced in his canonization of Pavlov and Lysenko[3] — reflects the polemic prejudices of Pisarev[4] more than the complex theories of Engels, let alone the thoughts of practicing scientists. His suspicion of all artistic activity without immediate social utility reflects the crude aesthetic theory of the sixties more than that of Marx.

All of the enforced artistic styles of the Stalin era — the photographic posters, the symphonies of socialism, the propagandistic novels, and the staccato civic poetry — appear as distorted vulgarizations of the predominant styles of the 1860s: the realism of the "wanderers," the programmatic music of the "mighty handful," the novels of social criticism, and the poems of Nekrasov. This artificial resurrection of long-absent styles brought a forced end to the innovations in form so characteristic of art in the silver age. Whole areas of expression were blighted: lyric poetry, satirical prose, experimental theater, and modern painting and music.

Art was, henceforth, to be subject not just to party censorship but to the mysterious requirements of "socialist realism." This doctrine called for two mutually exclusive qualities: revolutionary enthusiasm and objective depiction of reality. It was, in fact, a formula for keeping writers in a state of continuing uncertainty as to what was required of them: an invaluable device for humiliating the intellectuals by encouraging the debilitating phenomena of anticipatory self-censorship. It seems appropriate that the phrase was first used by a leading figure in the secret police rather than a literary personality. Publicly pronounced in 1934 at the First Congress of the Union of Writers by Andrei Zhdanov, Stalin's aide-de-camp on the cultural front, the doctrine was given a measure of respectability by the presence of Maxim Gorky as

[2] Nikolai Chernyshevsky — nihilist critic and writer of the mid-nineteenth century. — Ed.

[3] Ivan Pavlov, the psychologist; Trofim Lysenko, the quack geneticist. — Ed.

[4] Dmitri Pisarev — nihilist critic and writer of the mid-nineteenth century. — Ed.

presiding figurehead at the congress. Gorky was one of the few figures of stature who could be held up as an exemplar of the new doctrine. He had a simple background, genuine socialist convictions, and a natural realistic style developed in a series of epic novels and short stories about Russian society of the late imperial period.

Socialist realism no less than the revolution itself was to "dispose of its children." Gorky died under still-mysterious circumstances two years later in the midst of the terror which swept away imaginative storytellers like Pil'niak and Babel, lyric poets like Mandel'shtam, theatrical innovators like Meierhold, as well as the inclination toward experimentalism in such gifted young artists as Shostakovich. . . .

The peculiarities of Stalinist architecture lead us into a world very different from anything imagined by Lenin, let alone the materialists of the 1860s. The mammoth mosaics in the Moscow subway, the unnecessary spires and fantastic frills of civic buildings, the leaden chandeliers and dark foyers of reception chambers — all send the historical imagination back to the somber world of Ivan the Terrible. Indeed, the culture of the Stalin era seems more closely linked with ancient Muscovy than with even the rawest stages of St. Petersburg-based radicalism. One can, to be sure, find a certain bias in favor of bigness in the earlier period of rapid industrial development in the 1890s — evidenced in the preponderance of large factory complexes and in the building of the Trans-Siberian railway. There are also hints of classical Oriental despotism in the spectacle of giant canals and ostentatious public buildings thrown up by forced labor. Plans for a canal strikingly similar to Stalin's famous White Sea Canal of the early thirties had been mooted late in the Muscovite era at the court of Alexis Mikhailovich.[5] If this, the first major forced labor project of the Soviet era, had in some ways been anticipated in the Muscovite era, the site chosen in the twenties for the first of the new prison camp complexes of the USSR was one of the enduring symbols of Old Muscovy: the Solovetsk monastery. Ivan IV had been the first to use this bleak island monastery near the Arctic Circle as a prison for ideological opponents, and the Soviet government — by evacuating the monks — was able to accommodate large numbers.

Quietly heroic testimony to some survival of Old Russian culture

[5] Tsar, 1645–1676. — Ed.

into the twenties is provided in the works published with the apparent consent of camp authorities by intellectuals incarcerated on the archipelago. In the monthly journal *Solovetsk Islands*, "an organ of the directorate of the Solovetsk Camps of ordinary designation OGPU," we read during the twenties of new discoveries of flora, fauna, and historical remains; of the founding of new museums; of 234 theatrical performances in a single year; and of a nineteen-kilometer ski race between inmates, Red Army guards, and the camp directorate. One article writes with obvious sympathy about Artemius, the first prisoner in Solovetsk under Ivan IV, as "a great seeker of truth and an agitator for freedom of thought."

The camps of the Stalin era seemed at times to contain more scholars than the universities; but the relative freedom of Solovetsk in the early days was not to be maintained in the thirties; and only the terrible northern cold was to remain a constant feature of Stalin's concentration-camp empire. It seems eerily appropriate that the last publications to appear from Solovetsk (in 1934–1935, long after the monthly journal had ceased to appear) tell of discovering prehistoric relics on the archipelago and exploring the vast, uncharted labyrinths that had long fascinated visitors to the monastery.

At the very time when the emaciated prisoners of Solovetsk were plunging down to chart its frozen catacombs, thousands of laborers under various forms of compulsion were plunging even deeper beneath Moscow itself to build the greatest of all monuments of the Stalin era: the Moscow subway. From all over the empire party officials flocked to the capital like the faceless priests of some prehistoric religion to place ornate stalactites and stalagmites from the local republics into this giant communal labyrinth. The cult of the underground party also began in earnest at this time. Traditional idealistic leaders of foreign Communist parties began to be replaced by serpentine Stalinists: a cold-blooded species capable of fast, lizard-like movements in dark places and sudden chameleon-like changes of color.

Silenced prisoners in Solovetsk and authoritarian power in the Moscow Kremlin present a picture strangely reminiscent of ancient Muscovy. In some ways, the Stalin era calls to mind the compulsive Byzantine ritualism of those pre-Petrine times which had remained "contemporary" for so many Russians throughout the Romanov era. Icons, incense, and ringing bells were replaced by lithographs of Lenin, cheap perfume, and humming machines. The omnipresent prayers and calls to worship of Orthodoxy were replaced by the inescapable loud-speaker or radio with its hypnotic statistics and invocations to labor. The liturgy or "common work" of believers was replaced by the communal construction of scientific atheists. The role once played by the sending of priests and missionaries along with colonizing soldiers into the heathen interior of Russia was now assumed by "soldiers of the cultural army," who departed from mass rallies for "cultural relay races" into the countryside to see who could win the most converts for communism and collectivization in the shortest possible time.

Something like the role of the holy fools and flagellants of Muscovy was played by frenzied "heroes of socialist labor" ascetically dedicated to "overfulfilling their norms." Just as Ivan the Terrible canonized his favorite holy fool and built a cathedral later named for him, so Stalin canonized and built a national movement around Nicholas Stakhanov, a coal miner who in a fit of heroic masochism cut out 102 tons of coal (fourteen times his quota) in one shift. "Voluntary subscriptions to the state loan" replaced earlier tithes as a token of devotion to the new church; the "shock quarter" of the year replaced Lent as the periodic time of self-denial in the name of a higher cause. Like the zealous Old Believers, who sought to storm the gates of heaven by outdoing the Orthodox in their fanatical adherence to the letter of the old liturgy, the Stakhanovites sought to hasten the millennium by their "storming" (*shturmovshchina*) of production quotas. These were looked at in the way the Old Believers looked at sacred texts: as something not to be tampered with by bureaucratic innovators or scoffed at by Western skeptics, as a program of salvation if acted upon with urgency.

The Third Rome[6] had been succeeded by a new Third International; and the ideal cultural expression in the latter as in the former was the believer's cry of hallelujah in response to the revealed word from Moscow. The term *alliluishchik* ("hallelujah singer") was in fact widely used in the Stalin era. Russia, which had overthrown a discredited monarchy, suddenly fell back on the most primitive aspect of the original tsarist mystique: the idea that the *batiushka*, the father-deliverer in the Kremlin, would rescue his suffering children from malevolent local officials and lead them into the promised land.

---

[6] Nationalistic theory of the sixteenth century, holding that Moscow was the successor to the Roman and Byzantine empires. — Ed.

Thus, Stalin was able to succeed Lenin as supreme dictator not only because he was a deft intriguer and organizer but also because he was closer than his rivals to the crude mentality of the average Russian. Unlike most other Bolshevik leaders — many of whom were of Jewish, Polish, or Baltic origin — Stalin had been educated only in the catechistic theology of Orthodoxy. At Lenin's funeral, when the other Bolshevik leaders were speaking in the involved rhetoric and glowing generalities of the intellectual community, Stalin spoke in terms more familiar to the masses with his litany-like exhortations:

> *Departing from us, Comrade Lenin adjured us to hold high and keep pure the great title of member of the party. We swear to thee, Comrade Lenin, that we will fulfill thy bequest with honor! . . .*
>
> *Departing from us, Comrade Lenin adjured us to guard the unity of our party like the apple of our eye. We swear to thee, Comrade Lenin, that this obligation, too, we will fulfill with honor!*

The seminarian was clearly in a better position than the cosmopolitan to create a national religion of Leninism. He felt no sense of embarrassment as Lenin's embalmed body was laid out for public veneration with hands folded in the manner of the saints in the monastery of the caves of Kiev. The incongruous mausoleum in Red Square, which paid tribute to Lenin and the new order by exemplifying the purely proletarian "constructivist" style of architecture, was forced to pay a deeper tribute to an older order represented by the crypt beneath and the Kremlin walls above it. Stalin transformed the simple building into a shrine for pilgrims and the site of his own periodic epiphanies on festal days. He chose the traditional, theological way of immortalizing Lenin in contrast to the Promethean effort by the revolutionary intellectuals to discover after Lenin's death the material forces behind his genius through "cyto-architectonic" research (involving imported German scientists, innumerable microphotographs of his brain, and the projected comparative study of minute cranial slices from other leading thinkers).

For the rest of his life Stalin claimed to be nothing more than the rock on which Lenin had built his church. His theoretical writings were always presented as updated thoughts on "problems of Leninism." In the name of Lenin's theory of the past Stalin felt free to contradict both Lenin and himself and, of course, to suppress Lenin's final uncomplimentary assessment of Stalin.

Along with the forms of theological discourse went the new content of Great Russian patriotism. Stalin rehabilitated a whole host of Russian national heroes in the thirties and introduced ever sharper differentiations in pay and privilege to goad on production. The ingeniously Marxist and almost nameless sociological histories of Pokrovsky, which had dominated Soviet historical writing until his death in 1932, were "unmasked" two years later as a deviation from "true Marxism," which henceforth glorified such unproletarian figures as Peter the Great and General Suvorov. The fiercely proletarian novels of the period of the First Five-Year Plan, such as *Cement* and *How the Steel Was Tempered*, were replaced by a new wave of chauvinistic novels and films glorifying Russian warriors of the past.

By the late thirties, Stalin had produced a curious new mass culture that could be described by inverting his classic phrase "nationalist in form, socialist in content." The *forms* of Russian life were now clearly socialist: all agriculture had been collectivized and all of Russia's expanding means of production brought under state ownership and central planning. But socialization throughout the Stalin era brought few material benefits to the consumer, or spiritual benefits to those concerned with greater equality or increased freedom. The *content* of the new ersatz culture was retrogressively nationalistic. Under a patina of constitutions and legal procedures lay the dead hand of Nicholas I's official nationalism and some of the macabre touches of Ivan the Terrible. Stalin's proudly announced "wave of the future" looks, on closer analysis, more like backwash from the past: ghostly voices suddenly returning like the legendary chimes from the submerged city of Kitezh on Midsummer Eve — only to jangle on uncontrolled and out of tune.

. . .

Perhaps the best synoptic view of Russian culture under Stalin is provided by the development of the cinema, an art medium with little history prior to the Soviet period. The innumerable movie theaters large and small that sprang up all over the USSR in the twenties and thirties were the new regime's equivalent to the churches of an earlier age. Within the theaters, the prescribed rituals of the new order — its chronicles of success and promises of bliss — were systematically and regularly presented to the silent masses, whose main image of a world beyond that of immediate physical necessity was now derived from a screen of moving pictures rather than a screen of stationary icons. Like Soviet industry, the cinema produced in the age of Stalin a great quantity of films, including some of real quality. Yet despite the many new techniques and skilled artists involved, the Stalinist cinema represents a regressive chapter in the history of Russian culture. At best, it offered little more than a pretentious extension of the most chauvinistic aspects of prerevolutionary culture; at worst it was a technological monstrosity seeking to cannibalize one of the world's most promising theatrical traditions.

Hopes were high when idealistic young revolutionaries first wandered into the deserted studios of the infant Russian film industry during the revolutionary period. Here was an art medium closely linked to the liberating force of technology, uniquely suitable for spreading the good news of a new social order to all people. Here also was a relatively untouched world of artistic possibility: a cultural *tabula rasa*. For, since the first public movie theater had appeared in 1903, the Russian film industry had assumed no very distinctive character. It was an imitative, commercially oriented medium largely involved in producing never-never land sentimentality and melodramatic happy endings.

Placed under the commissariat of education by a Leninist decree of August 1919, and faced with the emigration of almost all its artists and technicians, the Soviet film industry became a major center for on-the-job training in the arts and an arena for florid experimentation.

During the relatively relaxed period of the early twenties a variety of new styles appeared, and a vigorous discussion ensued about the nature of cinematic art and its relation to the new social order. The remarkable "movie eye" (*kinoko*) group flourished briefly, with its fanatical dedication to documentary accuracy and precise chronology; a former architect and sculptor, Leo Kuleshov, pioneered in the use of open-air scenes, untrained actors, and monumental compositions; and scattered efforts were made to break down the flow of pictures into expressionistic or abstract forms.

But as in all fields of Soviet culture, the rise of Stalin to absolute power in the late twenties led to the adoption of a propagandistic official style that brought an end to creative experiment. The new style was perhaps the best example of that blend of revolutionary message and realistic form that came to be called socialist realism. At the same time, the subject matter of the cinema in the thirties and forties illustrates the increasing drift toward chauvinistic traditionalism in Stalinist Russia.

There were many influences behind the new Soviet film style. In a sense it was a return to the old tradition of the illustrated chronicle (*litsevaia letopis'*) with which the heroic history of the Church Victorious had been popularized in the late Muscovy. It was also a continuation and vulgarization of the traditions of heroic historical painting and mammoth exhibitions that had been developed in the nineteenth century. To these traditions was added the dream of a new type of revolutionary mystery play originated during the exciting days of War Communism. Open-air mass theatrical pageants were improvised as thousands took part in a cycle which attempted to reenact seven major popular revolutions in Russian history; eighty thousand took part in Maiakovsky's *Mystery-Bouffe*, and more than one hundred thousand in the ritual reenactment of the storming of the Winter Palace. Michelet said that the French Revolution really began not with the storming of the Bastille on July 14, 1789, but with the symbolic reenactment of the event a year later. In like manner, one could say that the Russian Revolution — as a symbol of liberation — was born not in the turbulent events of November, 1917, but in these subsequent scenes of pictorial pageantry and mythic recreation.

Robert C. Tucker

A New Stage in the Revolution

Robert C. Tucker is Professor Emeritus of politics at Princeton University and a noted authority on Stalin and Stalinism. The following analysis of the Stalin Revolution as a new phase in the Russian revolutionary process is excerpted from Professor Tucker's contribution to a major symposium on Stalinism that he organized and edited.

Western scholarship has been tardy in fixing analytic attention upon Stalinism. A bulky historical literature on the Stalin period and many biographies and memoirs dealing with the man Stalin coexist with a dearth of interpretive discussion of the "ism," by which I mean not alone the body of thought but the entire Stalinist phenomenon as an historical stage in the development of the Russian and other Communist revolutions and of Communism as a culture.

From Robert C. Tucker, "Stalinism as Revolution from Above," in *Stalinism: Essays in Historical Interpretation*, 1977, pp. 77–78, 82–85, 87–92, 94–98, 102–104. Reprinted by permission of the author.

To some degree, this situation shows the impact of Soviet thought patterns upon our scholarship. From the mid-1920's, it became a firm article of doctrine in the Communist movement that the only legitimate "ism" was Leninism — or Marxism-Leninism, to use the subsequently adopted phrase. Stalin himself never countenanced the use of "Stalinism" because of the deviational implications it would consequently have carried. The forcible mass collectivization, the industrialization drive, and other events of the Stalinist revolution from above of the 1930's were officially described as Marxism-Leninism in action — the natural and logical unfolding of the original Leninist revolutionary impulse and program. There was a strong tendency in the Western sovietological literature of the 1940's and 1950's to give credence to this claim, albeit with a different moral judgment on the process. As a sample of — and perhaps epitaph on — the tendency in question, we may cite the following: "Stalinism can and must be defined as a pattern of thought and action that flows directly from Leninism. Stalin's way of looking at the contemporary world, his professed aims, the decisions he made at variance with one another, his conceptions of the tasks facing the communist state — these and many specific traits are entirely Leninist."[1] From such a standpoint, there was no special problem of interpretive understanding of "Stalinism."

Although Stalin never, not even at the height of his personality cult, tolerated the use of the term "Stalinism," he and his party allies of the mid-1920's employed (or, as Trotsky maintained, concocted) the term "Trotskyism" as the emblem of a system of political heresy against Leninism. For Trotsky and his followers, however, the heresy was the political line that Stalin and his associates were pursuing and the ideological tenets, like "socialism in one country," which they were using in justification of the line. So it is in the Trotskyist polemical literature that we find the earliest interpretive and critical discussion of Stalinism. In this interpretation, Stalinism appeared as the practice, and its reflection in theory, of a conservative bureaucratic takeover of the Bolshevik Revolution, a Soviet Thermidor, of which Stalin himself was merely the representative figure and symbol.

In contradistinction to the first of the two positions just mentioned, I hold that Stalinism must be recognized as an historically distinct and

---

[1] Alfred G. Meyer, *Leninism* (Cambridge, Mass., 1957), pp. 282–83.

specific phenomenon which did *not* flow directly from Leninism, although Leninism was an important contributory factor. In contradistinction to the second, I will argue here (1) that Stalinism, despite conservative, reactionary, or counter-revolutionary elements in its makeup, was a revolutionary phenomenon in essence; (2) that the Stalinist revolution from above, whatever the contingencies involved in its inception and pattern, was an integral phase of the Russian revolutionary process as a whole; and (3) that notable among the causal factors explaining why the Stalinist phase occurred, or why it took the form it did, are the heritage of Bolshevik revolutionism, the heritage of old Russia, and the mind and personality of Stalin. . . .

History, as we know, did not go the way that Lenin charted; it went the Stalinist way. This was radically different from the path delineated in those Lenin articles of the final period that Bukharin, in the essay that he published in *Pravda* in January 1929 for the fifth anniversary of Lenin's death, described as "Lenin's Political Testament." Stalinism in its time of self-assertion and triumph, the 1930's, was a revolution in exactly the sense that Lenin had defined it in warning against a revolutionary approach to the further building of Soviet socialism: "a change which breaks the old order to its very foundations, and not one that cautiously, slowly, and gradually remodels it, taking care to break as little as possible." Instead of transcending the NEP evolutionarily, Stalinism abolished it revolutionarily, by decree and by force. Instead of proceeding gradually and by means of persuasion, it proceeded at breakneck speed and wielded state power coercively to smash popular resistance by terrorizing the population. Instead of taking care to break as little as possible, it broke the spirit along with the bodies of a great proportion of the generation that had come of age during the first phase of the Revolution a decade before. It also consumed a very heavy proportion of those party leaders and members who had, in the 1920's, been Stalinists in the simple sense of supporters of the general secretary and his "general line" in the fight with the oppositions.

The rural revolution called "mass collectivization" illustrates these points. In the space of a few years and at the cost of untold suffering and a famine whose toll of lives ran into many millions, a countryside with about twenty-five million peasant farmsteads functioning on nationalized land was transformed into one in which the great majority of those peasants were organized into some 200,000 collective farms (*kolkhozy*) while many more were employed as hired workers on state farms (*sov-*

khozy). In the *Short Course* of party history (1938), which Stalin edited personally, the collectivization is described as "a profound revolution, a leap from an old qualitative state of society to a new qualitative state, equivalent in its consequences to the revolution of October 1917." The *Short Course* goes on: "The distinguishing feature of this revolution is that it was accomplished *from above*, on the initiative of the state, and directly supported *from below* by the millions of peasants, who were fighting to throw off kulak bondage and to live in freedom in the collective farms."

It was indeed a state-initiated, state-directed, and state-enforced revolution from above — as was the Stalinist revolution as a whole — but the *Short Course* lied when it spoke of mass peasant support from below. Historical evidence available to us now in great abundance attests that not alone the ones classified in kulaks, whose "liquidation as a class" was proclaimed as the banner of the collectivization drive, but the mass of middle peasants and even some of the rural poor were sullenly opposed to the rural revolution and joined the *kolkhozy* only under duress or because of fear. The claim in Soviet publicity of Stalin's time and after that the collectivization was Lenin's "cooperative plan" in action is groundless. Not only was there no patient, long-drawn-out educational effort ("cultural revolution") to prepare the peasantry's mind for voluntary acceptance of cooperative farming, and no antecedent industrialization sufficient to produce the hundred thousand tractors that Lenin had foreseen as a powerful inducement to the peasants to farm cooperatively; still more important, the *kolkhozy* were (and are) socialist cooperatives only in their formal façade.

The rural revolution from above of 1929–33 proceeded simultaneously with the heroic phase of the Stalinist industrial revolution from above: that state-directed, frantic, military-oriented industrialization drive whose very slogan, "Fulfill the Five-Year Plan in Four," reflected the gap between what actually happened and the Plan as officially adopted in 1929. The relationship between these two processes presents a highly complex problem on which scholarly opinion has evolved as new factual information has become available in the recent past. It was at one time widely believed that the forcible mass collectivization was a necessity for the desired high-speed super-industrialization in that the *kolkhoz* system enabled the Soviet state to extract otherwise unobtainable (or uncertainly obtainable) agricultural surpluses to finance such basic needs of industrialization as the importation of foreign machinery and technicians and to supply the urban population with food and industry with raw materials. Such, indeed, appears to have been the underlying conception on which Stalin acted at the time; collectivization was envisaged as the presupposition of a form of industrialization geared to the priority of heavy industry and war industry over the consumer-goods industries whose greater development would have been a *sine qua non* of a Soviet industrialization within the frame of a continued rural NEP. In the event, however, the economic consequences of collectivization were so catastrophic that recent researches by Western scholars, supported by archival data published in 1968 and 1969 by the Soviet historian A. A. Barsov, have reached the conclusions that (1) "mass collectivization of Soviet agriculture must be reckoned as an unmitigated economic policy disaster," and (2) "the oppressive state agricultural procurement system, rather than serving to extract a net contribution from agriculture as a whole, should be credited with preventing the collectivization disaster from disrupting the industrialization drive." . . .

According to a view which draws part of its inspiration from Trotsky's thinking and which achieved wide influence owing to its espousal by Isaac Deutscher, Stalinist industrialization-cum-collectivization (which Deutscher calls "the second revolution") was a necessitated response to a "grave social crisis" of the later 1920's. Citing Stalin's statistics, Deutscher states that in January 1928, in particular, government grain purchases fell short by two million tons of the minimum needed to feed the urban population.[3] Emergency measures were applied by the government to extract grain that was being withheld from the market. The peasants were not, for the most part, politically motivated against the Soviet regime, but were driven by economic circumstances, in that the small farms produced only enough to meet the peasants' own food needs while the "big farmers" with surpluses were charging prices beyond the ability of the town population to pay and also were demanding concessions to capitalist farming. In this dilemma, yielding to the peasants would antagonize the urban working class, and refusal to yield would also bring a threat of famine and urban unrest. A "radical solution" was demanded, and Stalin, having until the very last moment shrunk from an upheaval, acted "under the overwhelming pressure of events" and embarked upon the second revolu-

[2] James R. Millar, "Mass Collectivization and the Contribution of Soviet Agriculture to the First Five-Year Plan," *Slavic Review*, December 1974, pp. 764, 765.
[3] Isaac Deutscher, *Stalin* (New York: Oxford University Press, 1967), pp. 312–13.

tion in an "unpremeditated, pragmatic manner." He was "precipitated into collectivization by the chronic danger of famine in 1928 and 1929." Such, in Deutscher's classic version, is the "circumstantial explanation" (as we may call it) of the initial phase of the Stalinist revolution from above. . . .

It is a central thesis of the present essay that the circumstantial explanation, notwithstanding a certain specious plausibility, is fatally flawed, and that we shall not attain a tenable view of Stalinism in its fundamental aspect as revolution from above until this is understood. The circumstantial explanation is flawed, first, in the utterly unproven nature of its assumption that collectivization in the terroristic form that it took was the only realistic alternative for the Soviet regime in 1929, much less a *sine qua non* of its survival. . . . Even allowing that the regime was faced in 1927–28 with something like a peasant "grain strike" (to use the loaded *Short Course* terminology), there is no serious evidence of incipient political rebelliousness in the countryside at that time; and there is evidence of general peasant acceptance of the Soviet regime, whatever the specific grievances that caused peasants to grumble or to withhold grain from the market in expectation of more return. Nor, as already indicated, has it been shown, nor is it true, that the terroristic collectivization was a necessity. . . .

The circumstantial explanation of forced mass collectivization hardly squares with the now demonstrated conclusion . . . that this course proved in practice an "unmitigated economic policy disaster," nor is it cogent that a policy which directly and indirectly produced the worst famine in Russia's famine-plagued history, that of 1932–34, which cost a conservatively estimated five million lives, was necessitated by the need to avert a famine. Although historical "might-have-beens" are just as difficult to establish as are arguments of the "there-was-no-other-possible-course" type, the insistently emerging conclusion from scholarly researches based on the more abundant data now available from Soviet sources is that "a continuation of the New Economic Policy of the 1920s would have permitted at least as rapid a rate of industrialization with less cost to the urban as well as to the rural population of the Soviet Union."[4] In effect, informed and thoughtful historical hindsight is confirming the basic economic realism of the program for a balanced industrialization policy within the frame of continuing NEP that

[4]Millar, op. cit., p. 766.

Bukharin presented in his *Pravda* article of September 30, 1928, "Notes of an Economist." The Bukharinist non-revolutionary alternative for Soviet industrialization policy at the close of the twenties, an alternative inspired in large part by the Leninist thinking of 1921–23, . . . was real. Had it been adopted, it could well have worked; had it worked poorly, the cost to the Soviet economy could not have compared with that which had to be paid for the Stalinist solution. . . .

[N]umerous Bolshevik minds in Moscow and around the country, including some and possibly even a majority in the Politburo, *did not perceive the Stalinist course as the only possible action to take in the circumstances then obtaining.* Bukharin, in a clandestine conversation of July 1928 with Kamenev which became widely known in party circles, clearly foresaw the catastrophic consequences of Stalin's contemplated rural revolution from above. It was, he said, a ruinous policy course signifying a return to War Communism, a course leading to civil war, to an uprising that would have to be drowned in blood. His prevision proved well founded in essence if not in specific detail. . . .

[T]he ruling party was divided in its appraisal of the circumstances in 1928–29 and . . . an influential section of Soviet political opinion opted for a course in agrarian policy and industrialization that would have been evolutionary, in accordance with the later Lenin's counsel, rather than revolutionary. The inevitable next question — why did the evolutionists go down to defeat in the party struggle, or why did Stalinism win? — cannot be answered by reference to the socioeconomic circumstances over which the quarrel raged in Bolshevik circles. It can be answered only by reference to the factors that determined the *Stalinist response* to the circumstances and its political victory. The circumstances as such cannot furnish the explanation of the revolution from above.

One of the forces conducive to a Stalinist revolutionary response among Bolshevik politicians was the other Lenin — the still very influential revolutionary Lenin of the War Communism period and the heritage of Bolshevik revolutionism that the other Lenin symbolized. It is understandable that Bukharin, involved as he was in a political struggle against Stalin and the policies he was advocating in 1928–29, treated Lenin's last writings as his "political testament," and that is certainly what Lenin himself intended them to be. But for the Bolshevik movement and party, Lenin's political testament was the entire corpus of his thought and writing, the whole record of his revolutionary leadership of the movement up to, during, and after the October Revolution; and Lenin's political testament in this more comprehensive sense, or Leninism as a whole, contained very much that Stalin and Stalinism had good claim to as an authoritative text and warrant for the policies followed in the revolution from above.

The very idea of a process of "revolution from above," taken in the most general terms, has a Leninist pedigree. Even in one of his last articles cited above, Lenin spoke of overtaking other nations "with the aid of the workers' and peasants' government." But the idea of revolution from above has a deeper place in Lenin's thought. When he contended in *The State and Revolution* in 1917, and in such subsequent works as *The Proletarian Revolution and the Renegade Kautsky*, that the doctrine of proletarian dictatorship was the core idea of Marxism and that Marxism called for a seizure of power followed by dictatorial rule by violence against the internal bourgeoisie and associated social forces, he was saying: The revolution does not end with the party's taking of power; that is only a momentous point of historical transition beyond which the party continues its revolutionary destruction of the old order from above, i.e., by wielding the coercive instruments of state power against the revolution's class enemies. Leninist revolution from above meant the use of state power for the continuation of class war *after* the revolutionary party has achieved such power and formed its government under the title of "proletarian dictatorship." This basic idea found its sharpest, though by no means its only, later expression in Lenin's prospectus of 1919 for a work (never completed) on the proletarian dictatorship. Two passages are especially notable: "The dictatorship of the proletariat is the *continuation* of the class struggle in *new* forms. That is the crux of the matter; that is what they do not understand." And: "The state is only a *weapon* of the proletariat in its class struggle. A special kind of cudgel (*dubinka*), rien de plus." Whether Lenin ever used the phrase "from above" in arguing this notion of the proletarian dictatorship as a continuing revolutionary struggle from the vantage-point of state power is of no consequence; the idea was unmistakably present in his thought.

It is true that as early as 1919, at the height of the Civil War and War Communism, we find intimations in Lenin of the transition to the later reformist approach to the building of socialism. . . . This transition was associated with the idea that the fundamental obstacle to socialism was the body of habit left over from the past and that the revolutionizing of habit — in other words, of culture — was *au fond* an educational task rather than one to be resolved by coercive means. In his article of May 1919, "A Great Beginning," Lenin hailed a workers' initiative of voluntary unpaid Saturday work (the Communist *subbotnik*) as a development of enormous historical significance, and observed in this connection that "the dictatorship of the proletariat is not only the use of force against the exploiters, and not even mainly the use of force."

But it would not be proper to discount on this evidence the Lenin for whom revolution was, in his own later words, "a change which breaks the old order to its very foundations, and not one that cautiously, slowly and gradually remodels it, taking care to break as little as possible" — and for whom state power, once in the hands of the revolutionary party, should be used as a cudgel against the class enemy. When Stalin in December 1926 rhetorically asked the Comintern Executive what the building of socialism meant in class terms and answered that "building socialism in the USSR means overcoming our own Soviet bourgeoisie by our own forces in the course of a struggle," he was simply drawing upon the Lenin and Leninism of the Civil War period and earlier, the Leninism in which the fundamental question for a Marxist seeking to create socialism was *Kto-kogo?*, or who will vanquish whom in the class war? To this Leninism of *Kto-kogo*, he did subsequently add one proposition that was original with him: that the internal class struggle intensifies with the society's advance toward socialism. He was drawing upon the Leninism that had stood during 1918–21 for forcible food requisitioning from the peasant (*prodrazvërstka*), for stirring up of class war in the villages by means of the committees of the poor (*kombedy*), for the belief (to cite Lenin) that the proletarian dictatorship should mean "iron rule" and not a "jellyfish proletarian government," and for the ruthless resort to terror as an instrument of dictatorial rule. *This was Stalinist Leninism*, and the authenticity of Stalinism's claim to it is not seriously diminished by the important fact that what Leninism stood for in Lenin's own mind, as a conception of how to build socialism in Russia, underwent great modification in 1921–23.

Nor was this Stalinist Leninism Stalin's only. A considerable proportion of his generation, men who had become Bolsheviks when Bolshevism was still an anti-regime revolutionary movement and who politically came of age, as Stalin himself did, during the era of War

Communism, shared his outlook to one or another degree. I am not speaking here about general ideas alone or about Leninism simply as a system of political belief, but likewise about the ingrained habits of mind, ways of defining and responding to situations, styles of action, common memories, mystique, etc., that collectively constitute the culture of a political movement insofar as a given age cohort of its membership (and leadership) is concerned. As its name indicates, War Communism had militarized the revolutionary political culture of the Bolshevik movement. The heritage of that formative time in the Soviet culture's history was martial zeal, revolutionary voluntarism and *élan*, readiness to resort to coercion, rule by administrative fiat (*administrirovanie*), centralized administration, summary justice, and no small dose of that Communist arrogance (*komchvanstvo*) that Lenin later inveighed against. It was not simply the "heroic period of the great Russian Revolution," as Lev Kritzman christened it in the title of the book about War Communism that he published in the mid-1920's, but above all the *fighting* period, the time when in Bolshevik minds the citadel of socialism was to be taken by storm. . . .

But if the surviving spirit of War Communism influenced the way in which the drives for collectivization and industrialization were conceived and carried out, it does not follow that the Stalinist revolution repeated 1917–21 or that the new Stalinist order which took shape in the 1930's was a revival of the system of War Communism. To be sure, the start of the new decade saw such reminders of the heroic period as food rationing, and other resemblances appeared. As Moshe Lewin has pointed out, however, the early Stalinist process showed many distinctive traits that differentiated it from its pre-NEP predecessor: the feverish industrial expansion, the emergence of anti-egalitarian tendencies in contrast to the egalitarianism of the Civil War period, the rise of new elites combined with the loss of the relatively independent political role of the lesser leadership ranks at the earlier time, and the political muzzling of the party rank-and-file in relation to the leadership itself. Still other, major differences call for mention: the *kolkhoz* system itself, which bore small resemblance to the agricultural communes initiated during the Civil War period; the use of police terror as a prime instrument of government in a manner sharply differentiated from the Red terror sponsored by Lenin via the original Cheka; and the interrelationship between internal and external policy. *The basic underlying*

*fact confronting us is that when the Russian revolutionary process re-
sumed in the Stalinist stage, it had a different character from the revolutionary process of destruction of the old order and makeshift creation of
the new that had marked the earlier, 1917–21 stage; and this change of
character is to be understood in terms of a reversion to a revolutionary
process seen earlier in Russian history.*

It has been argued here that the idea of revolution from above had a
Leninist pedigree. While that is important for an interpretation of
Stalinism, it must now be stressed that the phenomenon of revolution
from above has a range of forms, and that the Leninist form — revolution from above as a victorious revolutionary party's violent use of the
"cudgel" of state power to repress its internal class enemies — represented only one element in Stalinism as a complex and many-sided
revolution from above. Where the Stalinist phenomenon went far beyond the Lenin heritage lay in its constructive aspect. Leninist revolution from above was essentially a destructive process, a tearing down of
the old order from the vantage-point of state power; Stalinist revolution
from above used destructive or repressive means, among others, for
what was, both in intent and in reality, a constructive (as well as destructive) process. Its slogan or ideological banner was the building of a
socialist society. But in substance, Stalinism as revolution from above
was a state-building process, the construction of a powerful, highly
centralized, bureaucratic, military-industrial Soviet Russian state. Although it was proclaimed "socialist" in the mid-1930's, it differed in
various vital ways from what most socialist thinkers — Marx, Engels,
and Lenin among them — had understood socialism to mean. Stalinist
"socialism" was a socialism of mass poverty rather than plenty; of sharp
social stratification rather than relative equality; of universal, constant
fear rather than emancipation of personality; of national chauvinism
rather than brotherhood of man; and of a monstrously hypertrophied
state power rather than the decreasingly stratified commune-state delineated by Marx in *The Civil War in France* and by Lenin in *The State
and Revolution.*

It was not, however, by mere caprice or accident that this happened. Stalinist revolutionism from above had a prehistory in the political culture of Russian tsarism; it existed as a pattern in the Russian past
and hence *could* be seen by a twentieth-century statesman as both a
precedent and legitimation of a political course that would, in essentials, recapitulate the historical pattern. . . .

Confronted in the aftermath of the two-century-long Mongol domination with hostile and in some cases more advanced neighbor-states in possession of portions of the extensive territories that had made up the loosely confederated Kievan *Rus'*, the princes — later tsars — of Muscovy undertook the building of a powerful "military-national state" capable of gathering the Russian lands under its aegis. Given the primacy of the concern for external defense and expansion and the country's relative economic backwardness, the government proceeded by remodeling the social structure, at times by forcible means, in such a way that all classes of the population were bound in one or another form of compulsory service to the state. "The fact is," writes Miliukov, "that in Russia the state exerted enormous influence upon the social organization whereas in the West the social organization conditioned the state system. . . . It was the elementary state of the economic 'base' (*fundament*) which in Russia called forth the hypertrophy of the state 'superstructure' (*nadstroika*) and conditioned the powerful counter-influence of this superstructure upon the 'base' itself."[5]

A salient expression of the tsarist pattern of revolutionism from above was the legalized imposition of serfdom upon the Russian peasantry in the sixteenth and seventeenth centuries, the peasant's attachment by law to the soil, together with the system of *barshchina* (the *corvée*) under which the peasant was bound to contribute a certain number of days of work on the landowner's (or state's) land during the agricultural year. The Russian village commune, itself an archaic institution, was transformed by governmental action into a "coercive organization" for ensuring each member's fulfillment of state-imposed obligations under the principle of mutual responsibility (*krugovaia poruka*). The Stalinist rural revolution from above was in essence an accelerated repetition of this tsarist developmental pattern. . . . The *kolkhoz* . . . was a cooperative only in its formal façade. Underneath, it bore a far from superficial resemblance to the landed estate in the period of serfdom; and it is a highly significant fact that the *kolkhoz* was actually perceived by many Russian peasants as a revival of serfdom. Westerners who traveled in rural Russia in the early 1930's have reported that it was a common peasant practice to refer to "V.K.P." (the initials of V*sesoiuznaia kommunisticheskaia partiia*, the All-Union Communist party) in the esoteric meaning of "second serfdom" (*vtoroe krepostnoe*

[5] P. Miliukov, *Ocherki po istorii russkoi kul'tury* [Sketches in the History of Russian culture]. Pt. 1, 5th ed. (St. Petersburg, 1904), pp. 133–34.

pravo). Two features of the *kolkhoz* system gave special point to this perception. One was that the *kolkhozy* came to operate according to arrangements under which the peasant owed the *kolkhoz* an annual obligatory minimum, specified by Soviet law, of "work-day units" (*trudodni*); this was a return to *barshchina*. Second, when the internal passport system, an institution of tsarist Russia, was revived in Soviet Russia by a government decree of December 31, 1932, as a means of bureaucratic control over the movements of Soviet citizens, the farm population was not issued passports. The deprivation of passports attached the peasant to the soil of the *kolkhoz* or *sovkhoz* as securely as his serf ancestor had been attached to the soil of the landed estate.

The culminating phase of tsarism as a dynamic political superstructure engaged in the transformation of Russian society and development of its economic base for state-ordained purposes came in the long reign of Peter I, that "crowned revolutionary," as Herzen[6] later called him. Now the pattern of revolution from above emerged most distinctly, one of its prominent aspects being an industrial revolution from above aimed at building a powerful Russian war-industrial base. Intensifying serfdom, Peter employed state-owned serfs along with prisoners of war and others for industrial projects as well as the construction of canals on Lakes Ladoga, Onega, and others; and on occasion moved entire townships of people to the construction sites of the new enterprises in what are described as "Peter's forced labour camps."

Again, the parallel with the Stalinist industrial revolution from above is striking, the major difference being the greatly expanded scale of the use of forced labor in the Stalinist case. To what has been said above about the relation between collectivization and industrialization, something of importance here needs to be added. During the First Five-Year Plan, the slogan about "liquidation of the kulaks as a class" was used as a pretext for deportation of peasant families en masse — a process made all the more massive by the extreme looseness with which the label "kulak" was applied — to remote areas like the Urals, Siberia and the far North where they were set to work in timbering or on the construction of plants, such as the Magnitogorsk iron and steel complex in the Urals. The vast expansion of the forced-labor camp empire dates from this time. To cite Solzhenitsyn,[7] "In 1929–1930, billowed and

---

[6] Alexander Herzen, a famous Russian social critic of the mid-nineteenth century. — Ed.

[7] Aleksandr I. Solzhenitsyn, *The Gulag Archipelago, 1918–1956* (New York: Harper & Row, 1973), Vol. I, p. 54.

gushed the multimillion wave of *dispossessed kulaks*. . . . In sheer size this nonrecurring tidal wave (it was an ocean) swelled beyond the bounds of anything the penal system of even an immense state can permit itself. There was nothing to be compared with it in all Russian history. It was the forced resettlement of a whole people, an ethnic catastrophe." But while in size there was nothing in Russian history to compare with it, this mass use of deportation and forced labor for industrialization had a definite historical precedent in Petrine Russia. In the Stalinist industrial revolution from above, therefore, just as in the rural revolution from above, there were elements of a revival of the tsarist pattern of revolutionism from above. In this respect, Stalinism showed the influence not simply of the historically recent Witte system of state-sponsored industrialization, but of the much earlier system of direct exploitation of servile labor in the Russian state-building process.[8]

Here a brief comment is called for on the view, sometimes encountered in Western thought, that sees the Stalinist revolution from above under the aspect of "modernization." The difficulty with this position — apart from the nebulous character of the very concept of modernization — is its obliviousness of the strong element of "archaization" in Stalinism, its resurrection of the historic tsarist pattern of building a powerful military-national state by revolutionary means involving the extension of direct coercive controls over the population and the growth of state power in the process. Unless "modernization" is reduced in meaning mainly to industrialization and increase of the urban population (in which case the term becomes superfluous), the use of it to characterize Stalinism is misleading. If a formula for the state-building process is needed, it might best be the one that Kliuchevsky provided in his summation of modern Russian history from the sixteenth to the nineteenth century: "The state swelled up; the people grew lean."[9] . . .

In addition to interpreting the Stalinist revolution in culturalist terms, this essay has attempted to explain it so. The circumstantial explanation of the revolution from above was rejected in favor of one which stressed, first of all, the way in which the circumstances of 1927–28 were perceived and defined by a political leadership many of whose members, including Stalin, had come of age politically in the era of the

---

[8] Sergei Witte was the Russian minister of finance from 1893 until 1903.

[9] V. O. Kliuchevsky, *Kurs russkoi istorii* [A Course in Russian History], (Moscow, 1937), Vol. 3, p. 11.

October Revolution and War Communism and responded to those circumstances in the revolutionary spirit of the earlier time rather than in the evolutionary spirit of NEP Soviet culture. Further, the form taken by the Stalinist revolution, the relation between its two major phases, and the nature of the new Stalinist order that it created have been treated as a recapitulation in essentials of the pattern of revolutionism from above that belonged to the political culture of old Russia and was visible in the tsarist state-building process from the fifteenth to the eighteenth centuries and the sociopolitical order it produced.

But the question inevitably arises, why did history recapitulate itself so in this instance? Cultural patterns out of a nation's past do not repeat themselves in the present simply because they were there. Nor can we explain the phenomenon by reference to like circumstances, such as NEP Russia's relative international isolation and economic backwardness, for we have argued that circumstances do not carry their own self-evident meaning, that what people and political leaders *act upon* is always the circumstances *as perceived and defined by them*, which in turn is influenced by culture. But also, we must now add, by personality. And so we come at the end to what was mentioned at the start as a third important explanatory factor underlying the revolution from above — the mind and personality of Stalin.

To a certain extent the personal factor is covered by the culturalist explanation itself. In general, there is no conflict between culturalist explanations and those that make reference to the special historical role of a leader-personality. As cultural anthropologists have pointed out, "culture" and "personality" are, to a considerable degree, two ways of viewing one and the same phenomenon, culture being something which has its being mainly *within* people. In terms more immediately pertinent to our argument, a leader-personality becomes politically acculturated through his life-experience both in early years and during manhood. Thus, 1917 and the Civil War were a formative acculturating life-experience for Stalin and many others of his party generation, leaving a deep residue of the revolutionary political culture of War Communism within them. On this level of explanation, Stalin's historical role in the late 1920's was to make himself, as effectively as he did, the leader and spokesman of an outlook that he shared with numerous others in the party leadership and not alone the men of his own faction.

The recapitulation of the tsarist pattern of revolutionism from above presents a more difficult problem of explanation in culturalist *or*

personality terms, if only because Russian tsarism, in all its manifestations, was what the Bolshevik revolutionary movement had taken
originally as its mortal sociopolitical enemy. However, the Russian
nationalist feeling aroused in a section of the party during the Civil War
years, the revolution-born spirit of "Red Russian patriotism" against
which a party delegate from the Ukraine protested at the Tenth Party
Congress in 1921, was an element in the culture that *could* predispose a
Bolshevik to perceive certain patterns out of the heritage of old Russia as
relevant to the circumstances of the present. On the other hand, it did
not do so in the generality of instances of which we know. It is true that
Bukharin grasped the direction of Stalin's policy thinking in 1928, with
special reference to forced collectivization, and alluded to its tsarist
inspiration by terming it "military-feudal exploitation of the peasantry."
But the party resolution of April 23, 1929, against the Bukharinist
group stigmatized Bukharin's charge as "a libelous attack . . . drawn
from the party of Miliukov."[10] This was hardly an admission that Stalin's
neo-tsarist Marxism (the use of such a phrase may sound monstrous to
Marxists, but the Marxist *Weltanschauung* is capable of many meta-
morphoses) had found favor with a substantial body of party opinion.
Hence, in this problem the explanatory emphasis must fall more on
"personality" than on "culture."

To put it otherwise, acculturation is not to be viewed simply as a
process in which an individual is affected by formative life-experiences
and thereby internalizes culture patterns, including patterns out of the
past, as dictated by his psychological needs or predispositions. Stalin,
the commissar for nationality affairs and as such the presumable protec-
tor of the rights of the minority nations in the Soviet federation, was in
fact, as Lenin discovered to his horror shortly before dying, one of those
Bolsheviks most infected by "Russian Red patriotism." Lenin showed
his realization of this in the notes on the nationality question which he
dictated on December 30–31, 1922 and in which he characterized
Stalin as foremost among those Russified minority representatives in the
party who tended to err on the side of "true-Russianism" (*istinno-russkie
nastroeniia*) and "Great Russian chauvinism." Unbeknown to Lenin,
Stalin's sense of Russian nationality, if not his true-Russianism, had

---

[10]The Constitutional Democratic party, suppressed after the Bolshevik Revolution. —
Ed.

dated from his youthful conversion to Lenin's leadership and to Bolshevism, which he saw as the "Russian faction" in the Empire's Marxist Party, Menshevism being the "Jewish faction." It was on this foundation that Stalin, during the 1920's, went forward in his thinking and appropriative self-acculturation, as the generality of his Russian-nationalist-oriented party comrades did not, to envisage the tsarist state-building process as a model for the Soviet Russian state in its "building of socialism." And it was the great personal power that he acquired by 1929, with the ouster of the oppositions from the party leadership, that made it possible for him to proceed to carry out his design.

If the thesis concerning the recapitulation of the state-building process places heavy emphasis upon personality even in the context of a culturalist approach, a final explanatory consideration concerning the Stalinist phenomenon narrows the focus onto personality to a still greater degree. Unlike any other Bolshevik, to my knowledge, Stalin, as we have noted, defined the Soviet situation in 1925 and 1926 in eve-of-October terms, implicitly presaging thereby a revolutionary assault against the existing order, i.e., the NEP, in the drive to build socialism. Then, looking back in the *Short Course* of 1938 on the accomplishments of the Stalinist decade, he described them, and collectivization in particular, as equivalent in consequence to the October Revolution of 1917. Underlying both the definition of the situation in the mid-1920's and the retrospective satisfaction expressed in the late 1930's was Stalin's compulsive psychological need, born of neurosis, to prove himself a revolutionary hero of Lenin-like proportions, to match or surpass what all Bolsheviks considered Lenin's supreme historical exploit, the leadership of the party in the world-historic revolutionary success of October 1917. The great revolutionary drive to change Russia in the early 1930's was intended as Stalin's October.

In practice it achieved certain successes, notably in industrialization, but at a cost of such havoc and misery in Russia that Stalin, as the regime's supreme leader, aroused condemnation among many. This helps to explain, in psychological terms, the lethal vindictiveness that he visited upon millions of his party comrades, fellow countrymen, and others in the ensuing years. It was his way of trying to come to terms with the repressed fact that he, Djugashvili, had failed to prove himself the charismatically Lenin-like Stalin that it was his lifelong goal to be. If this interpretation is well founded, he was hardly the most impersonal of great historical figures.

Roy A. Medvedev

The Social Basis
of Stalinism

One of the most remarkable texts to come out of the Soviet Union prior to
Gorbachev's reforms was the vast historical narrative and analysis by the
philosopher Roy Medvedev (twin brother of the biologist Zhores Medvedev), *Let History Judge.* In this work, long suppressed inside the USSR,
Medvedev brought a remarkable degree of insight, objectivity, and archival
knowledge to bear on the problem of how and why Stalinism came to be.
This excerpt from the newly revised version of the book presents the core of
his sociological explanation of Stalinism. (By 1989 Medvedev was being
published officially in the Soviet Union, and was elected a member of the
new People's Congress and Supreme Soviet.)

I have described the general character of the repression of the thirties
and discussed the reasons for it, but there are other questions of no less
importance. How did Stalin manage to deal such a terrible blow to the
party? Why didn't his actions encounter decisive opposition from the
people, the party and the leadership?

Marx and Engels often referred to the possibility, or even the inevitability, that a revolution would degenerate if it occurred in objective
historical conditions that did not correspond to its aims. Plekhanov[1] also
wrote about this several times in his arguments with the populists. If the
people, Plekhanov declared, approach power when social conditions
are not ripe, then the "revolution may result in a political monstrosity,
such as the ancient Chinese or Peruvian empires, i.e., in a tsarist
despotism renovated with a Communist lining." Some persons I have
spoken with see prophetic truth in these words. They argue that in the
Soviet Union of the twenties it was inevitable for the likes of Stalin to

---

[1] Georgi Plekhanov, first major Russian Marxist writer; later sided with the Menshevik
faction against the Bolsheviks. — Ed.

come to power. "If Lenin had lived another ten or twenty years," one opponent, V. K—— declared, "he would have certainly have been pushed out of the leadership by the 'new' people, whose embodiment was Stalin." "The system created after the October Revolution," said another opponent, the economist I. P——,

> *was based on outright dictatorship, on force, to an excessive degree. Disregard of certain elementary rules of democracy and lawful order inevitably had to degenerate into Stalinist dictatorship. It was Stalin who fitted this system ideally, and he only developed its latent possibilities to the maximum degree. The whole trouble was that a socialist revolution in a country like Russia was premature. In a country that has not gone through a period of bourgeois democracy, where the people in its majority is illiterate and uncultivated, in such a country genuine socialism cannot be built without the support of other more developed socialist countries. By prematurely destroying all the old forms of social life, the Bolsheviks raised up and turned loose such forces as must inevitably have led to some form of Stalinism. Approximately the same thing is happening today in China and Albania.*

I cannot agree with this point of view. Various possibilities exist in almost every political system or situation. The triumph of one of these possibilities depends on both objective and subjective factors, some of which are obviously accidental. Even the tsarist regime in early twentieth-century Russia could have developed in various ways, and the fragile system of bourgeois democracy that existed in Russia from February to October 1917 was not inevitably doomed. Of course, a question always arises about the *degree of probability* that events will take one turn rather than another, but even the smallest possibility should not be dismissed. . . .

From this point of view Stalinism was not at all inevitable. I do not think by any means that the political conception the Bolsheviks brought to the October revolution was free of defects. The system of Soviet rule in the early years of the revolution also had quite a few defects, but it had many merits as well. For the young Soviet state the road of development was not determined in such a way that it necessarily had to grow into the Stalinist system. Various possibilities existed, and Stalinism was not the only one or even the main one. I will discuss this question further in subsequent chapters.

Many foreign thinkers, including Communists, have studied this problem. After the Twentieth Congress, in March 1956, Palmiro Togliatti[2] published his famous objection to a simple inversion of the cult of personality: blaming all evil on the superman who had formerly been praised for all good. Togliatti suggested that the system called "Stalinist" was to be explained by reference to the development of bureaucracy, deriving from prerevolutionary conditions and from the desperate need for centralized power during the civil war. This context favored the rise of Stalin, a typical apparatchik.

Truly we are confronted with this question: How, in spite of the monstrosity of his crimes, did Stalin manage to retain not only his power but also the respect and trust of the majority of Soviet people? It is an unavoidable fact that Stalin never relied on force alone. Throughout the period of his one-man rule he was popular. Aleksandr Zinoviev, in his recent book *The Flight of Our Youth* correctly notes that it is wrong to describe the Stalinist system as one based solely on force and deception "when at bottom it was the voluntary creation of the many-millioned masses who could be organized into a single stream only by means of force and deception." The longer Stalin ruled the Soviet Union, cold-bloodedly destroying millions of people, the greater seems to have been the dedication to him, even the love, of the majority of the people. When he died in March 1953 the grief of hundreds of millions, both in the Soviet Union and around the world, was quite sincere.

How can this unprecedented historical paradox be explained? We must look more closely at the conditions that facilitated Stalin's usurpation of power.

One condition that made it easy for Stalin to bend the party to his will was the hugely inflated cult of his personality. Ilya Ehrenburg writes in his memoirs:

> For 1938 it is more correct simply to use the word "cult" in its original religious meaning. In the minds of millions Stalin was transformed into a mythical demigod; all trembled as they said his name, believed that he alone could save the Soviet Union from invasion and collapse.

The deification of Stalin left the party unable to control his actions and justified in advance everything connected with his name. The embodiment of all the achievements of socialism in his person tended

[2] Leader of the Italian Communist party, 1926–1964. — Ed.

to paralyze the political activism of the other leaders and of the party membership as a whole, preventing them from finding their own way in the welter of ongoing events, leading them to place blind faith in Stalin. The cult of Stalin, following the logic of any cult, tended to transform the Communist Party into an ecclesiastical organization, producing a sharp distinction between ordinary people and leader-priests headed by their infallible pope. The gulf between the people and Stalin was not only deepened but idealized. The business of state in the Kremlin became as remote and incomprehensible for the unconsecrated as the affairs of the gods on Olympus.

In the thirties and forties the social consciousness of the people took on elements of religious psychology: illusions, autosuggestion, the inability to think critically, intolerance towards dissidents, and fanaticism. As Yuri Karyakin[3] put it, a secular variant of religious consciousness arose in the Soviet Union. Perceptions of reality were distorted. It was difficult, for example, to believe the terrible crimes charged against the Old Bolsheviks, but it was even more difficult to think that Stalin was engaged in a monstrous provocation to destroy his former friends and comrades. . . .

. . . There was a two-way cause-and-effect relationship between the terror and the cult of Stalin's personality. Stalin's cult facilitated his usurpation of power and the destruction of inconvenient people, while his crimes, supported by the apparatus and also by the deluded masses, extended and reinforced the cult of personality.

The cult of personality does not automatically lead to mass repression; much depends on the personality. Not every deified emperor or pharaoh was a cruel and bloodthirsty despot. But the most dangerous feature of the cult of personality is that the leader's conduct depends not on laws or other rules but on his own arbitrary will. For the Soviet Union it is an intolerable situation if the personal qualities of the leader of the party and government are the only guarantee of citizens' rights, indeed of their very lives. . . .

The widespread belief in the existence of a fascist fifth column facilitated Stalin's realization of his criminal plans. His cruelty and

---

[3] Soviet historian, also elected to the People's Congress in 1989. — Ed.

mistrust even seemed desirable qualities to many people. Thus in the years of the terror Stalin continued to rely on the masses, keeping them deceived and exploiting their urge for a better future and love for their homeland. His apostasy regarding the ideals of the socialist revolution was always masked by ultrarevolutionary phrases, which prevented working people and the youth from discerning the real motives behind his actions. Thus he secured the support of the people, without which even such a despot as Stalin could not have maintained himself. At the same time he could not stray too far outside the framework of the socialist system; he could not destroy all the gains of the revolution. By deceiving the people, Stalin was able to direct his fire at the veterans of the revolution, portraying them as enemies, but he could not come out openly against the revolution itself, against Lenin and socialism. Stalin greatly slowed the wheel of history but he could not turn it back. . . .

The reconstruction of the Cheka-GPU went on for some years in the first half of the twenties. But it slowed down after the deaths of Lenin and Dzerzhinsky; indeed things started moving in an entirely different direction. The GPU gradually began to resume the functions that were appropriate only for a period of civil war. Under pressure from Stalin, a punitive organization reappeared, with the right to put people in jail and camps, to exile them to remote places, and later even to shoot them without any juridical procedure, simply as an administrative act.

Vyacheslav Menzhinsky, the head of the GPU after Dzerzhinsky's death, was an old party official, but he lacked the influence and authority of his predecessor. He was sick for long periods and rarely interfered in the day-to-day activity of the GPU. The real boss by the late twenties was his deputy, Yagoda, who was strongly influenced by Stalin. Stalin and Yagoda introduced a new style of work, for example, in the seizure of valuables from Nepmen by massive use of violence and arbitrary force. The GPU was also assigned the job of transporting hundreds of thousands of kulak families to the northern and eastern districts of the country. Stalin relied on the GPU to carry out the lawless repression of the intelligentsia in the late twenties and early thirties. At that time some GPU employees, with tacit support from above, were already creating false evidence, forcing prisoners to sign false interrogation records, inventing all kinds of plots and organizations, and beating and torturing prisoners. When one victim, Mikhail Yakubovich, told his interrogator at the end of 1930 that such methods would have been impossible under Dzerzhinsky, the interrogator laughed: "You've found someone to remember! Dzerzhinsky — that's a bygone stage in our revolution."

The GPU gradually increased in size and in 1934 it was reorganized as the NKVD (People's Commissariat of Internal Affairs), which included the "militia" (the regular police) and the border guards. After Menzhinsky's death in 1934 Yagoda was officially made head of the NKVD. Beginning in 1934 Yagoda monitored the work of the NKVD for the party's Central Committee, but long before that Stalin had in fact established his complete and undivided control over the GPU-NKVD.

In 1934 the powers of the NKVD were substantially enlarged. A Special Assembly (Osoboe Soveshchanie) was established within the NKVD by a decree of the Sovnarkom [Council of People's Commissars] and Central Executive Committee with the right to confine people in prisons or camps or to send them into internal exile for as much as a five-year term without any court proceedings. The Special Assembly consisted of the commissar of internal affairs, his deputies, the head of the militia, and the chief prosecutor of the USSR or his deputy. A decision of the Special Assembly could be reversed, in the event of a protest by the procuracy, only by the Presidium of the Central Executive Committee.

After the murder of Kirov and especially after the first two Moscow trials, Stalin and Yezhov carried out a "general purge" of the NKVD. . . . The pay of NKVD employees was approximately quadrupled. Previously a relatively low pay scale had hindered recruitment; after 1937 the NKVD scale was higher than that of any other government agency. NKVD employees were also given the best apartments, rest homes, and hospitals. They were awarded medals and orders for success in their activities. And, in the latter half of the thirties, their numbers were so swollen as to become a whole army, with divisions and regiments, with hundreds of thousands of security workers and tens of thousands of officers. NKVD agencies were set up not only in every oblast center but in each city, even in each ration center. Special sections were organized in every large enterprise, in many middle-size ones, in railroad stations, in major organizations and educational institutions. Parks, theaters, libraries — almost all gathering places (even smoking rooms) came under constant observation by special NKVD operatives. An enormous network of informers and stool pigeons was created in almost every institution, including prisons and camps.

Dossiers were kept on tens of millions of people. In addition to the sections that kept tabs on Cadets[4] and monarchists, SRs[5] and Mensheviks, and other counterrevolutionary parties, in the Fourth Administration (*upravlenie*) of the NKVD a section was created for the Communist Party. It maintained surveillance over all party organizations, including the Central Committee. All raikom, gorkom, and obkom[6] secretaries were confirmed in their posts only after the approval of the appropriate NKVD agencies. Special sections were also created to watch the Chekists themselves, and a special section to watch the special sections. The Chekists were trained to believe that Chekist discipline was higher than party discipline. "First of all," they were told, "you are a Chekist, and only then a Communist." Their training included learning the history of the trade, beginning with a very serious study of the Inquisition.[7]

Stalin paid special attention to surveillance of his closest aides, the members of the Politburo. "The secret service of the sovereign," says an ancient Indian book, "must keep its eyes on all the high officials, directors of affairs, friends and relatives of the ruler, and likewise his rivals." Stalin watched every step of his closest aides, using the notorious law "On the protection of chiefs," enacted after Kirov's murder. While Stalin personally selected and completely controlled his own bodyguard (headed by General Vlasik), the protection of other leaders was entrusted to the NKVD. They could not go anywhere without the knowledge of their guard, could not receive any visitor without a check by the guard, and so on.

Although the powers of the NKVD were unusually great in the early thirties, in the summer of 1936 the Central Committee passed a resolution, on Stalin's proposal, to grant the NKVD extraordinary powers for one year — to destroy completely the "enemies of the people." At the June Plenum of the Central Committee in 1937 these powers

---

[4]Members of the Constitutional Democratic party. — Ed.

[5]Members of the peasant-based Socialist Revolutionary party. — Ed.

[6]District committee, city committee, provincial committee. — Ed.

[7]Chekists also received practical training in torture and many other things that were condemned in theory. Posted prominently in NKVD offices, even on the local level, was a saying by Lenin, "The slightest illegality is a hole through which counterrevolution can creep in." This hypocrisy was fully in the spirit of Stalin.

were extended for an indefinite period. At the same time the NKVD's juridical functions were significantly expanded. Within a day after the June plenum eighteen Central Committee members were arrested.

In addition to the Special Assembly, an extensive system of troiki, or three-man boards, was created, subordinated to this Special Assembly. These illegal bodies, whose very existence violated the Constitution of the USSR, independently examined political cases and passed sentences, completely ignoring the norms of jurisprudence. In this way the punitive organs were exempt from any control by the party and the soviets, the courts, and the procurator [prosecutor]. Even when the NKVD investigators passed cases to the procurator's office or the courts, the latter obediently handed down verdicts prepared beforehand by the agency. In many oblasti [provinces] procurators issued back-dated sanctions several months after an arrest, or even signed blank forms on which the NKVD subsequently entered any names they wanted. In reality, only one man had the right to control the activity of the punitive organs — Stalin himself.

This kind of repressive system obviously had its own kind of inertia, since a large percentage of the privileged NKVD officers would naturally desire to continue in their positions and therefore had an interest in finding and imprisoning more and more "enemies of the people" to justify their own existence. Thus the ever-expanding punitive agencies, besides being a firm foundation of the Stalinist regime, became a source of never-ending repression. . . .

The development of the cult of Stalin and the Stalinist system was facilitated to a large degree by the social processes taking place in the Soviet Union after the revolution — processes that cannot be reduced solely to the struggle between the proletariat and the bourgeoisie. Of no less importance was the struggle between petty bourgeois tendencies and aspirations, on the one hand, and proletarian socialist ones, on the other, both inside the Communist Party and Soviet government and outside of them.

As Lenin once wrote:

> *Whoever expects a "pure" social revolution will never live to see it. . . .*
> *The socialist revolution . . . cannot be anything other than an outburst of mass struggle on the part of all and sundry oppressed and discontented elements. Inevitably, sections of the petty bourgeoisie and of the backward workers will participate in it — without such participa-*

tion mass struggle is impossible; without it no revolution is possible —
and just as inevitably will they bring into the movement their preju-
dices, their reactionary fantasies, their weaknesses and errors.

Marxist sociology includes in the petty bourgeoisie not only peasants, artisans, small merchants, and the lower sections of office workers
and professionals but also declassed elements at the bottom of society, a
large group in Russia and many other backward capitalist countries.
They are people who have lost or have never had even petty property;
they have not grown accustomed to labor in capitalist industry and live
by occasional earnings. The significant stratum of agricultural workers,
or hired hands (*batraki*), in old Russia also had little experience of
collective labor, although they were called the "rural proletariat." Despite great diversity, all these petty bourgeois strata have certain features
in common, including political instability and vacillation, a degree of
anarchism, and small-proprietor individualism. Because of their political instability they may provide the reserves for revolution or for reaction, depending on circumstances. Unsettled and disoriented after
World War I, for example, they supported fascist dictatorship in some
European countries.

Under the autocratic regime in Russia, which was waging an unpopular and burdensome war, the Bolshevik Party was able to win over
not only the greater part of the industrial proletariat but also a substantial section of the semiproletarian and petty bourgeois masses. It would
be naive to think, however, that the tens of millions of semiproletarian
and petty bourgeois elements would be completely transformed by several years of revolutionary struggle, freeing themselves from the short-
comings and limitations of their class backgrounds. It would also be a
mistake to idealize the proletariat, picturing it as purely virtuous. Not
only in Russia but also in many industrially developed countries a good
part of the proletariat was infected with ideas, convictions, and attitudes
quite far removed from the socialist ideal.

Thus, it was not possible for the Bolshevik Party to somehow isolate
itself from the surrounding petty bourgeois element. That environment
inevitably exerted great pressure on the party through the most varied
channels and had a significant effect on the revolutionary cadres, the
party and government apparatus of the young Soviet republic.

As is generally known, most of the professional revolutionaries,
who formed the backbone of the party, came not from the working class

but from the intelligentsia, the lesser gentry, the civil service, the lower strata of the merchant class, artisans and craftsmen, and the clergy. These origins did not prevent most of these people from merging heart and soul with the proletariat and thus becoming proletarian revolutionaries in the full sense of the word. But by no means all the party activists experienced a complete transformation. Besides, the revolution and the civil war produced many new leaders who had not gone through the rigorous school of underground struggle before the revolution. That many individuals who were not true proletarian revolutionaries became leaders of the party both under Lenin and after his death was therefore not an accident or the result of insufficient wisdom. It was the natural result of a proletarian revolution in a petty bourgeois country like Russia. Lenin's remarks about the need to build socialism out of the human material left by capitalism applied to the Bolshevik Party as well.

Lenin was well aware that one of the most difficult problems of the proletarian revolution in Russia was to safeguard the party cadres from bureaucratic degeneration, to overcome the increasing pressure from the petty bourgeois element on the proletariat and the Bolshevik Party. He saw that the transformation of the party from an underground organization to a ruling party would greatly increase petty bourgeois and careerist tendencies among old party members and also bring into the party a host of petty bourgeois and careerist elements that had previously been outside. As early as the Eighth Party Congress, in 1919, Lenin said:

> We must avoid everything that in practice may tend to encourage individual abuses. In some places careerists and adventurers have attached themselves to us like leeches, people who call themselves Communists and are deceiving us, and who have wormed their way into our ranks because the Communists are now in power, and because the more honest government employees refused to come and work with us on account of their retrograde ideas, while careerists have no ideas, and no honesty. These people, whose only aim is to make a career, resort to coercion in local areas and imagine they are doing a good thing.

A resolution adopted in 1921 on Lenin's initiative, which dealt with "cleansing" the party of alien elements, said the following:

> A situation is gradually taking shape in which one can "rise in the world," make a career for oneself, get a bit of power, only by entering the service of the Soviet regime.

Lenin argued that petty-bourgeois intellectuals would always:

> *worm their way into the Soviets, the courts, and the administration, since communism cannot be built otherwise than with the aid of the human material created by capitalism, and the bourgeois intellectuals cannot be expelled and destroyed, but must be won over, remolded, assimilated, and reeducated, just as we must — in a protracted struggle waged on the basis of the dictatorship of the proletariat — reeducate the proletarians themselves, who do not abandon their petty bourgeois prejudices at one stroke, by a miracle, at the behest of the Virgin Mary, at the behest of a slogan, resolution, or decree, but only in the course of a long and difficult mass struggle against mass petty bourgeois influences.*

In his last writings Lenin concentrated on this very problem: the interrelation of petty bourgeois and proletarian elements in Soviet society and government and the bureaucratization and degeneration of the party and government apparatuses. As late as 1922, after five years of the revolution, Lenin's opinion of the party's composition was not particularly high.

> *There is no doubt that our party, to judge from the bulk of its present membership, is not sufficiently proletarian. . . .*
>
> *If we do not shut our eyes to reality, we must admit that at the present time the proletarian policy of the party is not determined by the character of its membership, but by the enormous, undivided prestige of that very thin stratum which may be called the party's Old Guard. A small conflict within this stratum would be enough, if not to destroy this prestige, in any event to weaken it to such a degree as to rob this stratum of its power to determine policy.*

In his "Letter to the Congress" (part of what is called "Lenin's Testament") he wrote:

> *The apparatus we call ours is, in fact, still quite alien to us: it is a bourgeois and tsarist hodgepodge, and there has been no possibility of getting rid of it in the course of the past five years without the help of other countries. . . . There is no doubt that the infinitesimal percentage of Soviet and Sovietized workers will drown in that tide of chauvinistic Great Russian riffraff like a fly in milk.*

Similarly, Lenin's opinion was not particularly high in regard to the Soviet working class itself, at least in the form it took in the wake of the upheavals and catastrophes of world war and civil war.

There is no doubt that we constantly regard as workers people who have not had the slightest real experience of large-scale industry. There has been case after case of petty bourgeois, who have become workers by chance and only for a very short time, being classed as workers. All shrewd White Guardists are very definitely banking on the fact that the alleged proletarian character of our party does not in the least safeguard it against the small-proprietor elements gaining predominance in it, and very rapidly too.

Lenin's concern for the preservation of the socialist character of the Soviet government and the proletarian policy of the Bolshevik Party was fully justified. He was, however, speaking only of the *danger* of bureaucratic and petty bourgeois degeneration, not its fatal inevitability. For in addition to the impact of petty bourgeois ideology on the proletariat and its party, an opposite process was under way — a decisive reshaping of the psychology, ideology, and morals of the petty bourgeois masses and the backward strata of the proletariat itself. The party protected itself against degeneration not only by regular purges of its ranks but also by organizing the education and reeducation of the masses on an unparalleled scale. The civil war weakened the proletariat, but it left the power in Bolshevik hands. Through the Soviets, the trade unions, the press, the school system, through groups organized to eradicate illiteracy, through "reading-room huts" (*izby-chitalni*) set up in countless villages, through the Red Army, and by all other available means the Bolshevik Party sought to lodge socialist ideology firmly in the consciousness of the masses. Considerable progress was made in this area even during Lenin's lifetime. After his death the effort began to flag, because Stalin took the leadership of the party. Stalin's views and personality combined the outward features and terminology of a proletarian revolutionary with the character traits of a petty bourgeois revolutionary and careerist inclined toward degeneration. With his petty bourgeois background and his training in church schools Stalin lacked the qualities of a genuine proletarian revolutionary.

But the problem did not lie in Stalin alone. Moral decay and bureaucratic degeneration to one degree or another affected a section of the party's Old Guard, on which Lenin placed such high hopes and of which he spoke with such pride. First of all, within this Old Guard throughout the twenties, . . . there was a fierce ideological battle, which at the same time was a struggle for leadership of the party. Secondly, great progress in socialist construction and considerable power turned the heads of many members of the Old Guard. Further contributing to this process was the steadily increasing centralization of power in both party and government, not matched by any increase in control from below. Symptoms of arrogance, conceit, intolerance of criticism, and susceptibility to flattery began to appear among some who previously had seemed to be modest and reliable revolutionaries. In their way of life, behavior, and material comforts these men moved farther and farther away from the ordinary people, and they did nothing to hinder the immoderate praise that in the late twenties began to be heaped upon them.

It is only fair to note that degeneration of a part of the revolutionary cadres is the rule in every revolution, which attracts many people who are motivated by a desire for power or wealth. The French Revolution brought to the fore not only leaders like Marat but also careerists like Fouché, Talleyrand, Barras, and Tallien. The October revolution did not escape the same fate. "Every revolution has its scum," Lenin said once. "Why should we be any exception?"

Mikhail Razumov provides a typical example. A party member since 1912, secretary of the Tatar and then of the Irkutsk obkom [provincial committee of the party], he turned into a magnate before the startled eyes of Eugenia Ginzburg, who records the process in her memoirs. As late as 1930 he occupied one room in a communal apartment. A year later he was building a "Tatar Livadia" (reminiscent of the former tsar's palace at Livadia in the Crimea). In 1933, when Tatary was awarded the Order of Lenin for success in the kolkhoz movement, portraits of the "First Brigadier of Tatary" were carried through the city with singing. At an agricultural exhibition his portraits were done in mosaics of various crops, ranging from oats to lentils. . . .

There were various reasons for this lamentable turn of events. People's paths away from the ideals and moral standards of the revolution were as varied as the ways by which they had come to the revolution in the first place. It is easy to understand the degeneration of Vyshinsky,[8] the Menshevik turncoat: he had apparently always been an unprincipled, cowardly person, hungry for power and fame. (Thus, it is not surprising that he persecuted first his former Menshevik comrades and later his new comrades, the Bolsheviks.) It is harder to understand

---

[8] Andrei Vyshinsky, prosecutor in the main purge trials, later Foreign Minister and Chief Soviet Delegate to the U.N. — Ed.

why men like Yaroslavsky or Kalinin who had once been staunch Bolsheviks broke and became totally submissive to Stalin's will. Personalities aside, the general rule is apparent. It was not the struggle with the autocracy, not jail or exile, that was the real test for revolutionaries. Much harder was the test of power, having the vast and powerful resources of the state at one's disposal.

Of course the degree to which Bolshevik leaders degenerated also varied. Bureaucratic degeneration reached great extremes in the cases of men like Postyshev, Krylenko, Sheboldaev, and Betal Kalmykov, not to mention such intimates of Stalin as Molotov, Kaganovich, and Voroshilov.[9] The moral collapse of many other members of the Old Guard was not so profound. But they did acquire the habit of commanding, of administration by fiat, ignoring the opinion of the masses. Cut off from the people, they lost the ability to criticize Stalin's behavior and the cult of his personality; on the contrary, they became increasingly dependent on him. Their change in life-style aroused dissatisfaction among workers and rank-and-file party members. One result was the relative ease with which Stalin subsequently destroyed such people, for he could picture their fall as the result not only of a struggle against "spies" and "wreckers" but also of the proletariat's struggle against corrupt and degenerate bureaucrats, a struggle to purge the party of petty bourgeois elements.

Of course after Stalin's purges the composition of the higher echelons of party and government grew even worse. Most of the new officeholders were not young and honest revolutionaries but unprincipled careerists who were willing to carry out any order Stalin gave, with no concern for the interests of the people and socialism. Nevertheless, even after rising to the party leadership, such people could not operate with a free hand. The concrete conditions of the Soviet system were such that they had to declare, at least in words, their devotion to the proletariat and the Communist movement. Thus a whole stratum of "Soviet" philistines and "party" bourgeois took shape, differing from traditional bourgeois philistines only by their greater sanctimoniousness and hypocrisy. The influence of such petty bourgeois elements was especially strong in the union republics where the proletarian nucleus was not as great and the revolution not as profound as in the basic regions of Russia.

[9]N. V. Krylenko, Commissar of Justice; B. P. Sheboldaev and B. Kalmykov, provincial party secretaries; K. Ye. Voroshilov, Commissar of War and later Chief of State. — Ed.

Thus, we see that the Stalin cult was not just a religious or ideological phenomenon; it also had a well-defined class content. It was based on the petty bourgeois, bureaucratic degeneration of some cadres and the extensive penetration of petty bourgeois and careerist elements into the ruling elite of Soviet society. Stalin was not simply a dictator; he stood at the peak of a whole system of smaller dictators; he was the head bureaucrat over hundreds of thousands of smaller bureaucrats.

Some sociologists have voiced the hypothesis that in the Stalin era the proletarian socialist core of the party and government were completely destroyed and that with the advent to power of purely petty bourgeois bureaucratic elements a society of the state capitalist type was created. This is a mistaken conception and a distortion of reality, although it contains an element of truth.

The extremely complex social processes in the Soviet Union in the twenties, thirties, and forties are still waiting for genuine scientific analysis. But certain trends are apparent. On the one hand, the working class, growing with exceptional speed, absorbed the declassed urban bourgeoisie and petty bourgeoisie and the millions of peasant migrants to the cities. In 1929–1935 new workers of these types were several times more numerous than the working class of the past. This rapid change in the composition of the working class was bound to affect its psychology and behavior and also the composition of the party, thereby facilitating the degeneration of some parts of the apparatus.

As the veteran party member B—— wrote in his unpublished memoirs:

> *Virtually the most important of the changes that took place was the change in the composition of the working class. Beginning with the first five-year plan, enormous masses of peasants began flooding rapidly into industry (the construction industry first of all), including many dekulakized peasants. Is this a fact of small importance? From time immemorial the Russian proletariat had consisted of former peasants. But it had grown at a measured pace and had always managed to digest its new replenishments from the peasantry. Now, however, because of the stormy pace of industrialization, dictated by the revolution and vitally necessary for the revolution, another process began to occur in parallel. The elemental petty bourgeois peasant mass began to encroach on the inner essence of the proletariat, on the proletarian psychology and social outlook, its attitude toward the individual, toward property, toward its work and the cause of socialism. The petty bourgeois element was on the offensive from within, wearing worker's overalls and carrying*

worker's tools. . . . When the factory didn't have the strength to pro-letarianize the peasants (and it couldn't have happened any other way, because of the rapid peasant influx and its enormous numerical growth), there immediately began the "peasantization" of the workers. With this change in composition something also changed in the work-er's soul. And these changes could not help but affect the party.

At the same time, alongside these negative processes in the thirties and forties, an opposite process was taking place: the transformation of the ideology and consciousness of enormous masses through the propagation of socialist ideology and morality, even though the forms and formulations were significantly distorted. In the deep recesses of Soviet society processes were under way that ultimately strengthened rather than weakened the role and influence of socialist elements. Through the press, the army, and especially the school system socialist ideology was spread to vast numbers, including the nonproletarian population. A new generation of young people grew up and a new intelligentsia. The work of educating and reeducating the populace was done on a vast scale, and although many gave only lip service, a great many more, especially among the youth, adopted socialist ideology and morality as the basis of their conduct and inner convictions. And this process proved to be the most important.

It would be unjust to say that in the thirties the Soviet state apparatus represented nothing but bourgeois and tsarist philistinism. Its composition was changing. But this process of socialist transformation proceeded in various ways on various levels and among various strata of the party, government, and society. The spread of proletarian ideology and Communist morality was most intensive in the twenties and thirties among the new generations and on the lower levels of society. The greatest changes in this respect were observable in the lower echelons of the party, government, and economic apparatus, where the losses from the mass repression were fewer than in the upper echelons. In the leadership of base-level organizations of the party and Komsomol, of individual factories, shops, and farms, among teachers, doctors, sports organizations, and so on the majority were not bureaucrats and careerists but honest and devoted cadres.

Of course they too were affected by the distortions connected with the cult. Many wrong and even criminal directives were carried out by primary party organizations. But there was far more sincere error and honest self-deception on these lower levels than there was higher up. Most of the directives sent down to them breathed the spirit of revolution, speaking about struggle with the enemies of socialism, concern for individuals, the need to advance the cause of the revolution. The lower organizations, failing to see the gap between the words and deeds of Stalin and his associates, tried to adhere to political and moral norms that many people at the top did not consider binding on themselves. Rank-and-file Communists and Komsomol members and apparatus cadres on the lower level sincerely tried as much as they were able to put into practice the socialist slogans, which for many careerists and bureaucrats at the top were just empty words.

Even at the top, however, there was some variety. One group, the Stalinist guard, consisted of cruel, unprincipled men, ready to destroy anything that blocked their way to power. But since these people were incapable of managing a big, complex governmental organism, Stalin had to bring into the leadership people of another type, comparatively young leaders who supported Stalin in almost everything but were not informed of many of his crimes. Although they shared certain characteristic faults of Stalin's entourage, they also wanted to serve the people, the party, and socialism. They lacked sufficient political experience to analyze and rectify the tragic events of the Stalinist period, and some of them perished toward the end of it. But others survived, and after Stalin's death gave varying degrees of support to the struggle against the cult and the effort to establish more normal conditions for Soviet society.

The petty bourgeois degeneration of a section of the party and government cadres took such forms as self-seeking, careerism, bureaucratism, lack of principle, conceit, vainglory, and time serving. It was this degeneration that facilitated the rise of the Stalin cult, and it was from this milieu that Stalinism drew its main cadres.

Within the proletariat and the proletarian core of the party, however, there were also conservative and dogmatic tendencies that contributed to the extended hegemony of Stalinism.

According to Marxist doctrine, the proletariat is the most advanced class of bourgeois society, but neither Marx nor Lenin idealized it. Lenin made the following point in his *"Left-Wing" Communism — An Infantile Disorder:*

> *Within every class, even in the conditions prevailing in the most enlightened countries, even within the most advanced class, and even when the circumstances of the moment have aroused all the spiritual*

forces of this class to an exceptional degree, there always are — and inevitably will be as long as classes exist, as long as a classless society has not fully consolidated itself, and has not developed on its own foundations — representatives of the class who do not think and are incapable of thinking. Capitalism would not be the oppressor of the masses that it actually is, if things were otherwise.

A creative approach to both reality and theory is considered the chief claim of Marxism and scientific socialism to superiority over other systems, but it would be wrong to place one's trust solely in the creative aspect of socialist ideology and underestimate the strength of dogmatism. It would be naive to think that dogmatism always repels people, while a creative approach is always attractive. Unfortunately, the opposite has more often occurred.

For a large number of people who lack the necessary education and training, dogmatism proves to be more attractive because it frees them from the need to think, to take initiative, to continually raise the level of their own understanding. Instead of studying ever-changing reality, they use a few fixed rules. Human history in general and the history of religions and ideologies in particular have shown us the immense force of dogmatic thinking. Things are always harder for creative thinkers and innovators than for dogmatists. Although a revolution represents the victory of new ideas over old dogmas, in time any revolutionary movement becomes overgrown with its own dogmas. In tsarist Russia such a tendency was more likely than usual, for a great many revolutionaries lacked education. In such a situation Stalin's ability to make extreme simplifications of complex ideas was not the least factor in his rise. Many party cadres knew Marxism and Leninism only in its schematic Stalinist form, unaware that Stalin had impoverished and vulgarized Marxism, transforming it from a developing, creative doctrine into a kind of religion.

Thus it would be wrong to attribute every mistake of former revolutionaries to petty bourgeois degeneration. Many of their errors were due not to a change in their earlier views but to an incapacity for change — in other words, to dogmatism.

Many dedicated revolutionaries, indifferent to personal advantage, were nevertheless incapable of carrying the revolution forward when a new stage required new methods. More and more their thought revealed the doctrinaire rigidity, the sectarian ossification, that Thomas Mann had in mind when he spoke of "revolutionary conservatism."

Many leaders who excelled in the period of civil war were not effective at building a new society. Accustomed to resolving most conflicts by force of arms, they were incapable of complex educational work, which had to be the chief method in the new period. Instead of learning, some Communists even began to boast of their lack of education. "We never finished *gimnazii* [secondary schools], but we are governing *gubernii* [provinces]," a well-known Bolshevik declared in the late twenties, and his audience applauded. When such people ran into difficulties, they often turned into simple executors of orders from above, valuing blind discipline most of all. The closed mind, the refusal to think independently, was the epistemological basis of the cult of personality. It was not only degenerates and careerists who supported the cult; there were also sincere believers, genuinely convinced that everything they did was necessary for the revolution. They believed in the political trials of 1936–1938; they believed that the class struggle was intensifying; they believed in the necessity for mass repression. They became willing or unwilling accomplices in Stalin's crimes, although subsequently many of them also became his victims.

Leon Trotsky

Soviet Bonapartism

Leon Trotsky (1879–1940), one-time second-in-command to Lenin, defeated by Stalin in the controversies of the 1920s, is the great tragic figure of the Russian Revolution. He was expelled from the Communist Party in 1927 and deported from Russia in 1929. He finally settled in Mexico, where, in 1940, he was assassinated by a Soviet agent. During the years of exile Trotsky published a steady stream of articles and books, attacking Stalin's rule in Russia as a bureaucratic and "Bonapartist" perversion of the Russian Revolution analogous to the rule of Napoleon Bonaparte in France. His most provocative critique is excerpted here.

From Leon Trotsky, *The Revolution Betrayed: What Is the Soviet Union and Where Is It Going?*, translated by Max Eastman (Garden City, NY: Doubleday, Doran and Co., 1937), pp. 5–8, 19–20, 45–47, 54–56, 275–279.

Owing to the insignificance of the Russian bourgeoisie, the democratic tasks of backward Russia — such as liquidation of the monarchy and the semifeudal slavery of the peasants — could be achieved only through a dictatorship of the proletariat. The proletariat, however, having seized the power at the head of the peasant masses, could not stop at the achievement of these democratic tasks. The bourgeois revolution was directly bound up with the first stages of a socialist revolution. That fact was not accidental. The history of recent decades very clearly shows that, in the conditions of capitalist decline, backward countries are unable to attain that level which the old centers of capitalism have attained. Having themselves arrived in a blind alley, the highly civilized nations block the road to those in process of civilization. Russia took the road of proletarian revolution, not because her economy was the first to become ripe for a socialist change, but because she could not develop further on a capitalist basis. Socialization of the means of production had become a necessary condition for bringing the country out of barbarism. That is the *law of combined development* for backward countries. Entering upon the socialist revolution as "the weakest link in the capitalist chain" (Lenin), the former empire of the tsars is even now, in the nineteenth year after the revolution, still confronted with the task of "catching up with and outstripping" — consequently in the first place *catching up with* — Europe and America. She has, that is, to solve those problems of technique and productivity which were long ago solved by capitalism in the advanced countries.

Could it indeed be otherwise? The overthrow of the old ruling classes did not achieve, but only completely revealed, the task: to rise from barbarism to culture. At the same time, by concentrating the means of production in the hands of the state, the revolution made it possible to apply new and incomparably more effective industrial methods. Only thanks to a planned directive was it possible in so brief a span to restore what had been destroyed by the imperialist and civil wars, to create gigantic new enterprises, to introduce new kinds of production and establish new branches of industry.

The extraordinary tardiness in the development of the international revolution, upon whose prompt aid the leaders of the Bolshevik party had counted, created immense difficulties for the Soviet Union, but also revealed its inner powers and resources. However, a correct appraisal of the results achieved — their grandeur as well as their inadequacy — is possible only with the help of an international scale of measurement. . . .

During the last three years the production of iron has doubled. The production of steel and the rolling mills has increased almost 2½ times. The output of oil, coal and iron has increased from 3 to 3½ times the prewar figure. In 1920, when the first plan of electrification was drawn up, there were ten district power stations in the country with a total power production of 253,000 kilowatts. In 1935, there were already ninety-five of these stations with a total power of 4,345,000 kilowatts. In 1925, the Soviet Union stood eleventh in the production of electroenergy; in 1935, it was second only to Germany and the United States. In the production of coal, the Soviet Union has moved forward from tenth to fourth place. In steel, from sixth to third place. In the production of tractors, to the first place in the world. This also is true of the production of sugar.

Gigantic achievements in industry, enormously promising beginnings in agriculture, an extraordinary growth of the old industrial cities and a building of new ones, a rapid increase of the number of workers, a rise in cultural level and cultural demands — such are the indubitable results of the October Revolution, in which the prophets of the old world tried to see the grave of human civilization. With the bourgeois economists we have no longer anything to quarrel over. Socialism has demonstrated its right to victory, not on the pages of *Das Kapital*, but in an industrial arena comprising a sixth part of the earth's surface — not in the language of dialectics, but in the language of steel, cement and electricity. Even if the Soviet Union, as a result of internal difficulties, external blows and the mistakes of its leadership, were to collapse — which we firmly hope will not happen — there would remain as an earnest of the future this indestructible fact, that thanks solely to a proletarian revolution a backward country has achieved in less than ten years successes unexampled in history. . . .

The national income per person in the Soviet Union is considerably less than in the West. And since capital investment consumes about 25 to 30 percent — incomparably more than anywhere else — the total amount consumed by the popular mass cannot but be considerably lower than in the advanced capitalist countries.

To be sure, in the Soviet Union there are no possessing classes, whose extravagance is balanced by an underconsumption of the popular mass. However the weight of this corrective is not so great as might appear at first glance. The fundamental evil of the capitalist system is not the extravagance of the possessing classes, however disgusting that may be in itself, but the fact that in order to guarantee its right to extravagance the bourgeoisie maintains its private ownership of the means of production, thus condemning the economic system to anarchy and decay. In the matter of luxuries the bourgeoisie, of course, has a monopoly of consumption. But in things of prime necessity, the toiling masses constitute the overwhelming majority of consumers. . . . Although the Soviet Union has no possessing classes in the proper sense of the word, still she has very privileged commanding strata of the population, who appropriate the lion's share in the sphere of consumption. And so if there is a lower per capita production of things of prime necessity in the Soviet Union than in the advanced capitalist countries, that does mean that the standard of living of the Soviet masses still falls below the capitalist level.

The historic responsibility for this situation lies, of course, upon Russia's black and heavy past, her heritage of darkness and poverty. There was no other way out upon the road of progress except through the overthrow of capitalism. To convince yourself of this, it is only necessary to cast a glance at the Baltic countries and Poland, once the most advanced parts of the tsar's empire, and now hardly emerging from the morass. The undying service of the Soviet regime lies in its intense and successful struggle with Russia's thousand-year-old backwardness. But a correct estimate of what has been attained is the first condition for further progress.

The Soviet regime is passing through a *preparatory* stage, importing, borrowing and appropriating the technical and cultural conquests of the West. The comparative coefficients of production and consumption testify that this preparatory stage is far from finished. Even under the improbable condition of a continuing complete capitalist standstill, it must still occupy a whole historic period. . . .

The material premise of communism should be so high a development of the economic powers of man that productive labor, having ceased to be a burden, will not require any goad, and the distribution of life's goods, existing in continual abundance, will not demand — as it does not now in any well-off family or "decent" boardinghouse — any control except that of education, habit and social opinion. Speaking frankly, I think it would be pretty dull-witted to consider such a really modest perspective "utopian."

Capitalism prepared the conditions and forces for a social revolution: technique, science and the proletariat. The communist structure cannot, however, immediately replace the bourgeois society. The material and cultural inheritance from the past is wholly inadequate for that. In its first steps the workers' state cannot yet permit everyone to work "according to his abilities" — that is, as much as he can and wishes to — nor can it reward everyone "according to his needs," regardless of the work he does. In order to increase the productive forces, it is necessary to resort to the customary norms of wage payment — that is, to the distribution of life's goods in proportion to the quantity and quality of individual labor.

Marx named this first stage of the new society "the lowest stage of communism," in distinction from the highest, where together with the last phantoms of want material inequality will disappear. In this sense socialism and communism are frequently contrasted as the lower and higher stages of the new society. "We have not yet, of course, *complete* communism," reads the present official Soviet doctrine, "but we have already achieved socialism — that is, the *lowest* stage of communism." In proof of this, they adduce the dominance of the state trusts in industry, the collective farms in agriculture, the state and cooperative enterprises in commerce. At first glance this gives a complete correspondence with the a priori — and therefore hypothetical — scheme of Marx. But it is exactly for the Marxist that this question is not exhausted by a consideration of forms of property regardless of the achieved productivity of labor. By the lowest stage of communism Marx meant, at any rate, a society which from the very beginning stands higher in its economic development than the most advanced capitalism. Theoretically such a conception is flawless, for taken *on a world scale* communism, even in its first incipient stage, means a higher level of development than that of bourgeois society. Moreover, Marx expected that the Frenchman would begin the social revolution, the German continue it, the Englishman finish it; and as to the Russian, Marx left him far in the rear. But this conceptual order was upset by the facts. Whoever tries now mechanically to apply the universal historic conception of Marx to the particular case of the Soviet Union at the given stage of its development, will be entangled at once in hopeless contradictions.

Russia was not the strongest, but the weakest link in the chain of capitalism. The present Soviet Union does not stand above the world level of economy, but is only trying to catch up to the capitalist countries. If Marx called that society which was to be formed upon the basis of a socialization of the productive forces of the most advanced capitalism of its epoch, the lowest stage of communism, then this designation obviously does not apply to the Soviet Union, which is still today considerably poorer in technique, culture and the good things of life than the capitalist countries. It would be truer, therefore, to name the present Soviet regime in all its contradictoriness, not a socialist regime, but a *preparatory* regime *transitional* from capitalism to socialism. . . .

Experience revealed what theory was unable clearly to foresee. If for the defense of socialized property against bourgeois counterrevolution a "state of armed workers" was fully adequate, it was a very different matter to regulate inequalities in the sphere of consumption. Those deprived of property are not inclined to create and defend it. The majority cannot concern itself with the privileges of the minority. For the defense of "bourgeois law" the workers' state was compelled to create a "bourgeois" type of instrument — that is, the same old gendarme, although in a new uniform.

We have thus taken the first step toward understanding the fundamental contradiction between Bolshevik program and Soviet reality. If the state does not die away, but grows more and more despotic, if the plenipotentiaries of the working class become bureaucratized, and the bureaucracy rises above the new society, this is not for some secondary reasons like the psychological relics of the past, and so forth, but is a result of the iron necessity to give birth to and support a privileged minority so long as it is impossible to guarantee genuine equality.

The tendencies of bureaucratism, which strangles the workers' movement in capitalist countries, would everywhere show themselves even after a proletarian revolution. But it is perfectly obvious that the poorer the society which issues from a revolution, the sterner and more naked would be the expression of this "law," the more crude would be the forms assumed by bureaucratism, and the more dangerous would it become for socialist development. The Soviet state is prevented not only from dying away, but even from freeing itself of the bureaucratic parasite, not by the "relics" of former ruling classes, as declares the naked police doctrine of Stalin, for these relics are powerless in themselves. It is prevented by immeasurably mightier factors, such as material want, cultural backwardness and the resulting dominance of "bourgeois law" in what most immediately and sharply touches every human being, the business of insuring his personal existence. . . .

While the growth of industry and the bringing of agriculture into the sphere of state planning vastly complicates the tasks of leadership, bringing to the front the problem of *quality*, bureaucratism destroys the creative initiative and the feeling of responsibility without which there is not, and cannot be, qualitative progress. The ulcers of bureaucratism are perhaps not so obvious in the big industries, but they are devouring, together with the cooperatives, the light and food-producing industries, the collective farms, the small local industries — that is, all those branches of economy which stand nearest to the people.

The progressive role of the Soviet bureaucracy coincides with the period devoted to introducing into the Soviet Union the most important elements of capitalist technique. The rough work of borrowing, imitating, transplanting and grafting, was accomplished on the bases laid down by the revolution. There was, thus far, no question of any new word in the sphere of technique, science or art. It is possible to build gigantic factories according to a ready-made Western pattern by bureaucratic command — although, to be sure, at triple the normal cost. But the farther you go, the more the economy runs into the problem of quality, which slips out of the hands of a bureaucracy like a shadow. The Soviet products are as though branded with the gray label of indifference. Under a nationalized economy, *quality* demands a democracy of producers and consumers, freedom of criticism and initiative — conditions incompatible with a totalitarian regime of fear, lies and flattery.

Behind the question of quality stands a more complicated and grandiose problem which may be comprised in the concept of *independent, technical* and *cultural creation*. The ancient philosopher said that strife is the father of all things. No new values can be created where a free conflict of ideas is impossible. To be sure, a revolutionary dictatorship means by its very essence strict limitations of freedom. But for that very reason epochs of revolution have never been directly favorable to cultural creation: they have only cleared the arena for it. The dictatorship of the proletariat opens a wider scope to human genius the more it ceases to be a dictatorship. The socialist culture will flourish only in proportion to the dying away of the state. In that simple and unshakable historic law is contained the death sentence of the present political regime in the Soviet Union. Soviet democracy is not the demand of an abstract policy, still less an abstract moral. It has become a life-and-death need of the country.

If the new state had no other interests than the interests of society, the dying away of the function of compulsion would gradually acquire a painless character. But the state is not pure spirit. Specific functions have created specific organs. The bureaucracy taken as a whole is concerned not so much with its function as with the tribute which this function brings in. The commanding caste tries to strengthen and perpetuate the organs of compulsion. To make sure of its power and income, it spares nothing and nobody. The more the course of development goes against it, the more ruthless it becomes toward the advanced elements of the population. Like the Catholic Church it has put forward the dogma of infallibility in the period of its decline, but it has raised it to a height of which the Roman pope never dreamed.

The increasingly insistent deification of Stalin is, with all its elements of caricature, a necessary element of the regime. The bureaucracy has need of an inviolable super-arbiter, a first consul if not an emperor, and it raises upon its shoulders him who best responds to its claim for lordship. That "strength of character" of the leader which so enraptures the literary dilettantes of the West, is in reality the sum total of the collective pressure of a caste which will stop at nothing in defense of its position. Each one of them at his post is thinking: *l'état — c'est moi.* In Stalin each one easily finds himself. But Stalin also finds in each one a small part of his own spirit. Stalin is the personification of the bureaucracy. That is the substance of his political personality.

Caesarism, or its bourgeois form, Bonapartism, enters the scene in those moments of history when the sharp struggle of two camps raises the state power, so to speak, above the nation, and guarantees it, in appearance, a complete independence of classes — in reality, only the freedom necessary for a defense of the privileged. The Stalin regime, rising above a politically atomized society, resting upon a police and officers' corps, and allowing of no control whatever, is obviously a variation of Bonapartism — a Bonapartism of a new type not before seen in history.

Caesarism arose upon the basis of a slave society shaken by inward strife. Bonapartism is one of the political weapons of the capitalist regime in its critical period. Stalinism is a variety of the same system, but upon the basis of a workers' state torn by the antagonism between an organized and armed soviet aristocracy and the unarmed toiling masses.

As history testifies, Bonapartism gets along admirably with a universal, and even a secret, ballot. The democratic ritual of Bonapartism is the *plebiscite*. From time to time, the question is presented to the citizens: *for* or *against* the leader? And the voter feels the barrel of a revolver between his shoulders. Since the time of Napoleon III, who now seems a provincial dilettante, this technique has received an extraordinary development. The new Soviet constitution which establishes *Bonapartism on a plebiscite basis* is the veritable crown of the system.

In the last analysis, Soviet Bonapartism owes its birth to the belatedness of the world revolution. But in the capitalist countries the same cause gave rise to fascism. We thus arrive at the conclusion, unexpected at first glance, but in reality inevitable, that the crushing of Soviet democracy by an all-powerful bureaucracy and the extermination of bourgeois democracy by fascism were produced by one and the same cause: the dilatoriness of the world proletariat in solving the problems set for it by history. Stalinism and fascism, in spite of a deep difference in social foundations, are symmetrical phenomena. In many of their features they show a deadly similarity. A victorious revolutionary movement in Europe would immediately shake not only fascism, but Soviet Bonapartism. In turning its back to the international revolution, the Stalinist bureaucracy was, from its own point of view, right. It was merely obeying the voice of self-preservation.

Nikolai Shmelyov and Vasily Seliunin

Economics Versus Bureaucracy

Nikolai Shmelyov is an economist on the staff of the Institute of the USA and Canada in Moscow; Vasily Seliunin is a frequent commentator on economic topics. In articles in the liberal literary monthly *Novyi Mir* (New World) excerpted here, they put forth the most penetrating criticism yet heard in the Soviet Union of the blind alley into which Stalinism led the country.

From Nikolai Shmelev, "Avansy i dolgi," *Novyi Mir*, no. 6, 1987, and from Vasilii Seliunin, "Istoki," *Novyi Mir* no. 5, 1988, translated by Robert V. Daniels.

SHMELYOV: "LOANS AND DEBTS"

The condition of our economy satisfies no one. Two of its central, built-in defects, so to speak — the monopoly of the producer under conditions of general shortage, and the lack of interest of enterprises in scientific and technological progress — are no doubt clear to everyone. But how to get rid of these defects, what to do, not just in theory but in practice — I am sure that there are no sages today high or low who could affirm that they know in full the recipe that would work for us. Right now we have many more questions about everything than answers to them. And we still have to talk, argue, propose and reject a great deal before we all of us discover the answers that we need so badly.

With blazing hopes, with deep, frank, and bold discussion of our problems, the past two years have been a time of genuine rebirth of our social thought, of our national self-knowledge. The Twenty-Seventh Congress of the CPSU [February–March, 1986] laid the foundation for revolutionary changes in the life of our society. And the direct, honest discussion spreading around the country about our painful economic problems is one of the most important manifestations of this process.

The basic causes of the blockage of vessels and slowing of blood circulation in our economy have already been revealed. The principle has been proposed, "from produce requisitioning to the produce tax," meaning that administrative methods of management should be replaced by economic accountability stimuli and levers. Certainly one can say that the road has been opened to common sense, at least on the ideological and theoretical plane. However, it is obvious that perestroika is impossible to accomplish on the scale that we would like in one stroke. Commands have ruled our economy instead of the ruble for too long. For so long that we have practically forgotten: there was a time, there really was, when the ruble ruled our economy rather than commands, i.e., common sense rather than speculative armchair arbitrariness.

I understand what reproaches I am inviting, but the question is too serious, too vitally important, to soften one's statements and take refuge in silence. Unless we recognize the fact that the rejection of Lenin's New Economic Policy complicated the building of socialism in the USSR in the most serious way, we will again as in 1953, as in 1965,[1]

---

[1] References to the economic reforms attempted by Prime Minister Georgi Malenkov after the death of Stalin and Prime Minister Alexei Kosygin after the fall of Khrushchev. — Ed.

condemn ourselves to halfway measures; and the halfway approach, as we know, is often worse than doing nothing. The NEP with its economic stimuli and levers was replaced by the administrative system of management. This system by its very nature cannot provide for growth in the quality of output or for raising the efficiency of production or for achieving the greatest result with the least expenditure. It aimed at the necessary gross quantity, not in accord with objective economic laws, but contrary to them. And "contrary" simply means, at the cost of inconceivably high expenses of material and especially human resources.

Meanwhile there still prevails among us the notion that the system of economic relations that took shape in our country, including the structure of property, is the embodiment of Marxism-Leninism in practice, a system fully corresponding to the nature of socialism as a social structure. They say you can perfect it and correct it, but that in its basic principles it is inviolate. However, if learned conclusions are to be governed not by directives but by facts, not by nostalgia for the recent past but by the honest wish for essentially revolutionary changes, then the question of the historical roots of our economic model is far from settled.

We know that at the moment of the victory of the revolution in Russia, none of its recognized theorists or its most authoritative practitioners had (nor could have) a more or less complete picture of the shape of the future socialist economic system. Marx and Engels worked out the theoretical foundations of revolution and substantiated its objective necessity, but as to what kind of economy there would be after victory, they only had guesses. Their point was primarily the general social-economic goals of socialism. They actually left us nothing that could be considered practical advice as to methods of attaining these goals. V. I. Lenin's prerevolutionary work was also basically devoted to pure politics (how to destroy the old social structure) and not at all to the question of what concretely had to be done to get full-blooded economic life going after the revolution.

The revolution thus caught us unarmed with any well-thought-out, complete economic theory of socialism. However, there is reason to believe that in the early months after October, when circumstances still permitted it, Lenin gave this problem very serious attention. It was just at this time that he formulated his celebrated idea that socialism is Soviet power plus Prussian order on the railroads, plus American technology and organization of trusts, plus American mass education, etc.

He wrote then that it was necessary to learn socialism from the organizers of the trusts. He also attached great significance to monetary policy and to a healthy, balanced financial system. It is evident that in the initial period of the revolution Lenin proceeded from the fact that capitalism had already created all the necessary economic forms for socialism and that we only needed to fill them with a new, socialist content.

However, the events following this period called into being the policy of "War Communism," with its exclusively administrative, strong-willed methods of organizing the economy. At some point, apparently, Lenin himself, caught up in this struggle to the death, began to believe that command methods were the basic methods of socialist economics. Here it should be pointed out that there was undoubtedly a conviction that Russia would not long remain alone, that it was not we but the rich industrial West who would lay down the road to the new economic system, that revolution in the West would enable us to resolve many of our sharpest economic problems. The Kronstadt Revolt, the Antonov movement,[2] and the falling off of the revolutionary wave in Europe compelled us, as we know, to reconsider these views and calculations. The NEP signified . . . a revolution of sorts in economic thinking. The question was asked in full measure for the first time, What kind of a socialist economy should we have, not under extraordinary conditions, but under normal human ones?

Many people still believe that the NEP was only a maneuver, only a temporary retreat. There was, of course, a retreat: the Soviet power allowed some space for private enterprise in the cities. But the basic, lasting significance of the NEP was something else. For the first time the basic principles were formulated for a scientific, realistic approach to the tasks of socialist economic construction. From heated, emotional pressure tactics (which we were compelled to resort to by extraordinary circumstances) we shifted to routine, considered, constructive work, to the creation of an economic mechanism that would not weigh down all the creative forces and energy of the toiling population, but would mobilize them instead. The NEP essentially meant a transition from "administrative socialism" to "accountability socialism." In Lenin's plan for shifting the country's economy to normal, healthy conditions, three practical ideas were of key importance. First was the development

[2] Anti-Communist revolt at the Kronstadt naval base and the peasant uprising in central Russia, early 1921. — Ed.

in every way of commodity-monetary market relationships in the economy and the beginning of self-financing and paying one's own way with maximum utilization of cost leverage in the administration of economic processes: prices, a sound gold ruble, profit, taxes, bank credit, and interest. In other words, complete, all-around accountability in all economic relationships from top to bottom. Second was the creation of trusts as units of accountability and the voluntary combination of them into syndicates as the basic worker links in the organizational structure of the economy. Third, the development of cooperative property and cooperative relationships, not only in the village but also in the city — in industry, in construction, in trade, and in what today is called the sphere of social services.

Under the conditions of the NEP, Lenin wrote, trusts (combinations of enterprises) should work "on the basis of the greatest financial and economic autonomy and independence from the local Siberian, Kirgiz, or other authorities, but directly under the Supreme Economic Council."

We know well the very bitter character of the struggle that Lenin and those who were at the time putting this new course into effect waged against overcentralization, bureaucratism, and monopolies of any agency. In the economic and organizational independence of trusts and syndicates they saw the main guarantee against monopoly, which is the instrument of the captains of industry against the constantly threatening demands of the market.

The dismantling of Lenin's policy of "accountability socialism" is often linked even today with the rise of Fascism and the stark appearance in the 1930s of the threat of a new war. This is incorrect: the dismantling began in 1927–1928. The arbitrary reduction of purchase prices for grain forced the village to curtail not only the sale of grain to the state, but even its production. Then it was decided to assure collections for the state by methods of compulsion. It was just at this point that the return to the administrative economy, to the methods of "War Communism," began. These steps were manifested most visibly in collectivization. But such arbitrary relationships were very quickly extended to the city as well. Industry began to get planned assignments from on high, and it is no accident that the basic goals were not fulfilled in any of the prewar five-year plans.

At the price of the utmost exertion of its strength, the country endured the 1930s, and the most terrible war in its history, and the hardship of postwar restoration of the economy. We can understand those who believe that it is useless to compare this price and the results today. But one thing is obvious: it could only be explained, though not justified, by extraordinary, inhuman circumstances which had ceased to exist no later than the mid-1950s. Meanwhile the consequences of rejecting the NEP were not only not being eliminated but were accumulating, and the ailments of the economy were not being cured but only driven in deeper.

The objective demands of contemporary scientific and technological progress, of new conditions and new tasks in the economic competition with capitalism, revealed even more the historical nonviability of this voluntaristic system of managing the economy, that sometimes was simply the brainchild of armchair economists. From the very beginning this whole system was distinguished by economic romanticism, well mixed with economic semiliteracy, and by incredible exaggeration of the efficacy of the so-called administrative, organizational factor. This system was not inherent in socialism, as many people still believe — on the contrary, under normal conditions it is contradictory to it.

It is necessary to see clearly that the cause of our difficulties is not merely and not so much in the heavy burden of military expenditures and the extremely costly scale of the country's global responsibilities. With reasonable spending even our remaining material and human resources would fully suffice to sustain a balanced economy oriented toward technological progress and at the same time satisfy the traditionally modest social needs of our population. However, persistent and prolonged attempts to break the objective laws of economic life, and to suppress work stimuli formed over the centuries in conformity with human nature, led in the last analysis to results directly opposite of what we had calculated. Today we have a planned economy of shortages that is, in fact, unbalanced on all counts and in many respects unmanageable, and to be brutally frank, almost refuses to budge. It still does not accept scientific and technological progress. Industry today rejects up to 80 percent of new, approved inventions and solutions to technical problems. We have one of the lowest levels of labor productivity among the industrialized countries, in particular in agriculture and construction, for during the years of stagnation the mass of the toiling population almost completely lost any incentive for full-blooded, conscientious labor.

However, the consequences of the "administrative economy" that are the most painful to cure do not even lie in the economic sphere.

The excessively administrative view of economic problems, the almost religious "faith in organization," the dislike and incapability of seeing that you never do anything sensible in economics by force, pressure, appeals and goading, became deeply rooted. As both our own and worldwide experience show, the main condition for the viability and efficiency of complex social systems is self-tuning, self-regulation, autonomous development. Attempts to completely subordinate social-economic "Brownian movement"[3] with its inevitable but ultimately acceptable costs, to some kind of central point of management have been fruitless from time immemorial, and the further we go the more obvious this becomes.

Apathy and indifference, theft, disrespect for honest work together with aggressive envy of those who earn more even if they are earning it honestly, have reached a mass scale. Signs have appeared of an almost physical degradation of a significant part of the people in the form of drunkenness and idleness. And finally there is disbelief in proclaimed goals and intentions, in the possibility of a more rational organization of economic and social life. As Academician T. I. Zaslavskaya judiciously observed in the journal *Kommunist* (no. 13, 1986), "Frequent confrontations with various forms of social injustice, and the futility of attempts at individual struggle with its manifestations, became one of the main reasons for the alienation of some of the toilers from our social goals and values."

Obviously it is unrealistic to suppose that all this can quickly be overcome — years, perhaps generations, are necessary. To fully construct "accountability socialism" is much more complicated than simply getting rid of cumbersome individual bureaucratic structures. This does not mean, however, that we can sit with folded arms. There is no way for us, considering today's internal and international realities, to go back to "administrative socialism." . . .

SELIUNIN: "SOURCES"

In the 1920s one man, knowing well its value, effectively concentrated unlimited power in his own hands — the unforgettable Stalin. He was little disturbed by the disputes at all the congresses and meetings of those days. He understood the main thing: the people who really run

[3]An analogy to the random motion of individual particles in chemistry. — Ed.

the country are those who actually take control of the executive apparatus of the state, who direct this apparatus. He guessed something else correctly: as the model for a hierarchical apparatus it was best to use the organization of the military, with its discipline and individual authority. In 1921, in a draft of the plan of a brochure "On the Political Strategy and Tactics of the Russian Communists" that was unusual in its frankness, he wrote, "The Communist Party is a kind of Order of Knights of the Sword inside the Soviet state, directing the organs of the latter and animating their activity." (I recall that the Knights of the Sword were a militarized religious unit that preceded the Livonian Order.[4]) Any kind of struggle of opinions inside the order, obviously could not be allowed; factionalism was criminal.

According to the decision of the Tenth Party Congress, adherence to any grouping would subject a member to "unconditional and immediate expulsion from the party." Many meritorious party members complained: a hierarchy of secretaries had arisen, they said, who decided every question, and the congresses and conferences had become mere assemblies to carry out decisions, where party and public opinion were stifled. At the Thirteenth Party Conference in January 1924, Stalin answered that the party could not be a coalition of groups and factions but must become "a monolithic organization, hewed from a single stone."

In a second speech there Stalin declared that all other institutions (the Soviets, the trade unions, the Komsomol, women's organizations, etc.) were transmission belts, "feelers in the hands of the party, with the aid of which it transmits its will to the working class, and the working class is turned from an atomized mass into the army of the party." Thus, we many say, the Soviets are in no way a power, but only a transmission belt. "The dictatorship of the proletariat," Stalin taught, "consists of the guiding instructions of the party plus implementation of these instructions by the mass organizations of the proletariat, plus their application by the populace."

What sort of "guiding instructions"? Concretely, whose? It is enough to pose such questions to make it clear that the party itself was also being transformed into a transmission belt, the main one in the transmission mechanism. The mechanism of power sketched out by

---

[4] Successive organizations of the Teutonic Knights of the Middle Ages. — Ed.

Stalin presupposes only one operator who actually runs the whole thing.

There were people who understood the threat of all this. In a private letter to Kuibyshev, Dzerzhinsky perspicaciously predicted: "I am fully convinced that we can handle all our enemies if we find and take the correct line in the practical management of the country and the economy. If we don't find this line and tempo, the country will then find itself a dictator, a grave-digger of the revolution, whatever fine feathers he wears." But clairvoyants did not determine the course of events.

Of course, in the plan of Preobrazhensky and the other Leftists there were no direct appeals for the physical annihilation of the most active part of the rural population, for labor under noneconomic compulsion. But just as all the properties of the oak are stored up in the acorn, it was already contained here in embryo. Having liquidated, as usual, the authors of this theory, Stalin put their ideas into effect. Naturally it required measures corresponding to the intended goal. There was no divergence between end and means, as in general there is not in life. For the means is the end in action, in motion, in everyday practice; in other words, the end is not capable of manifesting itself except through the means.

The turn to industrialization began with the savage destruction of the mechanism of the NEP. In 1929 the apparatus of power tied up all aspects of private enterprise. They cut off the private trader's access to bank credit and smothered him with taxes; he paid the highest rates for transportation. The regime requisitioned or simply stole private mills, and canceled many agreements for the lease of state enterprises.

Methodically and purposefully the apparatus put the squeeze on the peasantry down to their fingernails, reviving the typical methods of "War Communism." Given deliberately unequal exchange and consciously lowered prices for grain, meat, milk, and other products, the peasant understandably did not wish to sell the fruits of his labor to the state. Stalin personally took charge of the collections. Early in 1928 a directive went out to the provinces ordering them to take the grain from the peasantry "no matter what." Stalin himself went to Siberia. At meetings with local activists he accused the kulaks of disrupting the collections and demanded that they be hauled into court for speculating. The property of those convicted was subject to confiscation. As under "War Communism," Stalin proposed giving a quarter of the confiscated grain to the poor peasants (in practice, to informers). Stalin ordered party and soviet functionaries who did not carry out these repressive measures removed from their positions.

A wave of mass searches rolled across the country, just as at the time of "War Communism." The regime forbade the sale of grain in markets, and in many places armed roadblocks were set up on the highways.

Forcible collectivization completed the destruction of rural commodity production.

A series of energetic measures destroyed the commercial model in state industry as well. The Seventeenth Party Conference in 1932 emphasized "the total incompatibility of the policy of the party and the interests of the working class, with bourgeois-NEPman perversions of the principle of accountability expressed in the squandering of nationwide state resources, and consequently in the disruption of established economic plans." Here wholesale trade and economic responsibility for the results of labor were being called perversions and squandering. It was just out of this that the basis of the bureaucratic system of distributing resources came, with a ruinous influence on the economy to this day.

They say that the victors are not judged. But comparison of results with the price paid for them is an obligatory thing in economics. Only by investigating this is it possible to understand what actually happened — was it a victory or a defeat? We will ask questions that are simple at first glance: what were the planned parameters of the First Five-Year Plan, and what were its economic results?

Beginning in 1926 Gosplan and the Supreme Economic Council began to prepare variants of the plan. The planners of that time should not be confused with those of the present, who don't predict the weather but prescribe what it should be. No, they did not yet have among the procedures of their discipline the exertion of every effort to pull the arrow of the barometer into the "clear" range in spite of the storm. They recommended maximum proportionality and balance in the plan — between accumulation and consumption, between industry and agriculture, between industry of group A and group B,[5] between monetary receipts and guarantees of goods.

---

[5] Producer-goods industry and consumer-goods industry. — Ed.

The careful specialists headed by Krzhizhanovsky made up two variants of the plan — a minimal one (or as they called it, the starting point) and a maximal one. According to the maximal plan, in five years industrial production should grow 180 percent (i.e., almost multiplied by three!), and production of means of production should grow 230 percent. Productivity of labor in industry was supposed to rise 110 percent. Agriculture was assigned a growth in total volume of 55 percent. They programmed a rapid growth in real wages and the doubling of the national income.

The assignments were not at all regarded as fantasy — these were approximately the real rates of development during the previous years. Still, the planners hedged: in the minimal variant the assignments were curtailed by 20 percent. This is understandable: as the authors of the NEP warned, the maximal variant proceeded from the assumption that there would be good harvests in all five of the coming years, that the outside world would provide technology and credit, and that expenditures for defense would decline. But Stalin intervened personally in the matter. By his decree only the maximal variant was to be considered.

In May 1929 the plan was confirmed by the Fifth All-Union Congress of Soviets. As a practical matter this act had no significance — the plan was already considered to have been in effect since October 1, 1928. But they didn't worry about that — they began to cut the plan up and reshape it. Stalin sounded the call, "the Five-Year Plan — in four years." In the second year of the Five-Year Plan they planned to increase industrial production by 31.3 percent, which exceeded by approximately one and a half times the maximum original draft. But little came of this. Stalin declared that in a whole series of industrial branches the Five-Year Plan could be fulfilled in three years.

It ended on January 7, 1933, when Stalin declared the Five-Year Plan fulfilled in four years and three months. From that time on, it seems, no one checked assignments against results. Let us do this. The growth of industrial production from 1928 to 1932 amounted not to 180 percent, as the specialists calculated, but to 100 percent. Average annual increases in comparison with the period of the NEP fell from 23.8 percent to 19.4 percent overall for industry, while the tempo of development in light industry fell almost by half. These are the official statistics.

Someone may object: so the plan was not fulfilled, so the tempo of industrial development slowed down in comparison with the preceding period, still the success was striking. Is it doing poorly to double industrial production in four years? It wouldn't be bad, but the question is how this figure was derived. Everything produced in industry is expressed in rubles (otherwise you can't compare a loaf of bread with a tractor, an airplane with an electric power plant), and then volumes of production are compared each year and the tempo of development is derived. This method is reliable only in that case where the value of one and the same product is calculated each year at constant prices. But during the First Five-Year Plan wholesale prices galloped away, which was not taken into account. Therefore the proclaimed totals of increases in production turn out to be too high.

It is simplest to evaluate the fulfillment of the First Five-Year Plan in physical indicators. Pig iron smelting was supposed to reach 10 million tons; the actual result was 6.2 million. Generation of electric energy did not reach 22 billion kilowatt hours, but only 13.5 billion; production of fertilizer — 0.9 million tons instead of 8 million, etc. If comparison is made with the period of the NEP (1923–1928), the average annual increase in iron smelting was down in the period 1929–1932 from 670 thousand to 400 thousand tons, and in the output of shoes, down from 8.5 million to 7.2 million pair per year. Production of textiles had previously risen each year by 400 billion meters, and of sugar by 179,000 tons, while in the First Five-Year Plan output of these goods, like many others, fell in absolute terms. How then can one understand Stalin's proclamation about fulfilling the Five-Year Plan at the end of 1932?

In the Second Five-Year Plan it was originally intended to raise production of electricity to 100 billion kilowatt hours, the extraction of coal to 250 million tons, the smelting of pig iron to 22 million tons. These limits were attained only in the 1950s. In 1938–1940 industry as a whole marked time — production of pig iron, steel, rolled plate and cement, and the extraction of petroleum actually did not increase, and in a series of branches retrogression was even observed.

Not long ago the economist G. Khanin used new methods to calculate the most important indicators of the development of the economy from 1928 to 1941. It appears that national income grew during this period not by 5.5 times, as the statistics assert, but by 50 percent; the productivity of social labor, not by 4.3 times but by 36 percent, etc. During these years crash construction of enterprises went on, and new branches of industry arose. The basic productive stock in the economy almost doubled, but at the same time the removal of production from subsidized accounts fell by a quarter. The expenditures of materials per unit of final product rose 25 to 30 percent, which substantially devalued the growth of production in the raw-material industries. It was just at this point that the disproportions arose that still torment our economy today: between heavy and light industry, between transport and the other branches of physical production, between monetary incomes and the goods to cover them.

The most serious consequence of the 1930s was the ruin of agriculture. In 1929 Stalin promised that the Soviet Union would "become in just three years one of the biggest grain-producing countries, if not the biggest grain-producer in the world." Three years later, as we know, famine had broken out, carrying off millions of lives. Only in 1950 did the grain crop finally exceed the level reached during the NEP. In 1933 compared with 1928 the number of cattle had been reduced almost by half. Only in the late 1950s did the quantity of large horned cattle and sheep reach the level of 1926, and then thanks only to the personal auxiliary plots.

Simultaneously with the destruction of commodity production it was objectively necessary to replace economic stimuli of labor with crude compulsion, and to strengthen significantly, as the journal *Bolshevik* wrote, that side of the dictatorship "which is expressed in the application of violence unrestricted by law, including the application in necessary cases of *terror* in regard to class enemies." Much has already been written about the violent character of collectivization. In March 1930, when it became clear that the collective farms would spoil the sowing campaign, Stalin came out with his article "Dizzyness with Success." Putting the blame, as usual, on "distortions" in implementation, he allowed withdrawal from the collective farms. However, cattle and tools were not returned to those who left, and they received only the most unsuitable land. On the other hand, in the summer of 1930 Stalin declared: "There will be no more returning to the old ways. The kulaks are doomed, and will be liquidated. Only one path remains, the path of the collective farms." Years later in an interview he said that in the process of collectivization millions of peasants were physically annihilated. Up to now the true figure is unknown.

As one wise person observed, the year 1929 has been justly called the year of the great break, without saying what was broken: the backbone of the nation.

In economic construction, essentially the methods of "War Communism" were revived. In the choice of concrete methods the personality of the leader certainly exerted an influence. It was in character for Stalin to approach any innovation with distrust, and he did not wish to carry out Trotsky's brilliant plan for the militarization of labor. He had in his heart more the classical form of force — convict labor. It was used to develop Kolyma and the Northern Urals, Siberia and Kazakhstan, to construct Norilsk, Vorkuta, Magadan, to dig canals, to build roads in the North — altogether more than you can count up. . . .

"War Communism" had its roots in our national history. Formerly the central power in Russia for long periods gave orders directly to everything that lay, stood, crawled, walked, swam, or flew. Historical science is always a field of combat. Fulfilling their social command, our historians looked for proof that it was just in these periods that our economic, military, and every other kind of success were achieved. Until recently, for example, Ivan the Terrible was highly regarded. The performer of the leading role in the famous Eisenstein movie film,[6] Nikolai Cherkasov, threw some light in his memoirs on important details of a meeting Stalin had with leading figures in the arts: "Alluding to the mistakes of Ivan the Terrible, Joseph Vissarionovich noted that one of his mistakes was that he was not able to liquidate the five remaining powerful feudal families, that he did not carry the struggle with feudalism to the end — if he had done this, then Russia would have had no Time of Troubles."[7] And then Joseph Vissarionovich added humorously that "Here God got in Ivan's way: The Terrible liquidates one feudal family, one noble clan, and then for a whole year repents and atones for his 'sin' by prayer, when he should have acted even more decisively." . . .

In one exceptionally important sphere of life the heritage of the centuries was especially heavily imposed on our postrevolutionary history and formed a solid wall that we have still not been able either to penetrate or to surmount. This is bureaucratic management, which is showing itself to be the main obstacle on the path of change. . . .

The breakup of the old state machinery after October 1917 did not mean that the roots of bureaucratism had been dug out. Indeed, the

---

[6] *Ivan the Terrible.* — Ed.
[7] The period of rebellions, invasions, and dynastic struggles, 1605–1613. — Ed.

danger even increased to the extent that the whole economy was again included in the sphere of state management. The colossal work of regulating the economy, which, even though imperfectly, was accomplished under commodity production by the market, had to be transferred at once to the administrative apparatus. The situation was complicated by the fact that the economic model of "War Communism" excluded any independence whatsoever of economic units. Industry, for example, constituted, in essence, one superenterprise, administered from the center.

To decide urgent tasks it was necessary to create innumerable organizations. A well-known economist of that time, Yury Larin, called the prevailing system of economic management "All-Russian chekvalapism," from the name of the Extraordinary Commission for Felt Boots and Bast Sandals (Chekvalap). It is important to understand that for all the implausibility of similar institutions, they could not help but spring up. Armies and labor camps needed footwear. But imagine the envoy from the center with extraordinary authority in this matter. He has a concrete task, and to fulfill it he tries to take people away from other production, about which, in turn, another manager is concerned. As a result the need appears for a new superextraordinary commission. Labor under noneconomic compulsion requires an apparatus of overseers. Here we add in apparatuses for collecting food requisitions, for distributing vital goods, and a multitude of others.

V. I. Lenin was the first to understand the danger, and declared war on bureaucracy — otherwise the revolution would have drowned in ink. Ilyich's great merit was that he abruptly turned the country towards the NEP, under which the objective conditions arose for curbing bureaucratism. By the summer of 1922, out of 35,000 employees in the central economic organs, 8,000 remained, in the provincial economic councils, 18,000 out of 235,000.

But as early as 1927, when the NEP was giving out, the status of the enterprise was changed by legislation. According to the new statute the goal of the enterprise became the execution of the plan sent down from above, instead of earning a profit, as was set by the statute of 1923. From now on the higher organ gave out assignments in construction, appointed and removed administrators, and dictated prices. Beginning in January 1932 the vertical managerial chain began quickly to take shape (the Commissariat — the Chief Administration — the enterprise), ideally suited for management by decree. . . .

When the economic mechanism took in as an obligatory element labor under noneconomic compulsion ("subsystem terror" . . .), management by command had an influence on every aspect of our life, although it worked at the time with terrible inefficiency. Today this is the apparat, knowing its inadequacies but not knowing how to correct them. . . .

The social interest is the opposite side of bureaucratism. From the point of view of the bureaucrat, individual or collective income belongs to the treasury, which can return it to its owners in whole or in part, but can also refuse to return it. The hope for benevolent bosses became a norm of conduct.

The conservatism of the bureaucracy coincided with the mood at the bottom, i.e., we and you. There you find sentimental recollection of the past, the yearning for a boss and for order, the instinctive preference for the habitual and traditional, attempts bodily to close the embrasures through which innovation seeped in; here you find fear of independence, hope for manna from heaven. Both here and there you find a fear of life, of the harsh realities of economics. In this situation one serious failure is enough, whether economic or foreign policy, it doesn't matter what, to morally isolate the reformers. . . .

History will not forgive us if we again let slip our chance. A chasm can be crossed in one leap; it cannot be done in two.

Zagorka Golubović

Stalinism Against Socialism

Zagorka Golubović is a sociologist at the University of Belgrade, Yugoslavia. Barred from teaching by Marshal Tito because she was member of the reformist Praxis group, she and her colleagues were nevertheless able to continue their studies at the Institute of Social Sciences. Their journal

From Zagorka Golubović, "Stalinism and Socialism," excerpts from pp. 126–136, *Praxis International*, v. 1, no. 2, London, 1981.

Praxis (Practice) was suppressed and continues only in its English-language version published in London, but Professor Golubović was ultimately able to publish the book on which the article excerpted here was based (*Staljinizam i Socijalizam* [Belgrade: Philosophical Society of Serbia, 1982]). She argues that Stalin's "revolution from above" represented a fundamental break with the socialist principles of 1917.

Democracy and Socialism are not two separate concepts. Rather, the development of democratic relations has served as the basic premise for both the original idea of socialism and all authentic socialist movements, dating from the Paris Commune through twentieth century socialist revolutions. In regard to socialist relations, the presence or absence of democratic foundations has always been and continues to be the basic criterion for an assessment of the character of communist movements. The criticism of revolutionary movements of the past two centuries, from Bakunin's critique of Marxist ideas to Rosa Luxemburg's criticism of revolutionary practices after the Russian Revolution, and including destalinization in the last three decades, has been inspired by the same idea: socialism and democracy must become one, otherwise there will be no socialism.

Until recently it has been common to identify the system created in the USSR, i.e., Stalinism, as socialism. This has been done, not only by those who claimed that Stalinism was the inevitable consequence of Marxism, but also by those scholars who analyze reality only in terms of that which is empirically given, casting aside ideas and possibilities into the sphere of "utopia" that may be dealt with by philosophers but which cannot be considered by serious social scientists. Using the actual existing conditions as their point of departure, while forgetting their historical genesis and their real potential which were inaugurated by the October Revolution but were later destroyed in so-called "really existing socialism," they acknowledge as socialism that which empirically exists. They have not posed the question of whether it really is socialism. From this position they criticize socialism as a movement which is undemocratic by its very nature.

It is for these reasons that an investigation of the historical genesis of Stalinism has not lost its relevance, even after numerous studies which have dealt with the issue from various aspects. The differences between many other well-known studies and my inquiry lies, first and foremost, in the use of the method of historical and comparative analysis with the objective of determining the roots and sources of Stalinism in the Russian Revolution. By comparing the early period with the period of Stalinist consolidation at the end of the 1920's, my objective has been to determine whether Stalinism simply continues tendencies started during the October Revolution or whether it constitutes a break and destruction of initial revolutionary forces. Following the fate of new revolutionary institutions in the context of the consequences which they provoked, I argue that it is possible to determine the boundary line between the revolutionary phase, in which the ideas of socialist revolution were active (if not always carried out accordingly), and the phase which is representative of a break-off with the socialist revolution. The latter phase is expressive of counter-revolutionary tendencies since it stifles the most significant achievements of the previous revolutionary period while establishing an order which represents its opposite.

The term "Stalinism" is used to indicate implementation of a policy that stands in opposition to the basic tendencies of the socialist revolution which came about by either abolishing or arresting those tendencies in the late 1920's. Stalinism was determined by a number of specific choices. Had Stalinist policy been only the result of a prolongation of those tendencies which had already appeared during the 1920's due to the presence of unforeseen difficulties, or of certain inconsistencies of Leninism, one could have spoken of a greater or lesser degree of "deviation" from revolutionary policy. However, several decisive steps that were taken by Stalin as soon as he became Secretary General of the Party, especially beginning in 1928–29 (a period commonly labeled as the "revolution from above"), confirm the thesis that Stalinism did not emerge through gradual deviations but rather through forceful intervention upon the course of revolution that was vigorously paving its way up until the end of the 1920's, while Stalinism was then still being confronted by a strong opposition. It cleared its path by means of the following measures: total state control of ownership over the means of production in industry which led to the absolute monopoly of decision-making from one center; accelerated industrialization based on exploitation of the laboring classes; enforced collectivization of land property and establishment of feudal relationships between the State and the peasantry (the new laws forcibly kept peasants tied to collective farms and limited their freedom of movement).

Thus Stalinism is obviously a *turning-point* and not a further development of the revolution despite the continuity with certain ambivalent policies determined by the great difficulties that confronted the October Revolution. Therefore it is necessary to provide an answer to the question regarding which revolutionary processes were extinguished by the Stalinist counter-revolution.

First, instead of continuing with revolutionary transformations of property relations through their socialization (which assumes not only changes in ownership over the means of production, but also more profound alterations in the status of producers as regards the means and conditions of work as well as the distribution of the products of labor), *state ownership* was established and proclaimed as the only and highest form of "socialist property." Thus the revolutionary transformation of the class mode of production into a new socialist form was prevented. In addition, the basic goals of socialist revolution were changed: a revolutionary transformation of the totality of social relations was replaced by strengthening the domination of the state and party apparatus both in the economy and politics. Thereby all other processes of transforming the mode of production were likewise suspended. This had its repercussions on the entire social structure including maintenance of the class division of labor and the hierarchical organization of the work process which arrested processes that were directed at abolishing wage labor and the class character of the mode of production. All of these changes were aimed at reproducing ruling class power and preserving the function of exchange value as the basic aim of economic development contrary to the goal which the proletarian revolution is supposed to reach, i.e., transforming production into a means for satisfying human needs.

Thus state ownership became the basis for building a system whose aims were contrary to those of socialism. Instead of ending the alienation of producers from the means and conditions of work, a rigid system separating managers from producers was established. Instead of abolishing exploitation, it was legalized under the name of "socialist accumulation." Instead of gradually eliminating class principles in the organization of production, class elements were restored (not only those of the capitalist type but the pre-capitalist as well).

Second, decisive political steps were taken that strengthened the Stalinist line. Factory committees, as a form of direct worker participation in management, along with city and village soviets, represented the main obstacles to complete state control and bureaucratization of the system. Stalin had either to abolish them or reduce them to mere "form," contrary to the Marxist thesis regarding the need for the withering away of the state and the necessity for democratization of management processes. On the one hand, the soviets were transformed into a state power organization, while on the other, all institutions and organizations were subject to state control. Leadership was concentrated in one center (located at the top of the party apparatus). The next step — merging party and state power — led to the absolute alienation of power and caused a breach between the state and society (as a matter of fact, society was replaced by the state).

Third, in order to make this possible, it was necessary to arrest all democratic processes within the party, turning the party organization into an easily manipulated machine. For this reason the party was replaced by an apparatus that acts as the only active force, and to which principles of class organization are applied: the hierarchical and authoritarian principle, appointment rather than election, the elitist principle of the "nomenclature system," the principle of manipulating membership, etc. The party apparatus thus became the real power center whose instructions direct the entire life of society and its individuals. At the same time, the party profile was altered and what was once a proletarian party (on the basis of statistics showing that workers comprised the party majority up until the end of the 1920's) became a party of the bureaucracy and the middle class.

Fourth, the process of liberating the individual was cut short. During the 1920's, this process was manifest in the pursuit of diverse forms of living and creativity. Conversely, during the epoch of Stalinism, the concept of "directed personality" was imposed. An individual had to forfeit his/her own personality and become entirely subservient to the demands of the system and commands from the top. However, at the same time, petty bourgeois tendencies and privatization of the individual were encouraged, especially during the last years of the 1930's when a strong middle class had already been constituted. It had to be satisfied and won over, while Stalinism always carried on its main battle against the "revolutionary character." Ideological indoctrination was not sufficient in reaching this goal. This is why Stalin introduced mass terror against non-conformist and libertarian conduct. True to the tradition, present day Soviet leadership strictly penalizes non-conformist writers and the members of revolutionary workers' groups who attempt to rejuvenate revolutionary traditions since this manner of conduct represents a serious threat to the existing system.

In order to squelch any possibility of reviving revolutionary tendencies and to secure the creation of a stable order of power for the party apparatus, two steps were of greatest significance: first was the fostering of social stratification and the development of a privileged middle stratum; second was the organization of an extensive bureaucratic apparatus network subjugated to the supreme leader who holds the entire power network in his hands and sovereignly controls the future of all his subjects. Such ramifications of the bureaucratic system were the main obstacles to restoring the revolutionary tradition. It was also responsible for the longevity of this regime that functioned almost automatically for decades according to rigidly determined routine rules, paying no attention to the negative results it was producing. Taken as a whole these measures signified a counter-revolutionary policy — the results of which were not the consequences of chance error, or deviations, but rather were integral parts of a preconceived plan. . . .

It does not follow that the revolutionary course (as it is known to have existed during the 1920's with all of its uncertainties, inconsistencies, and its accent on authority and centralism) would necessarily have led straight away to socialism. The challenges were great while the limitations of the Bolshevik party already threatened to end or turn the revolution away from its sources. However, a variety of circumstances acted as a dam against the break-off with the revolution. Despite Lenin's ambivalence, he always returned to revolutionary goals. Some of Lenin's ideas and practices were rightly criticized by Kautsky and Rosa Luxemburg.[1] Other strong revolutionary figures also impeded a drift away from revolutionary goals. Inner-party democracy curbed both the party and state apparatus from total bureaucratization. New revolutionary forms of workers' movements were still active. It is also significant that certain revolutionary principles still stood inviolable: abolition of exploitation and social inequality, adherence to the election principle for functionaries, and a sense of responsibility to the working class.

[1] Karl Kautsky, theoretician of the German Social-Democratic party; Rosa Luxemburg, co-founder of the German Communist party, killed during the revolution of 1918–1919. — Ed.

Based on all analyses of the 1920's revolutionary period it can be claimed that during Lenin's time certain basic boundaries marking how far it was possible to tread and not transgress revolutionary practices of the proletarian revolution were still not overstepped. All of this supports the thesis that the Russian socialist revolution did indeed have a chance to gradually transform key institutions of the old class society and to develop new socialist relations. The Leninist period can be characterized as a period during which the revolution was still underway. The deviations already appearing at that time did not yet eliminate the possibility of continued transformation, while the Stalinist period signifies a sharp break with the revolution. These basic differences cannot be overlooked as was done by Leszek Kolakowski[2] who has sought to prove that Stalin was only faithful in realizing Lenin's doctrine. Standing behind the contradictions and conflicts of the 1920's was a revolutionary fervor that brought forth an abundance of ideas and possibilities which were not comparable to the sterile Stalinist period when everything was already predetermined, sealed shut, and all controversies "stamped out" and driven from the visible horizon.

If Stalinism was not the inevitable end result of the 1917 Revolution, what then decisively influenced its victory? The answer which is usually given from the standpoint of strict determinism primarily takes into consideration the objective circumstances of Russia's economic underdevelopment in the second decade of the century. The conclusion is, then, that no other outcome was possible since the necessary conditions which Marx had in mind when foreseeing socialist revolutions in developed industrial countries were missing. The *a priori* assumption here is that industry and modern technology, as developed in capitalism, represent prerequisites for socialism because they foster the realization of mass production which is able, in itself, to satisfy human needs. The question is not posed whether it is possible, or even necessary, to create a different technical foundation or a different conception of production which would really have the function of satisfying human needs and would constitute a more adequate basis for the creation of a new socialist civilization. The assumption must be challenged that only the capitalist way of development can serve as the necessary prerequisite for socialist economic and political development. Otherwise, the possi-

[2] Polish philosopher, now a professor in the United States. — Ed.

bility of the Soviet government following a different, more appropriate policy of social development is thereby entirely eliminated.

The claim that it is not possible to carry out a socialist revolution in the framework of an underdeveloped society is based on the presupposition that socialism can only be achieved in one way: through capitalism and industrialization of the capitalist type as complete and pre-existing accomplishments. Contrary to this, Marx also foresaw other possibilities, having in mind societies which could not be categorized in the scheme of the five socioeconomic formations [slave, Asiatic, feudal, capitalist, socialist]. . . . This allowed for the possibility of a socialist revolution in Russia on the basis of traditional rural communes. A different policy, one better adapted to conditions in Russia, could have initiated significantly sounder preparations for the revolutionary transformation of the old Russian society were it not for the Bolshevik leadership's adherence to a stereotyped project construed to operate under entirely different conditions. Had this been the case, support of the revolution would no doubt have been more extensive. Policy regarding the peasant population would have been different, giving it quite a significant role instead of pushing it into the margins of revolutionary events. This would also assume the more gradual and more moderate development of industry during which time the economic, political, and cultural development of the working class would take a more systematic course. In this way it might have been possible to avoid detours taken by the Russian Revolution and used later by Stalin. The myth of the necessity of accelerated industrialization, which many authors justify on the ground that the USSR could not have otherwise survived fascist attacks, cannot be empirically proven. Technical supremacy was certainly not the decisive factor leading to victory in the Soviet Civil War (nor was it essential in the war of liberation carried out by the Vietnamese people against US aggression). . . .

Bolshevism suffered from serious inner limitations which paved the way to Stalinism. The first such limitation was the Leninist conception of the party which placed the vanguard in opposition to the working class and opened the possibility of the party's victory over the working class. Hence a turnabout from the dictatorship of the proletariat to a dictatorship of the party, and, subsequently, the transformation of the party into an instrument of personal dictatorship, were not difficult to carry out. However, when it is suggested that Lenin had already created a complete dictatorship run by the party apparatus, significant facts are simply overlooked: first, Lenin was not the only individual responsible for decision-making; second, an opposition did not cease to function until the very end of the 1920's, despite a ban against factions made at the Tenth Party Congress in 1921; and, finally, there still was the possibility of critically reviewing party policy. Lenin himself engaged in it, especially toward the end of his life.

Perhaps the most significant factor that made possible the victory of Stalinism was the acceptance of a one-party system as a necessity. This justified the liquidation of political pluralism and significantly limited socialist alternatives, especially with the abolition of all other socialist parties. In the chain reaction of consequences that were to follow, the specific position taken toward the party is significant, namely, the party as a metaphysical entity with the attribute of infallibility. Thereby the party was transformed from an organized *means* of revolutionary struggle into an *end in itself* and became the only legitimate "demiurge" of revolutionary transformation. This explains the indecisiveness of the opposition in agreeing to an organized battle against the growing tide of Stalinism of which the representatives of the opposition were already aware in the mid-twenties (in 1923 Trotsky also very clearly anticipated this in his work "New Course"). "Factional battle" was considered as treason by the party. Discipline and loyalty toward the party had top priority running ahead of revolutionary candidness and love of the truth. (This led to an unprincipled merging of certain oppositional groups with the ruling Stalinist stream so as not to weaken "party unity" which simultaneously weakened the opposition movement and enhanced its atomization.) The opposition did not even attempt to seek support from the public nor to explain its standpoint in an open political struggle — all in fear that the myth of a "monolithic party" might be destroyed. Therefore its actions remained individual, isolated, frequently pitted one against the other, provoked distrust, and thus contributed to the acceptance of Stalin's policy as the way out of a confused situation which the opposition was not prepared to solve through a more decisive policy. Stalin's personality should also not be overlooked even though the viewpoint presented here stands opposed to the conception of a "personality cult" whereby all determinants of Stalinism are reduced to one personal factor. . . .

Stalinism started with Stalin but does not terminate with his death. It refers to a sequence of constituted objective conditions and characteristics that are not associated only with Stalin's personality. Although it labels itself "socialist," it is in fact a new social order, a specific class society characterized by the following features:

1. A specific class method of production based on state property, the extension of wage labor conditions onto the entire employed population, state dictation of work conditions, and arbitrary, central control of all social resources and social surplus-products.
2. The specific class division between the class managing all labor conditions existing as the only autonomous subject, and the remainder of society that is subject to inviolable directives and is divested of the opportunity to decide upon the conditions and results of labor. The ruling bureaucratic class is surrounded by "satellite strata," a specific middle class, which supports the system and shares certain social privileges.
3. Concealed and ideologically masked with the myth of the "leading role of the working class," social conflicts take place in a less obvious manner (either in the form of passive resistance to the work process manifest in low productivity, or poor discipline, or the form of opposition to official ideology which is especially characteristic of the post-Stalin period). Class conflicts are disguised by the official ideology which admits only the existence of "non-antagonistic classes" (which is nonsense, since according to Marx, classes exist only if they are in conflict with opposing classes). Only the ruling class possesses all means necessary for establishing class identity and for leading class struggles, including means of repression. All other classes cannot express themselves as a class or defend their interests since they have neither their own organizations nor are allowed to develop their own ideology.
4. A totalitarian political structure — since all social and human relations are politicized and placed under the absolute control of a state and party mechanism — that allows no room for the existence of political (or cultural) pluralism, freedom of thought or action, or respect for human rights. Repression is thus an integral part of the system. Only its form can be changed. In the post-Stalin period mass terror was no longer acceptable (not only because Stalin's crimes were disclosed by Khrushchev in his "secret" speech, but also because of the insecurity that it instilled in the ruling class circles). However, the ruling class did not renounce the use of terror; it was merely applied in a more refined, "legalized" manner. (Some

"ideological friends" of the Soviet Union see in this great progress, claiming that today's Soviet government convicts individuals "only on the basis of deeds committed." However, all forms of non-conformist conduct qualify as punishable activities: participation in demonstrations, publication of manuscripts abroad that have been rejected by official censorship in the USSR, refusal to accept work imposed on the individual, attempts to engage in "free-lance professions" which have been condemned as "parasitism.")

5. Stalinist ideology as a necessary, integral part of the Stalinist order with its special place — legitimating role — in the system. The ruling class presents itself as the "vanguard of the working class," as the only real historical subject that can bring about the realization of socialism. Another purpose of ideology is to maintain some semblance of unity in a basically divided and disunited class society that has been deprived of the classical mechanism of class conflict and mutual compromise. In order to function, this society needs certain common symbols that gather dissipated elements of society (for example, "socialist patriotism").

Taking into consideration these essential characteristics, this type of social order can be identified as a *bureaucratized political society*, the name itself indicating basic elements of such a system: the existence of the political bureaucracy as the independent, legitimate social force which, by fusing economic and political power, is the only element with the right to direct economic and social processes and to dispose of social surplus-products; and the absolutization of political institutions which subordinate to it all forms of social life. . . .

The objectives set up by Stalinism as its practical program are diametrically opposed to socialist goals as they were defined by Marx. The primary end of Stalinism is *consolidation and maintenance of power* (which is characteristic of the entire socialist epoch according to Stalinist terminology) contrary to the Marxist understanding that the basic goal of socialism is *emancipation of the working class* in order to bring about general *human emancipation*. The latter requires liberation of individuals as humans not only as the members of one class but of persons emancipated from all the imposed conditions of sociability in order to freely create a new model of sociability through self-action and self-realization of unfolding personalities.

By reducing the basic goal to that of strengthening the state (power), alterations were necessarily made in other derived ends. The Stalinist system could not strive to strengthen the working class in the sense of its becoming an autonomous social subject. On the contrary, the system needs a numerous but disintegrated working class subordinate to the state and party. Thus the following demands were placed before the working class: achievement of higher labor productivity (production as an end in itself or, more precisely, in the function of strengthening state power); submission to strict discipline; competitive Stakhanovism (that was proclaimed as the highest form of socialist competition while, in fact, being a powerful means of exploitation).

Power, and *production* as the self-purpose of Stalinist social developmental policy, mutually reinforce one another and foster absolutization of the power of the political bureaucracy. The *idea of social equality* as an aim was rejected. The inequitable distribution of social income for diverse unequal contributions was justified by criteria of "social usefulness" determined by the political bureaucracy.

The goal of multilateral development of the creative capacities of each individual has been replaced by the one-sided training of work abilities of the mass population of producers. The development of spiritual faculties is reserved for the cultural elite while supervisory expertise is left exclusively to the political elite. This shows that the person, as a whole, is regarded as an instrument and that the development of the human individual is subordinate to the tasks and needs of the existing social system which strives to maintain the given order (to keep it functioning) and not to support the revolutionary transformation of social relations which would otherwise open qualitatively different possibilities for the development of human potentials.

Analogous to the inversion caused by Stalinism in the sphere of social goals, a change also ensues in the conception of values. The banner of every socialist revolution would surely have to carry the words "freedom," "equality," "solidarity," and "social justice," denoting the basic values in whose name all great social revolutions have been sparked but to which those classes that triumphed gave their own interpretation. All analyses of the Stalinist value system confirm that the Stalinist ruling class did not retain these symbols of revolution, not even as slogans. Rather it defined its values in accordance with the modified social goals which have been most briefly formulated as: a system of individual obligation to the collective and the state ("socially useful work" and patriotic duties); loyalty to the party and its "leader"; discipline (obedience and compliance to work assignments); the nurturing of a collectivistic ethos opposed to individuality (which is interpreted as a negative category); modesty instead of a plentitude of human needs. In short, Stalinism prefers a value system that incorporates a *heteronomous* rather than an *autonomous* orientation and perpetuates the *alienation* and *reification* of humans instead of values which would foster emancipation in all spheres of human life.

Suggestions for Further Reading

The quantity of literature on Soviet Russia and Communism now available in English is staggering. No attempt will be made to cover it all; listed are suggestions to the interested reader of some of the most important books dealing with Soviet Russia in general or with particular topics that are especially relevant to the subject of the Stalin Revolution.

The works represented by selections in this book, all fundamental sources for understanding Soviet Russia and its crucial development in the 1930s, are not repeated in the following list.

For a general view of Soviet history there are numerous good texts, of which a few of the best are Donald Treadgold, *Twentieth Century Russia*, 5th ed. (Chicago: Rand McNally, 1981); Basil Dmytryshyn, *USSR: A Concise History*, rev. ed. (New York: Scribner's, 1981), which includes a useful documentary appendix with the full text of Khrushchev's Secret Speech of 1956; Martin McCauley, *The Soviet Union since 1917* (London: Holden, 1983); and the interesting émigré interpretation by Alexander Nekrich and Mikhail Heller, *Utopia in Power: The History of the Soviet Union from 1917 to the Present* (New York: Summit Books, 1986). A comprehensive history centering on the Communist party as an institution is Leonard Schapiro, *The Communist Party of the Soviet Union*, rev. ed. (New York: Random House, 1970). The official Stalinist history was *The History of the Communist Party of the Soviet Union (Bolsheviks): Short Course* (New York: International Publishers, 1939), the preparation of which was reportedly supervised by Stalin himself. (See the comments in the selection in this book by Giuseppe Boffa.) The most recent translation of an official history is Boris Ponomarev et al., eds., *History of the Communist Party of the Soviet Union* (Moscow: Foreign Languages Publishing House, 1960); this has been completely outdated by the Gorbachev reforms and is due to be superseded in the near future. A selection of key statements by the Soviet leaders is contained in Robert V. Daniels, ed., *A Documentary History of Communism* (rev. ed., 2 vols., Hanover, NH: University Press of New England, 1984 and 1988); see also Robert H. McNeal, general editor, *Resolutions and Decisions of the Communist Party of the Soviet Union* (4 vols., Toronto: University of Toronto Press, 1974), especially vol. 3, *The Stalin Years: 1929–1953*.

Good studies of the Russian historical and economic background as it relates to the Stalin Revolution include Robert Bideleux, *Commu-*

nism and Development (New York: Methuen, 1985); Cyril E. Black, *Understanding Soviet Politics: The Perspective of Russian History* (Boulder, CO: Westview Press, 1986); Tim McDaniel, *Autocracy, Capitalism, and Revolution in Russia* (Berkeley, CA: University of California Press, 1988); and Teodor Shanin, *Russia as a Developing Society* (New Haven, CT: Yale University Press, 1987). The more immediate background of Russia from 1917 to 1929 has been studied exhaustively by E. H. Carr in his *History of Soviet Russia* (9 vols. in 11 parts, New York: Macmillan, 1951–1959), continued in R. W. Davies, *The Industrialization of Soviet Russia* (2 vols., Cambridge, MA: Harvard University Press, 1980). See also Roger Pethybridge, *The Social Prelude to Stalinism* (New York: St. Martin's, 1974) and Theodore von Laue, *Why Lenin? Why Stalin? A Reappraisal of the Russian Revolution* (New York: Harper & Row, 1971).

Stalin has been the subject of many excellent biographies — in particular, Isaac Deutscher, *Stalin: A Political Biography* (New York: Oxford University Press, 1949); Robert C. Tucker, *Stalin as a Revolutionary, 1879–1929* (New York: Norton, 1973); and Adam B. Ulam, *Stalin: The Man and His Era* (New York: Viking, 1973). Leon Trotsky's *Stalin: An Appraisal of the Man and His Influence* (New York: Harper, 1946) was compiled from notes left by the author when he was killed. The official edition of Stalin's *Works* (sanitized in places) is available in translation (13 vols., Moscow: Foreign Languages Publishing House, 1952–1955). T. H. Rigby, *Stalin* (Englewood Cliffs, NJ: Prentice-Hall, 1966), brings together selections of Stalin's writing and comments on him by various contemporaries and historians.

The political events of the 1920s and 1930s are dealt with in detail in Robert V. Daniels, *The Conscience of the Revolution: Communist Opposition in Soviet Russia* (Cambridge, MA: Harvard University Press, 1960, and Boulder, CO: Westview Press, 1988); Merle Fainsod, *Soviet Rule in Smolensk* (based on the party archives captured by the Germans during World War II, Cambridge, MA: Harvard University Press, 1958); Sheila Fitzpatrick, *The Russian Revolution, 1917–1932* (New York: Columbia University Press, 1982); and Boris Nicolaevsky, *Power and the Soviet Elite* (Ann Arbor, MI: University of Michigan Press, 1975), essays by a Menshevik émigré with the purported record of a long talk with Nikolai Bukharin in Paris in 1936.

There are many journalistic and autobiographical accounts of the Stalin Revolution. Representative books by correspondents are Walter

Duranty, *Duranty Reports Russia* (New York: Viking, 1934); William Henry Chamberlin, *Russia's Iron Age* (Boston: Little, Brown, 1937); Maurice Hindus, *Humanity Uprooted* (New York: Cape & Smith, 1930, and *Red Bread* (New York: Cape & Smith, 1931). John Scott's *Behind the Urals* (Boston: Houghton Mifflin, 1943) is the account of an American who worked in the Soviet steel industry. *The Bells of the Kremlin: An Experience in Communism* by Arvo Tuominen (Hanover, NH: University Press of New England, 1983) comprises the recollections of a Finnish ex-Communist. Two recent Soviet memoirs are Anton Antonov-Ovseyenko, *The Time of Stalin* (New York: Harper & Row, 1983) and A. I. Mikoyan, *The Path of Struggle* (Madison, CT: Sphinx Press, 1988), Vol. I of *The Memoirs of Anastas Mikoyan*, the recollections of a top Stalinist official who turned critic when he served under Khrushchev as the nominal Soviet president. Two moving accounts of the purge era by widows of purge victims are Evgenia Ginzburg, *Journey into the Whirlwind* (New York: Harcourt, Brace & World, 1967) and Nadezhda Mandelshtam, *Hope Against Hope* (New York: Atheneum, 1970).

For background on socialist and Communist theory, see Wolfgang Leonhardt, *Three Faces of Marxism* (New York: Holt, Rinehart and Winston, 1974) and Alfred G. Meyer, *Communism* (4th ed., New York: Random House, 1984). The old official interpretation of Marxism-Leninism (now outdated) was expounded in O. V. Kuusinen et al., *Fundamentals of Marxism-Leninism* (Moscow: Foreign Languages Publishing House, 1961). Stalin's ideology is investigated in Robert C. Tucker, *The Soviet Political Mind* (New York: Praeger, 1963).

The development of the Soviet government before, during, and after the Stalin Revolution is treated in many texts, one of the best of which is Merle Fainsod, *How Russia Is Ruled* (rev. ed., Cambridge, MA: Harvard University Press, 1963, updated by Jerry Hough as *How the Soviet Union Is Governed*, Cambridge, MA: Harvard University Press, 1979). Soviet totalitarianism is analyzed in Carl J. Friedrich and Zbigniew K. Brzezinski, *Totalitarian Dictatorship and Autocracy*, rev. ed. (Cambridge, MA: Harvard University Press, 1965), and in the collection edited by Paul T. Mason, *Totalitarianism: Temporary Madness or Permanent Danger?* (Boston: D.C. Heath, 1967), a volume in the "Problems in European Civilization" series. The events of the Great Purge are recounted in Zbigniew Brzezinski, *The Permanent Purge* (Cambridge, MA: Harvard University Press, 1956) and in Robert Conquest, *The Great Terror* (New York: Macmillan, 1968). Particular aspects of the terror are treated in Boris Lewytzky, *The Uses of Terror: The Soviet Secret Police, 1917–1970* (London: Sidgewick & Jackson, 1971); in Simon Wolin and Robert M. Slusser, eds., *The Soviet Secret Police* (New York: Praeger, 1957, and Westport, CT: Greenwood Press, 1975); and in Alexander Solzhenitsyn's classic, *The Gulag Archipelago, 1918–1956* (3 vols., New York: Harper & Row, 1973–1979). Other interesting commentaries on Soviet politics include Archie Brown and Jack Gray, eds., *Political Culture and Political Change in Communist Societies* (New York: Holmes & Meier, 1977); Pavel Campeanu, *The Origins of Stalinism: From Leninist Revolution to Stalinist Society* (Armonk, NY: M.E. Sharpe, 1986); *Eurocommunism and the State*, by the former leader of the Spanish Communist party, Santiago Carrillo (Westport, CT: Greenwood Press, 1978); and Stephen White, *Political Culture and Soviet Politics* (New York: St. Martin's, 1979). A broad comparative study is Samuel P. Huntington, ed., *Authoritarian Politics in Modern Society: The Dynamics of Established One-Party Systems* (New York: Basic Books, 1970).

The economic side of the Stalin Revolution and of Soviet Russia generally has been subjected to more careful analysis than any other aspect of these events. The principles of the Soviet economy are ably explained in Robert W. Campbell, *The Soviet Type Economies: Performance and Evolution* (Boston: Houghton Mifflin, 1973), while the main economic institutions and problems are described in Marshall Goldman, *The Soviet Economy: Myth and Reality* (Englewood Cliffs, NJ: Prentice-Hall, 1968). Economic progress is assessed in Raymond Hutchings, *Soviet Economic Development* (New York: New York University Press, 1983) and in Eric Hoffman and Robbin Laird, *The Politics of Economic Modernization in the Soviet Union* (Ithaca, NY: Cornell University Press, 1982). The controversies leading up to the Stalin Revolution are explained in Alexander Erlich, *The Soviet Industrialization Debate, 1924–1928* (Cambridge, MA: Harvard University Press, 1960) and in Moshe Lewin, *Political Undercurrents in Soviet Economic Debates* (Princeton, NJ: Princeton University Press, 1974). More specialized analyses are Hiroaki Kuromiya, *Stalin's Industrial Revolution* (Cambridge, England: Cambridge University Press, 1988); Eugene Zaleski, *Stalinist Planning for Growth, 1933–1952* (Chapel Hill, NC: University of North Carolina Press, 1980); and Abram Bergson, *The Real National Income of Soviet Russia Since 1928* (Cambridge, MA:

Harvard University Press, 1961). The organization and problems of industry are treated in Joseph S. Berliner, *Soviet Industry from Stalin to Gorbachev* (Ithaca, NY: Cornell University Press, 1988), and in David Granick, *The Red Executive: A Study of the Organization Man in Russian Industry* (Garden City, NY: Doubleday, 1960, and Salem, NH: Ayer, 1979). Arvid Brodersen, *The Soviet Worker* (New York: Random House, 1963), and Leonard Schapiro and Joseph Godson, eds., *The Soviet Worker: Illusion and Realities* (New York: St. Martin's, 1984), cover the history of labor conditions and organization. Collectivization and its consequences are appraised in Harry Shaffer, ed., *Soviet Agriculture* (New York: Praeger, 1977); in Robert Conquest, *Harvest of Sorrow* (New York: Oxford University Press, 1986); and in Moshe Lewin, *Russian Peasants and Soviet Power* (Evanston, IL: Northwestern University Press, 1968).

Two books on the social policies of Stalin's government that are still important are Nicholas Timasheff, *The Great Retreat* (New York: Dutton, 1946), and Max Eastman, *Stalin's Russia and the Crisis in Socialism* (New York: Norton, 1940). Particular areas of social and cultural policy have been treated in a series of good works in addition to those represented in the present volume: on law, Harold Berman, *Justice in the USSR*, rev. ed. (Cambridge, MA: Harvard University Press, 1963); on religion, John S. Curtiss, *The Russian Church and the Soviet State* (Boston: Little, Brown, 1953); on national attitudes and the minorities, Frederick Barghoorn, *Soviet Russian Nationalism* (New York: Oxford University Press, 1956); on philosophy and Marxist doctrine, Gustavo Wetter, *Dialectical Materialism* (New York: Praeger, 1958), and Klaus Mehnert, *Stalin vs. Marx* (London: G. Allen & Unwin, 1952); on the writing of history, George M. Enteen, *The Soviet Scholar-Bureaucrat: M. N. Pokrovsky and the Society of Marxist Historians* (University Park, PA: Pennsylvania State University Press, 1978); on science, David Joravsky, *Soviet Marxism and Natural Science, 1917–1932* (New York: Columbia University Press, 1961); on literature, Edward J. Brown, *Russian Literature since the Revolution* (3rd ed., Cambridge, MA: Harvard University Press, 1982), and Gleb Struve, *Russian Literature under Lenin and Stalin, 1917–1953* (Norman, OK: University of Oklahoma Press, 1971); on social science, Raymond A. Bauer, *The New Man in Soviet Psychology* (Cambridge, MA: Harvard University Press, 1952). The overall social impact of Stalinism is assessed in Alex Inkeles, *Social Change in Soviet Russia* (Cambridge, MA: Harvard University Press, 1968); Basile Kerblay, *Modern Soviet Society* (New York: Pantheon, 1983); Roy Medvedev, *On Stalin and Stalinism* (New York: Oxford University Press, 1979); Alex Nove, *Stalinism and After* (Winchester, MA: Allen & Unwin, 1980); and George R. Urban, ed., *Stalinism: Its Impact on Russia and the World* (New York: St. Martin's, 1982).

Fiction is an important source for understanding the Soviet social and political climate of the 1930s. Among the best-known Soviet novels of the period are Mikhail Sholokhov, *Virgin Soil Upturned* (London, 1935, and Moscow, 1979), American edition entitled *Seeds of Tomorrow* (New York: Knopf, 1935); and Nikolai Ostrovsky, *How the Steel Was Tempered* (Moscow: Foreign Languages Publishing House, 1959). A more recent novel attacking Stalinism is Anatoly Rybakov, *Children of the Arbat* (Boston: Little, Brown, 1988). Arthur Koestler, *Darkness at Noon* (New York: Macmillan, 1941, and Bantam Books, 1984) is the classic story of the purge trials by a noted Western ex-Communist.